Palgrave Studies in European Union Politics

Edited by: **Michelle Egan**, American University, USA, **Neill Nugent**, Visiting Professor, College of Europe, Bruges, and Honorary Professor, University of Salford, UK, and **William Paterson OBE**, University of Aston, UK.

Editorial Board: **Christopher Hill**, Cambridge, UK, **Simon Hix**, London School of Economics, UK, **Mark Pollack**, Temple University, USA, **Kalypso Nicolaïdis**, Oxford, UK, **Morten Egeberg**, University of Oslo, Norway, **Amy Verdun**, University of Victoria, Canada, **Claudio M. Radaelli**, University of Exeter, UK, and **Frank Schimmelfennig**, Swiss Federal Institute of Technology, Switzerland

Following on the sustained success of the acclaimed *European Union Series*, which essentially publishes research-based textbooks, *Palgrave Studies in European Union Politics* publishes cutting edge research-driven monographs.

The remit of the series is broadly defined, in terms of both subject and academic discipline. All topics of significance concerning the nature and operation of the European Union potentially fall within the scope of the series. The series is multidisciplinary to reflect the growing importance of the EU as a political, economic and social phenomenon.

Titles include:

Oriol Costa and Knud Erik Jørgensen (*editors*)
THE INFLUENCE OF INTERNATIONAL INSTITUTIONS ON THE EU
When Multilateralism hits Brussels

Falk Daviter
POLICY FRAMING IN THE EUROPEAN UNION

Renaud Dehousse (*editor*)
THE 'COMMUNITY METHOD'
Obstinate or Obsolete?

Kenneth Dyson and Angelos Sepos (*editors*)
WHICH EUROPE?
The Politics of Differentiated Integration

Michelle Egan, Neill Nugent, and William E. Paterson (*editors*)
RESEARCH AGENDAS IN EU STUDIES
Stalking the Elephant

Theofanis Exadaktylos and Claudio M. Radaelli (*editors*)
RESEARCH DESIGN IN EUROPEAN STUDIES
Establishing Causality in Europeanization

Jack Hayward and Rüdiger Wurzel (*editors*)
EUROPEAN DISUNION
Between Sovereignty and Solidarity

Wolfram Kaiser and Jan-Henrik Meyer (*editors*)
SOCIETAL ACTORS IN EUROPEAN INTEGRATION

Christian Kaunert and Sarah Leonard (*editors*)
EUROPEAN SECURITY, TERRORISM AND INTELLIGENCE
Tackling New Security Challenges in Europe

Christian Kaunert and Kamil Zwolski
The EU AS A GLOBAL SECURITY ACTOR
A Comprehensive Analysis beyond CFSP and JHA

Marina Kolb
THE EUROPEAN UNION AND THE COUNCIL OF EUROPE

Finn Laursen (*editor*)
DESIGNING THE EUROPEAN UNION
From Paris to Lisbon

Karl-Oskar Lindgren and Thomas Persson
PARTICIPATORY GOVERNANCE IN THE EU
Enhancing or Endangering Democracy and Efficiency?

Daniel Naurin and Helen Wallace (*editors*)
UNVEILING THE COUNCIL OF THE EUROPEAN UNION
Games Governments Play in Brussels

Dimitris Papadimitriou and Paul Copeland (*editors*)
THE EU's LISBON STRATEGY
Evaluating Success, Understanding Failure

Emmanuelle Schon-Quinlivan
REFORMING THE EUROPEAN COMMISSION

Roger Scully and Richard Wyn Jones (*editors*)
EUROPE, REGIONS AND EUROPEAN REGIONALISM

Yves Tiberghien (*editor*)
LEADERSHIP IN GLOBAL INSTITUTION BUILDING
Minerva's Rule

Asle Toje
AFTER THE POST-COLD WAR
The European Union as a Small Power

Liubomir K. Topaloff
POLITICAL PARTIES AND EUROSCEPTICISM

Richard G. Whitman and Stefan Wolff (*editors*)
THE EUROPEAN NEIGHBOURHOOD POLICY IN PERSPECTIVE
Context, Implementation and Impact

Richard G. Whitman (*editor*)
NORMATIVE POWER EUROPE
Empirical and Theoretical Perspectives

Sarah Wolff
THE MEDITERRANEAN DIMENSION OF THE EUROPEAN UNION'S
INTERNAL SECURITY

Jan Wouters, Hans Bruyninckx, Sudeshna Basu and Simon Schunz (*editors*)
THE EUROPEAN UNION AND MULTILATERAL GOVERNANCE
Assessing EU Participation in United Nations Human Rights and Environmental Fora

---

Palgrave Studies in European Union Politics
Series Standing Order ISBN 978–1–4039–9511–7 (hardback) and
ISBN 978–1–4039–9512–4 (paperback)
(*outside North America only*)

You can receive future titles in this series as they are published by placing a standing order.
Please contact your bookseller or, in case of difficulty, write to us at the address below with
your name and address, the title of the series and one of the ISBNs quoted above.

Customer Services Department, Macmillan Distribution Ltd, Houndmills, Basingstoke,
Hampshire RG21 6XS, UK

The European Union and the Council of Europe

Marina Kolb

Post-Doctoral Research Fellow at the Salzburg Centre of European Union Studies, University of Salzburg, Salzburg, Austria

Supported by the Faculty of Social Science
of the University of Vienna

Faculty of Social Sciences

First published 2013 by
PALGRAVE MACMILLAN

Palgrave Macmillan in the UK is an imprint of Macmillan Publishers Limited, registered in England, company number 785998, of Houndmills, Basingstoke, Hampshire RG21 6XS.

Palgrave Macmillan in the US is a division of St Martin's Press LLC, 175 Fifth Avenue, New York, NY 10010.

Palgrave Macmillan is the global academic imprint of the above companies and has companies and representatives throughout the world.

Palgrave® and Macmillan® are registered trademarks in the United States, the United Kingdom, Europe and other countries.

ISBN 978–1–137–02362–9

This book is printed on paper suitable for recycling and made from fully managed and sustained forest sources. Logging, pulping and manufacturing processes are expected to conform to the environmental regulations of the country of origin.

A catalogue record for this book is available from the British Library.

A catalog record for this book is available from the Library of Congress.

10   9   8   7   6   5   4   3   2   1
22 21 20 19 18 17 16 15 14 13

Contents

Figures and Tables

Figures

Tables

Acknowledgments

Research is formalized curiosity. It is poking and prying with a purpose.

Zora Neale Hurston (1942)

This book is the product of a long and exciting exploration, which started in 2007, of the relationship between the European Union and the Council of Europe. Numerous people and institutions supported me in undertaking this research and thus enabled me to gain insights into what *really* drives cooperation between organizations. I would like to take this opportunity to express my gratitude to all of them.

The study was funded by the Institute for Advanced Studies in Vienna in 2010. Besides the Institute for Advanced Studies, the University of Vienna and the University of Salzburg financially supported the research and enabled me to attend various conferences and present my work at different stages of the research process. The Faculty of Social Science of the University of Vienna supported this publication by funding the linguistic editing.

A big 'thank you' goes to Johannes Pollak, who oversaw this study from the very beginning to the end. I am grateful for his unlimited support, enthusiasm, and readiness to provide me with future academic guidance well beyond the completion of this research. I would also like to thank Oliver Treib at the Institute for Advanced Studies for his continuous support and assistance. I am also grateful to all my peers, in particular Bernhard Zeilinger and Sarah Meyer, for providing a stimulating and pleasant environment and thereby making this an interesting and worthwhile research journey.

I am indebted to many colleagues and friends who generously commented on related presentations and papers. In particular, I would like to thank Alexandru Grigorescu for his invaluable feedback at the MPSA conference in Chicago in 2012.

In addition, I profited from the friendly atmosphere, encouragement, and helpfulness of many colleagues of the University of Salzburg and the Salzburg Centre of European Union Studies in the process of writing this book. Michael Blauberger was particularly helpful and provided me with feedback and useful advice.

I would like to thank the reviewer and the editors of the Palgrave Studies in European Union Politics Series for their thorough review. I highly appreciate their comments and suggestions, which significantly contributed to improving the quality of the publication at hand.

My sincere thanks also go to all interview partners and experts from the empirical cases. This work would not have been possible without their dedicated time and insightful perspectives.

For her careful editing and proof reading I am indebted to Julia Reynolds. She did a fabulous job in reading through the whole manuscript.

Finally, the book would not have been written without the never-ending encouragement and ongoing support by my friends and family. A big thank you to all of you!

Notwithstanding all of the above support for this project, all shortfalls and errors are solely my own.

Abbreviations

CAHDI	Committee of Legal Advisers on Public International Law
CATS	(Troika of the) Article 36 Committee
COCEN	Council Working Party on Central Europe
CM-SUIVI3	Follow-up Committee on the Third Summit
CODEXTER	Committee of Experts on Terrorism (COE)
COE	Council of Europe
COM	Committee of Ministers (COE)
COREPER	Committee of Permanent Representatives
COSCE	Council Working Party on the Organization for Security and Co-operation in Europe and the Council of Europe
COTER	Working Party on Terrorism (EU)
CJ-PD	Project Group on Data Protection (COE)

Secretariat of the COE

DER	Directorate of External Relations (COE)
DGHL	Directorate General of Human Rights and Legal Affairs
DG III	Directorate General of Social Cohesion

General Secretariat of the Council of the EU

DG E	Directorate-General External Relations and Political–Military Affairs
DG G	Directorate-General Economic and Social Affairs
DG H	Directorate-General Justice and Home Affairs

European Commission

DG ELARG	Directorate-General for Enlargement
DG EMPL	Directorate-General for Employment, Social Affairs and Equal Opportunities
DG HOME	Directorate-General for Home Affairs (since July 2010)
DG JLS	Directorate-General for Justice, Freedom and Security (until July 2010)

DG JUSTICE	Directorate-General for Justice (since July 2010)
DG RELEX	Directorate-General for External Relations
DSG	Deputy Secretary General
EEAS	European Union External Action Service
EC	European Communities
ECJ	Court of Justice of the EU
ECHR	Convention for the Protection of Human Rights and Fundamental Freedoms (COE)
ECtHR	European Court for Human Rights (COE)
ECRI	European Commission against Racism and Intolerance (COE)
EEC	European Economic Community
EP	European Parliament (EU)
EU	European Union
EUMC	European Monitoring Centre on Racism and Xenophobia (EU)
FRA	Fundamental Rights Agency (EU)
GMT	Multidisciplinary Group on International Action against Terrorism (COE)
ICG	Informal Contact Group of International Organizations and Institutions dealing with Roma issues
IO	International Organization
IOR	Interorganizational Relations
IR	International Relations
I-XX	Expert interview number XX
JHA	Justice and Home Affairs
MG-S-ROM	Committee of Experts on Roma and Travelers (COE)
MOU	Memorandum of Understanding between the COE and the EU
NGO	Nongovernmental Organization
OECD	Organization for Economic Co-operation and Development
OSCE	Organization for Security and Co-operation in Europe
PACE	Parliamentary Assembly of the Council of Europe
PNR	Personal Name Records
SG	Secretary General
TEC	Treaty establishing the European Community

TEU	Treaty on European Union
T-PD	Consultative Committee of the Convention for the Protection of Individuals with Regard to Automatic Processing of Personal Data (COE)
UK	United Kingdom
UN	United Nations
UNHCR	United Nations High Commissioner for Refugees

Part I
Introduction

1
Introduction

'Fundamental rights at the heart of policy making' was the title of a press release sent from the newsroom of the European Commission in April 2012 (Commission 2012b), illustrating the increasing prominence of fundamental rights within the European Union (EU). This fact is reflected, most importantly, in the Charter of Fundamental Rights of the European Union in force and legally binding for over two years now. With the ratification of the Lisbon Treaty, EU member states obliged the EU to accede to the European Convention for the Protection of Human Rights and Fundamental Freedoms (ECHR) of the Council of Europe (COE). To this end, the European Commission (henceforward, Commission) and the COE kicked off joint talks on the EU's accession to the ECHR in July 2010. Two years later, technical negotiations have concluded and a draft accession agreement has been drawn up. However, the accession process is still far from the finish line: the accession, based on an international treaty among all 47 COE member states, will only enter into force upon ratification by all parties, which – this goes without saying – is a rather lengthy process.

The idea of EU accession to the ECHR did not appear out of the blue during negotiations over the Lisbon Treaty; on the contrary, it is part of ongoing and long-standing reflections and discussions dating as far back as the 1970s. At its core, the accession process examines the question of how the EU's accession to the ECHR should be tackled while simultaneously implying at the much broader question of how to deal with the increasing overlap between the EU and the COE must be looked at: the more competence the EU has gained over the past two decades, especially in the field of Justice and Home Affairs (JHA), the more urgent it has become to reflect upon the relationship between these two regional organizations that both deal with human rights in Europe. The Action

Plan adopted at the so-called Warsaw Summit of the COE in 2005 recognizes this overlap in the legal field and stresses the need for increased cooperation (COM 2005b: Chapter IV.1):

> Considering the important contribution of the Council of Europe to democracy, cohesion and stability in Europe, we call on the Council of Europe to:
>
> strengthen its relations with the European Union so that the Council of Europe's and the European Union's achievements and *future standard-setting work are taken into account, as appropriate, in each other's activities* (emphasis added).

Originally, however, the COE and the slightly younger EU (at that time the European Economic Community and the European Atomic Energy Community, respectively) were founded as alternatives that aimed at European integration (Schneider 1977: 217; Rittberger 2001: 687, 694; Petaux 2009: 274–8). They have run parallel for most of their existence, each within its very own field of activity and each forging different paths for integration (Mitterand 1982: 31; Commission 1989: 2; Juncker 2006: 1; Joris and Vandenberghe 2008/2009: 4). The COE, as the main European organization for the protection of human rights, has fostered European integration through the protection of human rights, pluralist democracy, and the rule of law since 1949. The slightly younger EU, founded in 1957 (except in Chapter 3 dealing with the historical development of the EU–COE relations, the term EU is used to enhance readability; hence the names of EU's predecessors, namely the European Coal and Steel Community, the European Economic Community, the European Atomic Energy Community, and the European Community (EC) are omitted), took another road and tried to bring the European countries closer by focusing on coal and steel. Since then, the EU has grown in both its competencies and the number of its member states. At present, the EU is far from being the coal and steel organization of the 1950s (see, for example, Wallace et al. 2005), and through its development it intrudes into competence spheres of other European organizations. By putting 'the human rights issue at the forefront' (Commission 2012d), the EU's engagement in the field of human rights is becoming increasingly visible. While the EU had started combining trade agreements with human rights requirements as early as in the 1970s, it was only in 1993 that the EU adopted its first specific human rights norm, which incidentally strongly resembled the COE criteria for membership: the so-called Copenhagen Criteria, which accession countries have to fulfill before becoming members of the EU (Chalmers et al. 2006: 243–4). The EU's interest in human rights has steadily increased from the 1990s

(Brosig 2006a: 9–16), the most visible consequences of which include – other than the Charter of Fundamental Rights of the EU (2000) – the Fundamental Rights Agency (FRA) (2007) and, in terms of staff restructuring, the new Commissioner post for Fundamental Rights (2009). Having exhausted the Common Market as a vision for further integration, the EU has been intrigued by human rights as a new raison d'être and longs to portray itself as a human rights organization (Von Bogdandy 2000). As a result, the EU is eager to (retrospectively) construct a foundational human rights myth that would suggest that the EU and human rights are, and always have been, intrinsically linked (Smismans 2010).

This compels the COE, previously the exclusive regional organization in the field of human rights protection, to confront a new competitor now heavily involving itself in the COE's core task. As a result, the EU and the COE now (partly) occupy the same policy space, and their relationship is a contentious one, a problem that has not yet been resolved. On paper, they like to picture themselves as complementary partners that reinforce each other and consequently improve human rights protection in Europe. Yet, the inflicted principles of complementarity (that is, no parallel structures) and cooperation seem to remain empty claims when it comes to practice, as the to-the-point report by Jean-Claude Juncker (2006: 2), Prime Minister of Luxembourg, states on the relations between the EU and the COE:

Although each has enriched the other, the two organisations remain at best a shaky team. Although each has borrowed from the other, they have never been able to make themselves permanently complementary.

How international organizations (IOs) react when confronted with such organizational overlap, which is, an intersecting mandate (overlapping competencies), possibly accompanied by a common membership, is the core interest of this book. An organizational overlap can either lead to conflictive situations such as turf wars and duplication of tasks, or can allow IOs to cooperate and strive for common goals. Starting from the organizational overlap, the *central research questions* are the following: Do overlapping competencies lead to cooperation or conflict between IOs? What are the conditions conducive to either cooperation or conflict between IOs?

In the context of the steadily increasing number, importance, and complexity of IOs over the past decades, it is astonishing that existing political science literature has failed to sufficiently address and explain interorganizational relations (IOR). IOR were largely neglected by theoretically informed scholars rooted in international relations (IR), who considered the study of IOs as 'the ugly duckling' within the discipline and bypassed IOs on the basis of their notion of 'international regimes'. Particularly in the aftermath of the Cold War, one can see IOs widening in their scope and membership, and the policy space at an international level becoming increasingly filled with IOs. As a result, earlier clear-cut arrangements between IOs on the question of who (unilaterally) deals with which policy issue have become blurred. In such complex settings, '[t]here are few social problems that still can be dealt with, let alone solved, within or by one or a few organizations working alone' (Hanf and O'Toole 1992: 165). As the number of overlaps between IOs has risen and is still rising, it has become increasingly important to ask how they interact. Especially in the light of scarce resources and constraints of empty coffers, one has to scrutinize whether these overlaps between IOs hamper the efficient use of their finances. Will organizational overlaps lead to a waste of resources, be it through turf wars or duplication of tasks, or do IOs work efficiently and combine forces in order to achieve their goals? Implicit in these arguments is the practical assumption, which is – unsurprisingly – quite common among researchers dealing with IOR, that cooperative relations are more likely to lead to optimal (policy) outcomes than conflictive ones. However, from a market-oriented perspective, one could argue the opposite: the more IOs compete for resources and policy solutions, the better it would be for the states, since only those IOs that are successful in providing a specific service can survive (lower costs). At the same time, enhanced competition (for resources and policy solutions) improves IOs' responses to current challenges as competition spurs innovation and, as a result, IOs are constantly trying to outdo each other. Applied to this book's focus on human rights protection in Europe, it is argued that cooperative relations, and not conflictive relations, are more likely to lead to the better protection of human rights, since conflict brings forth conflictive norms and thereby the possibility of 'forum shopping', which means that actors (states) can select from each forum what suits them best.

Along with IR, organization theory can also possibly answer the question of which factors influence relations between IOs. Yet, for a long time, issues of an interorganizational nature were ignored by organization scholars. It was not until the 1970s that IOR became a topic worth researching, especially to those advocating the resource dependency approach, which suggests that IOs seek to accumulate resources via relations with one another. This book argues that the resource dependency approach offers one explanation as to why IOs engage in relations with each other in the first place, and is particularly adequate for analyzing networks (a multiplicity) of IOs and singling out the goods of exchange processes (money, expertise, and so on). However, it is less suitable for analyzing dyadic relationships, and it does not explain what, or which, factors trigger cooperative (or conflictive) IOR.

Given the above-mentioned research gap within the literature, one needs to look elsewhere to determine which factors influence the state of an interorganizational relationship. Managers make up one group that has long been preoccupied with IOR, since they have had to cope with larger systems (for example industries or societies) and, for practical reasons, have needed to think about diverse internal and external factors faced when operating within larger systems. Therefore, IOR are tackled most importantly in the field of applied management studies and in the literature on implementation. However, the literature emerging on IOR from 1970s onwards has been broad-ranging and heterogeneous. This is where this book's research comes in: drawing on the fragmented literature, an innovative and coherent framework is constructed in Section 2.2 of Chapter 2, bringing together interest-based, organizational, physical, and cultural factors that may have an impact on interorganizational cooperation or conflict. According to the book's guiding thesis, *the biggest threat to interorganizational cooperation is organizational self-interest, despite a shared policy interest.*

1.1 The focus of the book

To answer the guiding research questions given earlier, this book looks into the issue of setting human rights standards, an area in which the overlap is most visible and in which the COE's role is the most potentially challenged by the EU. The COE's 'membership increasingly overlaps with that of the EU and the EU has, by taking on greater responsibility in the area of human rights, strayed into the COE's area of technical specialization' (Stivachtis and Habegger 2011: 170) and threatens the COE's role as the standard-setter *par excellence* in Europe. From a geographical point of view, the study therefore focuses on the internal dimension, that is, human rights protection within the EU-27. Those interested in the external dimension, such as the joint programs between the Commission and the COE targeted at non-EU member states, may wish to consult Brosig (2010).

The literature is divided into whether relations between the EU and the COE are expected to be cooperative or conflictive. Given the large number of member states (currently 47) and the sophisticated ECHR control system, the scenario of the EU replacing, or rather absorbing, the COE – ' "the" watchdog for human rights in Europe' (Brummer 2010: 281) – is not very likely, at least not in the near future. Yet, one strand of the literature argues that the COE is rather skeptical about the EU's approach toward the human rights field and sees the expanding leverage of the EU with partial disapproval. In this context, De Schutter (2007: 3–5) refers to the COE's fear of marginalization and traces this fear back to the fact that due to the enlargement of the EU to 27 member states, the EU now forms a majority within the 47-member COE. As a result, the COE risks becoming a standard-receiver in cases for which the EU has taken legislative initiatives. In other words, no longer able to act independently, the COE often has to align itself with these new EU standards. Therefore, one would expect IOR to be conflictive. Another strand of literature argues that, while human rights form the core policy of the COE, the EU sees human rights only as a peripheral policy. In this line of reasoning, the EU does not threaten the COE's position, and IOR will be cooperative (Brosig 2010: 15–6). This book's research will show which of the two arguments is accurate for EU–COE relations.

1.2 The case studies

To find out whether the EU's incursion into some of the COE's core areas of competency has fueled the COE's fear of marginalization and, if so, if this fear is justified, this book analyzes the following five cases in depth: the establishment of the EU Fundamental Rights Agency (FRA) in Vienna, Austria; the negotiations regarding the joint cooperation agreement Memorandum of Understanding (MOU); and IOR in the three issue areas of data protection, the fight against terrorism, and the fight against Roma discrimination. From this list it is apparent that this research analyzes two kinds of relations: relations dealing with institutional issues on the one hand and those dealing with policy issues on the other hand. Relations dealing with institutional issues can be regarded as politically sensitive and high-level ones and those dealing with policy issues are expected to be rather operational and low-level ones.

Given that the FRA and the MOU are the two most important issues in the relations between the EU and the COE regarding institutional questions, they are selected to be part of this study. With data protection, the fight against terrorism, and the fight against Roma discrimination, this research has chosen policy issues fulfilling two criteria – first, issues that *both IOs are engaged in contemporaneously*, otherwise there is no overlap; and second, issues that *are high on the agenda* of both IOs, conducive for IOR to take place and offering an interesting *variance across policy field* (JHA and social policy) and *across time* (data protection starting in the mid-1990s, fight against terrorism after 2001, and fight against Roma discrimination after 2004). For details on the case selection, see Section 2.4 of Chapter 2 and Table 2.1.

1.3 Goals and deliverables of the book

This section highlights and summarizes the book's objectives and defines how the research contributes to the existing literature. This research is innovative in three aspects that are of theoretical as well as of empirical relevance.

- Its primary goal is to *shed light on IOR between the EU and the COE* by generating and providing primary data on five empirical cases dealing with policy and institutional issues in the realm of human rights.

Although the current literature acknowledges the role of the COE within the European human rights protection system, it barely subjects it to closer scrutiny, not to mention its lacking analysis of the IOR between the COE and its most important partner, the EU. There are two reasons why the COE exists, for the most part, only as a long footnote in the social science community and/or is absorbed under the heading 'EU': first, the COE tends not to hold too high of an opinion of itself and has a rather reticent attitude as opposed to other IOs, such as the EU; and second, the COE has acted very generously with regard to the EU, allowing it to hold its sessions in the COE Palais de l'Europe in Strasbourg, France, and adopt the COE's symbol (the COE flag adopted in 1955 shows 12 stars against an azure background) and anthem (the COE approved Ode to Joy as the European anthem as early as 1971). Given the 'blurring' of the two IOs and the joint use of symbols, the public, the media, and even major scholars are confused and do not distinguish between the EU and the COE. By providing a thorough account of the EU–COE relationship in the field of human rights and exploring instances of cooperation and conflict therein, the book aims at filling this research gap.

- Additionally, the empirical research (undertaken to fulfill this aim) has the second goal of providing information on *major trends in the development of the European human rights protection system,* asking whether the COE's fear of marginalization is justified and whether the EU has become an important standard-setter.

Will the COE, known as the standard-setter *par excellence,* become a standard-receiver in cases where the EU has taken legislative initiatives? Since the EU has grown to 27 member states, the EU now forms a majority within the 47-member COE. As a result, the COE – no longer able to act independently – might have to align itself with these new EU standards. Does the COE therefore rightly fear marginalization? How do the EU and the COE deal with the issue of standard setting? And what will be the future role of the COE?

- The third goal is to allow a better theoretical understanding of the relations between organizations, answering the question of what *implications the present study has for our understanding of IOs in general.* Therefore, the book ultimately draws and incorporates conclusions regarding the latter two aims.

When looking at the theoretical results of this study, namely, which factors trigger cooperative or conflictive relationships between IOs, how and to what extent is it possible to draw general conclusions for the relationships between other IOs as well? The concluding Chapter 9 engages in drawing potential conclusions, based on the study at hand, for the development of the human rights protection system in Europe and the understanding of relationships between IOs beyond the EU and the COE.

Given the empirical interest of this research, this book contributes to the literature on the EU and IOs, IOR in general, and human rights protection in Europe in terms of empirical focus. As previously outlined in Section 1.1, in-depth analysis of the COE is lacking in the (social science) literature. The exception is law scholars, who have published extensively on the COE in the past. However, the judicial analysis is often engaged with different empirical questions, that is, the EU–COE relationship's limitation to the two courts. The political science perspective at hand complements the (mainly judicial) analysis of the European human rights protection system by turning its attention to the question of how the COE reacts to the EU's increasing engagement with human rights.

Therefore, the book furthers the agenda set by the literature in this field by providing a new theoretical framework and an in-depth empirical study of two main actors in the field of human rights protection in Europe from a political science perspective. In sum, the book complements the literature, mainly edited volumes, such as Brosig's (2006b) overview on the current human rights developments in Europe within the structures of the EU, Organization for Security and Co-operation (OSCE), COE, and the multilayered court system, with a focus that is partly judicial and, geographically speaking, on Central Eastern and South Eastern Europe. Jørgensen (2009) seeks to explore the relationship between the EU and various IOs, with the aim of filling 'a remarkably wide gap in existing literature on the topic'. The edited volume offers eight case studies, with the EU–COE relationship not included as part of the book. Focusing on the areas of security, democracy promotion, and peace building, Galbreath and Gebhard (2010) examine how the EU, NATO (North Atlantic Treaty Organization), OSCE, and COE interact with one another and whether they provide a 'useful and unique service to regional stability' (security-oriented analysis). From Bond's publication (2012), which provides a basic introduction to the COE from its foundation to the status quo, it becomes apparent how much literature on the COE is needed. Starting from the 'dramatic increase in interaction between the EU and multilateral institutions', Costa and Jørgensen (2012) aim at specifically showing how different IOs shape EU policies and policy-making processes.

Summing up, one can say that this book complements and surpasses the existing literature.

Its theoretical framework is distinct from the work done earlier, and it also distinguishes itself by giving priority to the COE in its research interest and choice of policies and actors.

1.4 Methodology

Analyzing five cases dealing with institutional and policy issues in depth, the book is a qualitative study of the relationship between the EU and the COE. To uncover and explain which factors account for the state of IOR (cooperation/conflict) between IOs, the book adopts a process-tracing approach, which 'attempts to identify the intervening causal process – the causal chain and causal mechanisms – between an independent variable (or variables) and the outcome of the dependent variable' (George and Bennett 2005: 206). The concluding Chapter 9 engages in a discussion of whether and to what extent one can draw conclusions for the relationships of IOs in general from the results based on the EU–COE analysis.

In terms of data collection, the study draws on qualitative fieldwork involving semi-structured expert interviews as well as documentary research based on primary and secondary literature and official documents. The semi-structured expert interview considers experts to be the source of information; its advantages include its usefulness in cases in which the decisions and actions that lie behind an event need to be established, and this applies to the topic of IOR and its potential to compensate for lack and limitations of documentary evidence. The series of 40 in-depth interviews involves, first, officials who are directly engaged with EU–COE relations and, second, members of NGOs, national administrations, and researchers who closely follow the behavior of the IOs from the outside.

In conclusion, it needs to be established that this research follows scholars such as MacMullen (2004) and de Schutter (2008) in treating the EU and the COE as IOs. It goes without saying that the EU and the COE are of different natures, differing substantively in terms of institutional attributes – such as access to membership, policy coverage, institutional apparatus, decision procedures and processes, and mechanisms to ensure output compliance – and financial resources at their disposal. Ultimately, the EU is partly a supranational arrangement, whereas the COE is predominantly an intergovernmental entity. Nevertheless, both are considered IOs. Within this IO-centered view, this research concentrates on the respective bureaucracies of the two IOs, while omitting the intergovernmental bodies as well as other actors that might play a role in IOR, such as EU and COE member states. Accordingly, whenever this research refers to relations between the EU and the COE, this explicitly means relations between the Commission and the General Secretariat of the Council on the EU side and the Secretariat on the COE side. The idea of including the European Parliament (EP) as well as the Parliamentary Assembly of the COE (PACE) was contemplated in the beginning, but abandoned due to pragmatic reasons (problems of access). Equally, the relations between the two Courts, the Court of Justice of the EU (ECJ) and the European Court for Human Rights (ECtHR, COE) are not part of this research. See Scheeck (2005; 2007), for an extensive analysis of the relations between the two courts.

1.5 Outline of the book

Chapter 2 develops the conceptual and theoretical framework of the book. The chapter begins with a look at the existing IR literature on international regimes, and on institutions and organizations. It then moves on to different approaches of organization theory, namely, exchange theory, organizational ecology and contingency theory, and transaction cost theory. The chapter finds that IR literature and organization theory neglect the issue of relations between IOs or are not adequate for this empirical research (Section 2.1 of Chapter 2). In contrast, a vast but incoherent literature specifically on IOR has developed within the field of applied management and implementation studies. Drawing on this fragmented literature, an innovative and coherent theoretical framework is constructed, bringing together interest-based, organizational, physical, and cultural factors that may have an impact on interorganizational cooperation or conflict. Along these lines, four main research hypotheses are formulated (Section 2.2 of Chapter 2). The chapter then elaborates on the dependent variable, suggesting a distinction between the terms of cooperation and coordination and conceiving it as a continuum ranging from cooperation to conflict (Section 2.3 of Chapter 2). The final section of this chapter justifies the case selection as well as the methodological approach (Section 2.4 of Chapter 2).

The empirical Chapter 3 provides the reader with background information necessary for an understanding of the subsequent empirical case study. It reviews the important milestones in the history of IOR between the EU and the COE, ranging from a basic Exchange of Letters, the first one in 1987, to the more complex MOU adopted in 2007 (Sections 3.1.1–3.1.8 of Chapter 3). The EU and the COE are portrayed as IOs and their differences regarding their tasks, purpose, and size are discussed (Section 3.2.1 of Chapter 3). The actors scrutinized in the subsequent section consist of various bodies, institutions, and units of the two IOs. The aim of the chapter is twofold: first, to shed light on the question of who is in contact with whom and, second, when necessary, to explain the mandate of the specific actors (Sections 3.2.2–3.2.6 of Chapter 3). Information on the mechanisms related to meetings between the two IOs are presented in Section 3.3 of Chapter 3. The sections compile the existing meeting mechanisms by displaying the high-level contacts (Section 3.3.1 of Chapter 3) and meetings in the field of external relations (Section 3.3.2 of Chapter 3) and JHA (Section 3.3.3 of Chapter 3).

On the basis of qualitative fieldwork involving expert interviews (in Brussels, Strasbourg, and Vienna), the empirical Chapters 4–8 reconstruct in a detailed way how both organizations interacted in relation to several institutional and policy issues. Hence, they analyze IOR between the EU and the COE regarding the establishment of the EU's FRA (Chapter 8) the negotiations on the MOU (Chapter 7), and IOR in the issue areas of data protection (Chapter 4), fight against terrorism (Chapter 5), and fight against Roma discrimination (Chapter 6).

The empirical case studies all follow the same structure. The chapters start by providing the reader with a brief introduction to the respective issue area. Then they introduce the COE's role in the respective issue area by going through its legislative instruments and concerned bodies. Subsequently, they turn to the EU's role in the respective issue area. Equally, the chapters scrutinize the EU's legislative instruments and concerned bodies. Special attention is paid to the interorganizational contacts between the EU and the COE in the respective issue area. At the core of these chapters is the subsequent analysis of IOR between the EU and the COE in the respective issue area. By reviewing the corresponding issues of interest, the chapters reveal, in a detailed way, instances of conflict or cooperation between the EU and the COE. The empirical cases conclude by giving an overall summary of the respective chapters.

The empirical case studies identify instances of both conflict as well as cooperation within EU–COE relations. Conflictive relations involve differences in opinion, resulting in missing political support, such as hostile press releases and documents (for example FRA, the fight against terrorism), motivation of one's own 'lobby' (for example national parliaments and member states' politicians), and interventions in order to block the initiative of the other organization (for example FRA). Complaints about the behavior of counterparts on a personal level or organizational level (for example fight against terrorism, data protection, and general access of the COE to EU meetings and documents) have been made. The fight against terrorism reveals a kind of 'race' to be the first to come up with a legal initiative. Linked to this are discussions on duplication and the reinvention of the wheel (for example the fight against Roma discrimination). Also in dispute is the question of the 'Disconnection Clause' with which the EU defies control of the COE convention system.

As regards cooperative relations, information is shared through liaison offices and reciprocal representation. Nevertheless, the information sharing process is criticized as being one-sided (for example the COE cannot access restricted EU documents). The two IOs organize joint press conferences or initiatives (for example FRA), conduct joint projects (for example FRA), and conclude cooperation agreements (for example FRA, MOU). They also support each other politically, for example, by referring to each other's work or by bearing out a convention (for example the fight against terrorism). The study emphasizes the importance of informal features of cooperative relations: the fact that cooperation often depends on how well the counterparts get along with each other implies that relations are not institutionalized. Moreover, informal relations might be more successful precisely because the institutional framework of the two IOs does not always support formal cooperation (for example fight against Roma discrimination).

The findings show differences between policy areas: cooperation between the EU and the COE is much more advanced in the JHA field than in the social policy field, in which the COE is merely named as one of the four or five most important actors. Also, specific coordination meetings between the EU and the COE are in place in the JHA field, highlighting the importance of relations in this area.

The highest level of conflict can be observed in the FRA case. The fight against terrorism is the case that shows the second highest level of conflict, followed by the MOU case. Less conflict potential can be seen in the case of the fight against Roma discrimination, and hardly any can be observed in the data protection case. To some extent, all three 'conflictive cases' were transformed into more cooperative situations during the analyzed time period.

Chapter 9 concludes by discussing the empirical results against the background of the research question and the previously formulated theoretical expectations, and focuses on the broader implications of this research. The findings show that interest-based factors are the most relevant for explaining the relations between the EU and the COE. The biggest threat to interorganizational cooperation turns out to be organizational self-interest. Despite similar policy interests in the protection of human rights, serious conflicts between both sides arise whenever organizational self-interest is at stake. In particular, this is the case when the COE perceives the EU as intruding into some of its core areas of competence, thus threatening its organizational survival. Processes of socialization and intraorganizational capacities only play a secondary role; they only reinforce the main trend toward cooperation or conflict arising from the constellation of interests.

On the basis of these findings, this book argues that cooperation between IOs is most likely when neither side considers the other's activities as a threat to its own organizational survival. As a consequence, the relations between similarly large and powerful organizations should be easier to handle in a cooperative manner than those involving a significantly larger and more powerful organization that threatens to crowd out the inferior side. One can conclude that the EU – from the COE's point of view – has turned from friend to foe. The empirical cases show that the EU has taken its inspiration from COE conventions and recommendations and that it has transferred them in its own legal initiatives that often have the upper hand over COE initiatives in terms of binding character, follow-up, and monitoring. It is therefore argued that the COE rightly fears marginalization, given the steadily increasing activity of the EU in the human rights field. The empirical cases show that the EU has remarkably changed its attitude toward human rights over time, and is increasingly attempting to establish a human rights policy on its own. This development is accompanied by the retrospective set-up of a foundational EU fundamental rights myth and free-riding on the reputation of the COE. Summing up, one can conclude that the strand of literature suggesting conflictive relations between IOs occupying the same policy space is quite accurate for relations between the EU and the COE.

Finally, the book reflects on the future of the EU–COE relationship: above all, the question of whether the COE will remain the main standard-setter in human rights depends on the COE itself and the currently ongoing reform that aims to revitalize the COE. At the moment, the COE is a highly qualified, yet not very powerful organization. In contrast, the EU is powerful, and this power comes with an attitude: the organization feels strong enough to ultimately handle all agendas on its own. It is probably also for this reason that past attempts to enforce a stronger interorganizational cooperation ran into sand. For the time being, cooperation takes place as well, but only when the IOs manage to overcome their organizational self-interest. It remains to be seen whether the new attempts to bring the EU and COE closer together will be successful in the future. What can already be said is that recent developments in IOR between the two IOs – the Juncker report, the MOU, and FRA – have at the very least helped to increase their knowledge and raise their awareness of each other.

2
Interorganizational Relations – A Framework for Analysis

This chapter establishes a framework for the analysis of relations between (international) organizations and aims to acquaint readers with the methodology of this research. It goes on to examine the explanatory power and limits of IR literature and organization theory with regard to the focus of this study. The overview suggests that, while the research agendas in these two fields do provide some insights, they give only insights. It will be shown that IR literature, to a large extent, bypasses the notion of IOs and that organization theory only helps to explain why IOR occur in the first place. Therefore, the book moves away from these 'traditional approaches', and instead engages with implementation literature and management studies, which, it is argued here, are particularly suited for the focus of this study as they specifically list factors that trigger conflict/cooperation between organizations. On the basis of the existing corpus of literature dealing with implementation and management, this chapter constructs a model for IOR. Finally, it justifies the case selection as well as the methodology.

2.1 Inadequacy of IR and organizations theory for explaining IOR

2.1.1 IOs – the ugly duckling of international relations

Prior to researching within the field of IOR, one would expect theories in the area of IR to provide helpful findings for the study of interorganizational relationships. Yet, IR falls short of expectations: despite the steadily increasing number, importance, and complexity of IOs over the past decades, the IR literature has failed to sufficiently address and explain IOR. In fact, IOR has been largely neglected by theoretically informed scholars rooted in IR, who consider the study of IOs as 'the ugly duckling' (Verbeek 1998: 11) within the discipline. The explanation for this theoretical lacuna (the neglect of IOs) can be traced back to the introduction of the analytical concept of international regimes in the 1970s, which bypassed the notion of IOs (Verbeek 1998: 11–3; Biermann 2008: 153). Given the focus on international regimes, the '"hot" topic in the study of international relations' (Donnelly 1986: 599), this section, in a first step, analyzes research on international regime interaction. Subsequently, it complements the review by focusing on another strand of the existing IR literature that deals with international institutions and organizations from the 1990s onwards. By doing so, it shows whether the research on regime interaction bears fruitful insights for the interaction of IOs as well and whether the research on international institutions and organizations helps explain the relations between IOs.

The rich and fairly complex literature on international regime interaction deals with empirical as well as theoretical issues: empirically, scholars have mainly analyzed environmental (Young 2002; Gehring and Oberthür 2006) and economic regimes (Kohler-Koch 1989; Knodt 2005). Theoretical articles so far have focused on – not easily distinguishable – 'nested and overlapping regimes' (Aggarwal 1998; Alter and Meunier 2006), 'regime interaction' (Gehring and Oberthür 2004), 'regime complexes' (Raustiala and Victor 2004), and finally 'regime complexity' (Alter and Meunier 2009). The literature points to the problem of institutional reconciliation and asks how new or adapted institutions fit to existing ones (1998: 1–31). It highlights the potential risks of 'forum shopping', meaning that actors within a regime complex can select from each forum what suits them best (2004: 295–309), and it is argued that exactly these nesting and overlapping commitments triggered the Banana dispute between the EU and the United States (2006: 365). Turning to regime interaction, Gehring and Oberthür (2004: 250–79) illustrate how a source regime can exert influence pressuring the target regime to adapt. By treating overlap (and complexity) as an independent variable, Alter and Meunier (2009: 13–24) ask if the effects emanating from it enforce cooperation or inefficiencies. However, as this literature on regimes says little about the question of whether relations between IOs are cooperative or conflictive and which conditions are therefore determinants, its implications for the study at hand remain ambiguous.

In contrast, selected literature on international institutions and organizations explores the 'power and pathologies' of IOs (Barnett and

Finnemore 1999; Barnett and Finnemore 2004), the European security architecture (Peters 1995; Borchert 2001), and 'the external face of
Europeanization' (Lavenex 2006). The literature points out four types of
authority that make IOs powerful: rational-legal, delegated, moral, and
expert. These features are used by IOs to classify the world and establish meaning in the social world, as well as set and diffuse norms (1999:
715–32; 2004: 20–44). By looking at the situation after the Cold War,
Peters (1995: 277–304) investigates how European security institutions
cooperate (or compete) with one another in certain spheres of action.
With regard to the consultation and cooperation between the EU, Organization for Security and Co-operation in Europe (OSCE), COE, and
United Nations (UN) concerning preventive diplomacy, peacekeeping,
and peace building, it has been shown that 'in most cases cooperation and coordination rest not on formal but on ad hoc agreements'
(Borchert 2001: 183). The so-called 'EU-ization' of IOs refers to the fact
that, confronted with increasing EU action within their field of activities, IOs react in two different ways: either they narrow down their
competences to areas in which the EU is not engaged, or they involve
themselves in the EU's activities and become partners (or sometimes
subcontractors) of the EU (2006: 252–64).

This brief excursus demonstrates that the literature dealing with international regime interaction, the power and 'pathologies' of IOs, the
European security institutions, and the influence of the EU on IOs, to
some extent, speaks to the research at hand. In particular, the perception of IOs as bureaucracies, the cooperation between European security
institutions, and the reaction of IOs to increasing EU activities are of
interest and show similarities to some facets of this research's applica-
tions (some of the findings of Barnett and Finnemore (1999) find their
way into the theoretical model developed in Section 2.2). Nonetheless,
what are missing are insights into the question guiding this research,
namely which factors influence the state of an interorganizational relationship. Therefore, one can conclude that there is a research gap within
the literature at hand and that a new theoretical framework is needed.

2.1.2 Why do IOR occur – approaches of organization theory

By bridging the gap and treating IOs as organizations (Ness and Brechin
1988), organization theory could potentially answer the question of
which factors influence relations between IOs. Yet, for a long time,
the research interests of organization theory have lain elsewhere: Evan
(1966: 176) emphasizes 'the general neglect of interorganizational phenomena by organization theorists'. It was not until the 1970s that

IOR became a topic worth researching, especially to those advocating the resource dependency approach, which suggests that IOs seek to accumulate resources via relations with one another (Cropper et al. 2008: 7). While looking at selected contributions to the field of organization theory, one would expect the literature on organizations to tackle and include the environment of organizations (and possibly their relations with other organizations) as well. This section will specifically deal with various resource dependency approaches: exchange theory, organizational ecology and contingency theory, and transaction cost theory.

On the question of why IOR occur, one can draw on three strands of organization theories: first, the most traditional exchange theory; second, the more recent organizational ecology and contingency theory; and finally, the transaction cost theory (Alexander 1995: 7–14). Exchange theory – long regarded as the dominant theoretical perspective on what is called 'interorganizational coordination' (Hall et al. 1977: 457) – considers resource exchange (acquisition) as the most important factor influencing organizational relations and behavior (Benson 1975: 231). Exchange theory builds on the assumption that survival is the primary goal for all organizations. Given the assumed resource scarcity, organizations have to supplement their resources elsewhere, and therefore depend – to varying degrees – on other organizations for resources. Resource exchange (dependency) is thus proposed to be the main incentive for interorganizational coordination (Grandori 1987: 58–72; Pfeffer and Salancik 2003). Organizational ecology and contingency theory both put forward the idea of organizational adaptation to its environment. To survive and to be successful, organizations have to adjust appropriately to their changing environment. According to representatives of this theoretical perspective, organizational adaptation could also be a reason for interorganizational coordination. For example, organizations of the same 'ecological niche' might interact symbiotically for their reciprocal advantage, or new environmental developments could create interdependence between organizations, resulting in interorganizational coordination (Grandori 1987: 103; Alexander 1995: 10–2). Transaction cost theory has evolved from economics and has institutionalization at its core. This theoretical perspective implies that interorganizational coordination takes place in order to lower the transaction costs of unconcerted actions between independent partners. Moreover, transaction cost theory provides explanations for the different forms of interorganizational coordination structures (Alexander 1995: 12–4).

This book argues that the aforementioned resource dependency approaches offer one explanation as to why IOs begin to engage in relations with one another in the first place (the counterargument being that IOs avoid cooperation with one another as it limits their autonomy and increases their dependency). It is particularly adequate for analyzing networks (a multiplicity) of IOs and singling out the goods of exchange processes (money, expertise, and so on) (for example Biermann 2008; Gest and Grigorescu 2010). Yet, the resource dependency approach is less suitable for analyzing dyadic relationships, as one cannot expect the need for resources or the available goods to vary (drastically) within an organization. Additionally, it remains difficult to translate the theoretical perspectives into conditions that could determine whether IOR are cooperative or conflictive. From a research design point of view, one also has a problem of endogeneity, given that cooperation – for example in the form of joint projects implying exchange processes – would be explained by the need for resources (exchange processes).

2.2 Constructing a model for IOR – implementation literature and management studies

2.2.1 Explaining IOR – factors triggering cooperation/conflict

Having put to the test the literature on regime interaction, international institutions, and organizations, as well as organization theory in general, the results are unsatisfactory in terms of an appropriate theoretical framework for the focus of this study. This double neglect, from both organizational theory and IR, results in a situation in which IOR are tackled most importantly in the literature on implementation and in the field of applied management studies. According to Hanf and O'Toole (1992: 163), the early research on IOR was primarily adopted by management scholars and administrators, who as early as the 1970s assessed that 'both the formulation and implementation of public policy increasingly involve different governmental levels and agencies, as well as interactions between public authorities and private organizations' (Hanf 1978: 1). Since then, research has focused on the need for coordination and shortcomings of central control. Public choice theory presents a way to deal with the interorganizational settings for policy implementation. Within the field of applied management studies and implementation literature, the awareness 'that organizations typically operate in a relational context of environmental interconnectedness and that an organization's survival and performance often depend critically upon its linkages to other organizations' (Oliver 1990: 241) has increased steadily. However, given the heterogeneous nature of the field, the literature emerging on IOR since the 1970s is broad ranging and fragmented. Within this field, researchers such as Metcalfe (1978), Ostrom et al. (1994), and Scharpf (1997) apply game-theoretic approaches; other scholars concentrate on the concept of the 'network' (for reviews see Klijn 2008; Kenis and Oerlemans 2008). In addition, some literature has also focused on the practical question of 'what actors (managers) can do to induce interorganizational cooperation'. This type of questioning results from applied management studies, and not from organization theory. As early as 1960s, Evan (1966: 176) emphasized that – in contrast to organization scholars – 'managers are greatly preoccupied with interorganizational relations'. Throughout the years, scholars, departing from a management perspective, have identified factors that induce or hinder interorganizational cooperation: Schermerhorn (1975) sets up determinants of interorganizational cooperation that he groups into motivating conditions, associated costs, boundary permeability, organizational goals, and opportunities to cooperate. Slightly differently, Halpert (1982: 54–63) elaborates facilitators and inhibitors of interorganizational coordination, differentiating between interpretive and contextual factors. Interpretive factors, on the one hand, relate to the subjective image that organizations (namely the staff members) have of another organization. Contextual factors, on the other hand, are those that exist in the organization or the environment and affect the IOR. O'Toole and Montjoy (O'Toole and Montjoy 1984: 492; O'Toole 2003: 237) put forward three important forms of inducements for interorganizational cooperation; one of these inducements is successful exchange processes, as described, in particular in Hanf and O'Toole (1992: 172–80). Mattessich et al. (2004) review articles on factors influencing successful collaboration among organizations and compile 20 success factors that relate to the environment, membership characteristics, process and structure, communication, purpose, and resources of organizations. One criticism has been that – though aiming to provide a tool for practitioners – '[t]he factors tend to be a mix of uncontrollable environmental attributes that need to be accounted for in the management of collaboration and controllable attributes that are the essence of what needs to be managed' (2008: 400). On the basis of Lewin's (1964) idea of force fields, Sharfman et al. (1991) and Gray (2008) work with driving and restraining forces that determine interorganizational collaboration. In contrast to the other scholars mentioned earlier, they further classify the driving and restraining forces into strategic and institutional factors. This differentiation exactly takes into account that there are some factors over which participants have control (strategic factor) and others that lie beyond the partners' sphere of influence.

In sum, the previous section has shown that the literature on international regimes, institutions, and organizations as well as organization theory does not provide a theoretical framework for the analysis of IOR, as it does not address factors influencing the kind of the interorganizational relationship (be it cooperative or conflictive). In this respect, implementation and managerial literature is much more promising and will therefore form the basis of the theoretical framework (and hypotheses) to be developed further. However, it is also evident that the implementation and managerial literature is vast, uncoordinated, and, in part, difficult to operationalize for empirical research. The challenge inherent in this research is therefore filtering out the most important factors listed in the 'broad ranging and heterogeneous' (Oliver 1990: 241) literature. Without claiming to conceive a completely new theoretical model, but instead drawing from the existing literature, the merit of the present model is singling out and combining factors in a way that allows for empirical research. Accordingly, one of the deliverables of the following section lies in the construction of an innovative theoretical framework, primarily based on the general literature of IOR, bringing together interest-based, organizational, physical, and cultural factors that may have an impact on interorganizational cooperation or conflict. The following sections elaborate on the above-stated four potential explanatory factors.

2.2.2 Interest (policy and organizational self-interest)

The first factor tackles the most obvious inducement for cooperation, shared policy interest (organizations pursuing the same goal) (1984: 492; O'Toole 2003: 237). It should be pointed out, though, that the common interest incentive is not understood as a tautology. If both IOs agree on what needs to be done, for example on the division of tasks or competence sharing, there is no need for cooperation, and instead, there is a need for coordination. Consequently, this research project conceives common interest as the extent of shared interest in achieving a specific common, for example policy, goal. Following O'Toole and Montjoy, this research also considers two other forms of inducements for interorganizational cooperation: authority (an obligation for the organizations to cooperate) and exchange (organizations cooperate because they receive something in return). Regarding the first form of inducements (on this aspect see also Schermerhorn 1975: 849), one must add, though, that an authority (figure) across organizations is rare in practice (Hanf and O'Toole 1992: 172). Since in the case of EU and COE there is no such authority that is capable of enforcing interorganizational cooperation between them, this research passes over this aspect. Within the framework of this research, exchange is, in contrast, treated as a part of the interorganizational cooperation (for example IOs exchanging information) and not as an independent factor influencing it. Following this reasoning, the shared policy interest factor is left as being the most important form of inducement for interorganizational cooperation. Accordingly, this research hypothesizes that:

H 1. Interest (policy and organizational) influences interorganizational cooperation.
H 1.1. Shared policy interest increases the likelihood of interorganizational cooperation.

Closely linked to the question of shared interest in specific policy goals is the question of (multiple) competing goals that pose a threat to the policy interest of one organization. One goal that possibly competes with shared policy interest is the organizational self-interest. On the one hand, organizational self-interest may take the form of an IO aiming at extending its own sphere of competence. On this, scholars such as Downs (1967: 16) point out that 'all organizations have inherent tendencies to expand'. Therefore, it is likely that in some cases organizations give priority to distinguishing themselves over cooperating with another organization. On the other hand, organizational self-interest may materialize when IOs feel threatened by other organizations. Halpert (1982) sums up the scholarly results on this issue by stating that specifically organizational leaders may perceive that cooperation does not only 'threaten them in terms of loss or fragmentation of authority, but also does endanger their organizations in terms of loss of either total identity or program identity'. In cases of perceived loss of autonomy and turf, there is little likelihood for successful cooperation. Thus, one can hypothesize that:

H 1.2. The absence of organizational self-interest increases the likelihood of interorganizational cooperation.

2.2.3 Organizational characteristics

The second factor can be described as *organizational characteristics*. Scholars such as Downs (1967: 50), Allison (1971: 79–80,164–6), and

Scharpf (1978: 347) point out the need to decompose organizations into fragmented or multiple actors rather than treating them as unitary actors. Following Knoke (2008: 460), this research holds the view that 'inside every organization are interest groups with their own frequently conflicting, organizational goals that may make an organization clearly distinguishable from an assumed unitary rational actor'. Since organizational units (departments) involved in the IOR are most often not fully detached from other units and/or cannot act independently for themselves, IOR research has to bear in mind the possible constraints arising from these complex settings. By treating organizations as multiple actors, it follows that the 'complexity of joint action' (Pressman and Wildavsky 1974: 87) – expressed in the number of actors and decision points – increases. To put it bluntly, the more the actors involved, the more difficult the interorganizational cooperation; this of course applies to intraorganizational cooperation as well. Hence, this research proposes the following hypothesis:

H 2. As the complexity of joint action (number of actors and decision points) within an organization decreases, the likelihood of interorganizational cooperation increases.

2.2.4 Socialization

The third factor taken into account can be framed as the 'socialization' factor, which splits into two interactive aspects: ways of seeing the world and trust. First, since IOs are (and remain in spite of interorganizational interaction) independent and autonomous actors, 'the differing routines and specialized languages, not to mention distinct ways of seeing the world' (O'Toole 2003: 235) pose tremendous challenges to interorganizational cooperation. Following Barnett and Finnemore (1999: 719), one could also refer to it as the organization's culture, as 'an organization's culture, understood as the rules, rituals, and beliefs that are embedded in the organization (and its subunits), has important consequences for the way individuals who inhabit that organization make sense of the world' (Barnett and Finnemore 1999: 719). In order to better understand the other organization's culture, common settings for communication are needed. According to O'Toole and Montjoy (1984: 492), 'organizations tend to develop routines, or standard operating procedures, by which personnel interact in regular and predictable ways to solve regular and predictable problems'.

Second, the 'socialization' factor looks at the individual unit, that is, the persons involved in the IOR. A key topic in the literature, which strongly influences interorganizational settings, is trust (Bachmann and Zaheer 2008: 533). According to the contact hypothesis, this research assumes that trust can be fostered by interorganizational social interaction (Pettigrew 1998: 70; Schruijer 2008: 424), which is expected to 'blur the boundaries between organizational units and stimulate the formation of common interests that, in turn, support the building of new exchange or cooperative relationships' (Tsai 2002: 181). Informal social interactions might take the form of a joint lunch or a 'good-natured drink' after an official meeting. In the same token, Ring and Van de Ven (1994: 95) argue that 'in the temporal development of a cooperative IOR, social-psychological processes will create a separate set of pressures to preserve the relationship'. This of course applies only to situations in which assigned individuals do not change. Personnel turnover has the effect of restarting the development from a scratch (Ring and Van de Ven 1994: 103–5).

H 3. A high degree of socialization between two IOs (similar ways of seeing the world and trust between the personnel involved in the IOR) increases the likelihood of interorganizational cooperation.

2.2.5 Physical opportunity

The fourth factor, physical opportunity for interorganizational cooperation, alludes to the fact that the external environment and the existing internal capacities of IOs impact on the IOR. Based on Schermerhorn (1975: 852) and Egeberg (2003: 118), this research suggests that at the external environment level, the geographic proximity of potential partners is crucial to interorganizational cooperation. As technology (communication and transport) has advanced since the 1970s, the actual geographical distance might not be so important anymore; for example, a good transport system facilitates interorganizational cooperation. Nevertheless, the proximity between actors remains a factor (for example it is expected to make a difference whether the actors are located in different cities or are on-site). At the intraorganizational level, there is the question of whether slack resources are available – and can be easily mobilized – to build and explore interorganizational cooperation (Schermerhorn 1975: 852; Mattessich et al. 2004: 27). On this note, scholars such as Mattessich et al. (2004: 12) speak of environmental characteristics influencing the IOR: 'The group [of actors involved in the IOR] may be able to influence or affect these elements in some way, but it does not have control over them'.

H 4. The physical opportunity influences interorganizational cooperation.
H 4.1. Proximity (actual geographic distance or a good transport system) between actors involved in the IOR increases the likelihood of interorganizational cooperation.
H 4.2. Existing internal capacities (for example, slack resources) of an IO increase the likelihood of interorganizational cooperation.

2.2.6 Conclusion

This chapter has applied the perspective of implementation literature and management studies on IOR and has used this literature to derive empirical expectations on the main question addressed in this book: What explains whether relations between IOs are cooperative or conflictive? Below, Figure 2.1 summarizes the theoretical framework and sets out the factors that impact on the nature of the IOR, facilitating or hindering interorganizational cooperation. Although the factors are mutually dependent, it goes without saying that the factors are not assumed to be equally important; for example, the policy interest factor is expected to be more decisive in fostering interorganizational cooperation than the physical opportunity factor, which, of course, exerts influence but is rather (seen as) an intervening variable.

The hypotheses derived from the implementation literature and management studies will be subjected to empirical analysis in the case

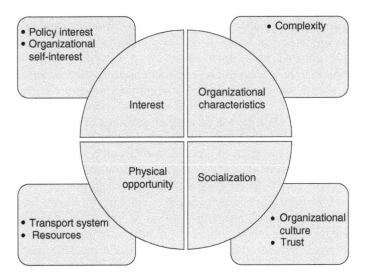

Figure 2.1 Factors influencing interorganizational relations

studies (Chapters 4–8). Each empirical chapter concludes with an evaluation of the empirical data through the theoretical lenses outlined earlier.

2.3 IOR – the dependent variable

While the previous section focused on the explanatory factors, this section briefly deals with this research's dependent variable. The dependent variable, the IOR, can be best displayed as a continuum ranging from cooperation to conflict. On an abstract level, this research understands *cooperation* (in its highest value) as a 'joint action by two or more parties for mutual benefit' (Bish 1978: 22). As distinct from cooperation, *coordination*, which is seen as 'the extent to which organizations attempt to ensure that their activities take into account those of other organizations' (Hall et al. 1977: 459), can therefore be understood as an essential pre-stage to or an integral part of cooperation. In the same way, Simon (1961: 72) argues for more clarity in this context and suggests using 'the term "cooperation" for activity in which the participants share a common goal, and "coordination" for the process of informing each as to the planned behaviours of the others. Hence, cooperation will usually be ineffective – will not reach its goal, whatever the intentions of the participants – in the absence of coordination'.

From a more practical point of view, one might ask what shape the interorganizational relationship can take. One end of the continuum forms the *cooperative interorganizational relationship*. Cooperation, on the one hand, can refer to the assignment of tasks, responsibilities, and competencies of the organizations. On the other hand, it can draw on different dimensions of one task, meaning that organizations deploy specific instruments complementarily to perform certain subtasks (Peters 1995: 277–9). Two other aspects of cooperation also seem worth highlighting: first, the process of cooperation may take place through formal or informal channels (Schopler 1987: 707–8). Second, the quality of cooperation or conflict can vary (Biermann 2008: 166) (for example information exchange may be substantial or formalistic).

The other end of the continuum forms the *conflictive interorganizational relationship*. This research conceives conflict as a broad category, comprising competitive elements (rivalry) as well. Organizations can compete for competencies, resources, and functional and political influence (Peters 1995: 278). It is also possible that one organization deprives the other organization of relevant information or even counteracts the rival. Although private profit-making firms are willing to engage in conflict with one another, scholars argue that organizations tend to avoid all-out struggles because they fear detailed investigations that would reveal their shortcomings (Downs 1967: 23). Concluding this section, it appears that organizations are eager not to call out conflictive elements in order to avoid 'bad publicity'. In the case of the EU and the COE, Stivachtis and Habegger (2011: 172) state that the 'desire to coexist is felt by both organizations'. Hence, this research follows Biermann (2008: 155) in presuming that conflict 'is more widespread than the cooperation rhetoric of organizations makes us believe'.

2.4 Methodology and data

Like many other research topics, IOR pose severe methodological challenges that must be overcome. Researchers concerned with interorganizational relationships have to define their level of analysis, which is either network or dyadic linkage (Whetten 1982: 107). In the present research, the level of analysis is the dyadic linkage between the EU and the COE. Subsequently, researchers need to decide on the methods. As early as 1970s, Hall (1977: 462) stated on this question: '[t]he measurement of social relationships has always been a nagging and unresolved problem for social scientists. Interorganizational relationships are no exception'.

To deal with this 'complex, variegated, multilevel phenomenon' (Benson 1975: 229), this research argues that a backward-looking, small-N, *qualitative case study* is best suited for the focus of this study, that is examining the interorganizational relationship between the EU and the COE regarding the internal human rights policy (human rights protection within the EU-27). As this research regards the IOR as a continuum, the dependent variable can occur in full variance, from cooperation (the one end of the continuum) to conflict (the other end of the continuum). The study is *backward looking*, as it seeks to explain this variance in its full complexity by analyzing the effects of a number of explanatory factors (and combinations thereof) on a single dependent variable (Scharpf 1997: 24–7). It adopts a *process-tracing* approach to uncover and explain which factors account for the state of IOR (cooperation/conflict) between IOs. In a nutshell, process tracing 'attempts to identify the intervening causal process – the causal chain and causal mechanisms – between an independent variable (or variables) and the outcome of the dependent variable' (George and Bennett 2005: 206). In terms of data collection, the study draws on qualitative field work involving *semi-structured expert interviews* (for example Burnham et al. 2004: 205–20;

Tansey 2007: 765–71; Rathbun 2008) as well as documentary research based on primary and secondary literature, and official documents. The semi-structured expert interview considers experts to be the source of information and it is particularly useful when the decisions and actions that lie behind an event need to be established, which applies to the topic of IOR. Another advantage is the possibility of expert interviews to compensate for lack and limitations of documentary evidence (Gläser and Laudel 2009: 12). See the end of this section for more information on the interviews conducted.

Empirically, this research analyzes five cases and thus can be classified as a *small-N study*. When thinking about the cases to be analyzed, two kinds of relations between the IOs are conceivable: relations dealing with institutional issues on the one hand, and relations dealing with policy issues on the other hand. Since these two types refer to different aspects of the relationship as a whole, it seems reasonable to differentiate for the sake of analytical clarity. *Relations dealing with institutional issues* can be regarded as politically sensitive and high level. *Relations dealing with policy issues* are expected to be rather operational and low level. Also it is plausible that different mechanisms (namely, different importance of specific factors) apply to these two kinds of relations, both of which are analyzed in this research. The remainder of this section gives some thoughts to the case selection.

Based on the (scarce) academic literature that exists on *relations between the EU and the COE dealing with institutional issues* (De Schutter 2007; Brummer 2008b), one can identify the following potential cases: EU FRA, the Central Intelligence Agency detention flights, the 'Disconnection Clause', and the EU Charter of Fundamental Rights. Besides the academic literature, at the more practical level is found the recent 'Memorandum of Understanding between the Council of Europe and the European Union' (COM 2007a), which can be understood as a new attempt to structure the cooperation between these two organizations. Therefore, though overlooked by the academic scholars, the MOU can also be seen as an important topic between the EU and the COE. Going through the entire population of institutional issues between the two IOs, one can see that some cases are less convenient than others for illustrating how IOR works and therefore will be omitted by this research. The Central Intelligence Agency detention flights had to be dropped due to pragmatic reasons (problems of access to interview partners). The 'Disconnection Clause' can be seen as a rather legal issue that per se does not allow for demonstrating cooperative or conflictive relations between the two IOs. However, practically applied, one will see the issue of the 'Disconnection Clause' in the COE Convention 196 recurring in the IOR in the field of fighting terrorism (see Chapter 5), one of the cases dealing with policy issues. Besides concerns and criticism of the COE toward the EU Charter of Fundamental Rights and the participation of COE representatives as observers in the Convention drafting the charter, this research classifies the EU Charter of Fundamental Rights as being a – more or less – internal issue within the EU, in which the COE was not (very much) involved; for example, there were no separate negotiations between the EU and the COE on this issue. It is therefore less convenient for illustrating how IOR works. In contrast, it proves useful to stick to the EU FRA and the MOU as they represent major issues in the EU–COE relations.

Besides the relations dealing with institutional issues, this research looks at *relations dealing with policy issues*. The population of cases is policy issues in which both organizations are engaged contemporaneously, a criterion that is crucial: there are policy issues that are irrelevant to the research project, since only the EU or the COE is tackling them. Thus, there is no organizational overlap and, hence, no interorganizational relationship between the EU and the COE that this research could possibly look at.

Within the policy fields dealt with by the EU alongside with the COE, one can further differentiate between policy fields that are relatively new to the COE and those that the COE has been handling for years, the latter of which are seen as the core competence of the COE. It would be a massive incursion in the core competences of the COE if the EU were to be successful in capturing the standard-setting tasks therein. Hence, this research argues for picking out these cases in order to assess if the fear of marginalization of the COE is justified. Following this reasoning, it is argued that, when the EU is threatening the standard-setting position of the COE in these specific core policy issues, it is most likely that the EU is able to do so in other policy issues as well. But the question one has to tackle is the following: Where to start and how to select these policy issues? Despite the fact that the COE is known as the main human rights organization in Europe and is often characterized as a highly specialized body (for example compared with the EU or the UN) dealing with human rights 'only', its range of activities is very broad (Petaux 2009: 17, 271–2). When looking at the most recent COE activity report (COE 2010a), one can witness the COE handling issues in the following categories: democracy and political affairs, human rights and legal affairs, social cohesion, education, culture, youth and sport, and public international law and the fight against terrorism. The categories consisting of human rights and legal affairs, social cohesion, and public international law and the fight against terrorism seem most promising in terms of policy substance and overlap with the EU; and the cases to be analyzed thus stem from these three broad categories. Given the empirical focus of this research, the aim is to select policy issues that are regarded to be core COE activities, policy issues that, first, the COE has been tackling for a long time, and, second, are high on the COE's agenda. On the EU side one has to pick issues that are, first, highly salient for the EU, and, second, the EU feels in charge of and has clear beliefs (that might be contrary to the COE's beliefs). The following cases selected are therefore issues both IOs are simultaneously dealing with. Additionally, they offer an interesting *variance across policy field* (JHA and social policy), and *across time*.

Within the human rights and legal affairs category, this research has singled out the issue of *data protection*, which is a highly salient issue for the EU. The EU Data Protection Directive goes back to the year 1995 (EU Directive 95/46/EC) and has remained on the agenda: data protection conflicting with counterterrorism measures (post-9/11), the FRA analyzing the impact of data protection measures (from 2007 onwards), and the Commission proposing a comprehensive reform of the data protection rules (April 2012). Nevertheless, while the EU has shown interest in data protection since the mid-1990s, the COE, pioneering this issue, opened its first convention on data protection in the early 1980s (COE 1981). Therefore, data protection can be seen as a core competence issue of the COE that is of equal interest to the EU and consequently is one of the empirical cases to be analyzed.

Within the social cohesion category, this research has selected an issue that has become particularly relevant to the EU with the 2004 enlargement: the *fight against Roma discrimination*. In 2004, the Roma became the largest ethnic minority in the EU, still facing massive discrimination and exclusion. The EU tackles the Roma discrimination on behalf of the EU anti-discrimination law (most importantly, Council Directive 2000/43/EC and Council Directive 2000/78/EC). The facts that the FRA inter alia addresses the situation of the Roma in the EU and that the EU has started organizing the Roma summits (see, for example, the 2010 Summit (Spanish Presidency 2010)), underline the importance of this issue within the EU social policy. The COE has been looking closely into the situation of the Roma since the mid-1990s, which coincides with the COE enlargement after the end of the Iron Curtain, when many former

Soviet countries joined (see, for example, COE (1995)). Therefore, both IOs are working now in the Roma field, which makes examination of the issue worthwhile.

Within the public international law and the fight against terrorism category, the choice for the fight against terrorism is obvious: to a certain extent since the mid-1990s, but at the latest since 9/11, the *fight against terrorism* has been a major issue for the EU, culminating in the appointment of a EU Counterterrorism Coordinator in March 2004 and two Council framework decisions (Framework Decision 2002/475/JHA and Framework Decision 2008/919/JHA). Given that the COE has addressed this phenomenon as early as late 1970s (COE 1977) and given that the issue can be regarded as a core competence with high activity post-9/11 (COE 2003, 2005a), this research project includes the fight against terrorism in the empirical analysis.

To sum up, since the organizational overlap is the starting point for this research, this study has selected only cases in which both IOs are contemporaneously engaged. Within the issues that are dealt with by both IOs (whether institutional or policy related), the research singles out topics that are high on the agenda for both IOs. Hence, the *institutional cases* selected are the EU FRA and the MOU between the EU and the COE. The *policy cases* offer an interesting *variance across policy field* (JHA and social policy), and *across time*. The policy issues under analysis include data protection, fight against terrorism, and fight against the Roma discrimination. It would be a massive incursion into the core competences of the COE if the EU were successful in capturing the standard-setting tasks in these policy issues. By analyzing these policy issues, this study assesses whether the fear of marginalization of the COE is justified. Table 2.1 names the cases for the IOR between the EU and the COE analyzed within this research.

Having discussed the tools of inquiry and the case selection, this paragraph gives more details on the research process. From November 2008 to April 2010, 40 semi-structured expert interviews were conducted in order to gain the relevant qualitative data for this research. Thirty-six interviews were carried out on-site in Strasbourg, Brussels, and Vienna; the remaining four interviews were conducted by telephone and e-mail. The time per interview ranges between 30 minutes and 1 hour 30 minutes. The series of in-depth interviews involves, first, officials who are directly involved with EU–COE relations and, second, members of NGOs, national administrations, and researchers who closely follow the behavior of the IOs from the outside. The officials come from the FRA,

Table 2.1   Cases and time frames of the research project

Case	Relations	Policy field	Time frame
Data protection	Policy	Justice and home affairs	1995–2009
Fight against terrorism	Policy	Justice and home affairs	2001–2009
Fight against Roma discrimination	Policy	Social policy	2004–2009
Memorandum of Understanding (MOU)	Institutional		2005–2009
EU Fundamental Rights Agency (FRA)	Institutional		2003–2009

the Commission, and the General Secretariat of the Council of the EU on the EU side, and the Secretariat General on the COE side (for more information, see Table A.1). After being carried out, the interviews were transcribed. The subsequent qualitative data analysis (Mayring 2003) was conducted through the software Atlas.ti. The theoretically informed judgments produced by this research shed light on the ways IOs react to organizational overlaps and seek to explain under which conditions cooperative or conflictive relations prevail. Since there are currently over 300 self-standing international governmental organizations operating around the world (Pevehouse et al. 2004: 106), the results are not only relevant to scholars of European integration, but also might be of relevance in their potential application to different IOs in other parts of the world (see Chapter 9 for a discussion on whether the results can be transferred to different contexts).

3
General Relations

3.1 Historical development of the relations between the two IOs – EU and COE

The legal foundations for the EU–COE relationship date back to the 1950s. While the statute of the COE (1949) itself did not provide a framework for relations with other IOs, the statutory resolution (51) 30 FE established that the 'Committee of Ministers may, on behalf of the Council of Europe, conclude with any intergovernmental Organisation agreements on matters which are within the competence of the Council' (COM 1951). This resolution can be seen as the institutional starting point for the relations of the COE with other IOs. Since then, the COE has been in touch with many IOs, the most important ones being the EU, the OSCE, and the UN (SG 2009: 2). Within the COE, informally, the EU has always been seen as the most important international partner (I-28). Formal documents referred to the COE and the EU as being 'important partners' (for example COM 2009b: 1), and the current COE Secretary General (SG) Thorbjørn Jagland has described the EU as being the COE's 'most important institutional partner' when meeting with the Commission President (COE 2009).

On the EU side, the treaty establishing the European Economic Community (EEC, 1957) already anticipated that the 'Community shall establish all suitable co-operation with the Council of Europe' (ex-Art. 230, TEC). At present, the EU's relations with IOs are laid out in article 220 Treaty on European Union (TEU) (ex-Art. 302–304, TEC). Article 220(1) TEU states:

> The Union shall establish all appropriate forms of cooperation with the organs of the United Nations and its specialized agencies, the Council of Europe, the Organisation for Security and Cooperation in Europe and the Organisation for Economic Cooperation and Development.

Hence, the EU maintains relations with IOs that may either have a worldwide membership (for example UN) or a regional membership (for example COE). Unlike COE's attitude toward the EU, the COE for the EU is only 'one organization among others' that the EU is dealing with.

Nevertheless, since the 1950s and the first relatively loose frameworks for contact with other organizations, the EU and the COE have deepened and institutionalized their relations, as can be seen in Table 3.1 which highlights the milestones of the IOR from 1959 onwards.

Following the interorganizational milestones set out in Table 3.1, the subsequent section describes the most important developments from 1959 onwards. It highlights all the existing arrangements regulating the EU–COE relations, namely, the exchanges of letters, the Joint Declaration, the MOU, and the Cooperation Agreement between the parliaments (missing from this list is the Cooperation Agreement between the FRA and the COE, which is the subject of Section 8.4.2 of Chapter 8). Additionally, it touches upon the joint programs and gives a review of the Juncker report on the EU–COE relations. For the high-level

Table 3.1   Milestones of the interorganizational relations between the EU and the COE

Year	Interaction mode	Subject matter
1959	Exchange of letters	Agreement on contact between COE, EEC, and Euratom
1987	Exchange of letters	Agreement on contact between COE and EC
1989	Quadripartite meeting	First high-level meeting between COE and EC
1993	Joint programs	Launch of codeveloped and cofinanced programs for cooperation with countries which have joined the COE since 1989
1996	Exchange of letters	Agreement on contact between COE and EU/EC
2001	Joint declaration	Agreement on contact between COE and EU/EC; first subject-related priorities
2006	Juncker report	Analysis of COE–EU relations
2007	Memorandum of Understanding	Agreement on cooperation between COE and EU/EC treating institutional- and subject-related questions
	Cooperation Agreement between PACE and EP	Agreement on increasing cooperation

Source: Adapted from Brummer (2008a: 230).

political dialogue, which took the form of the so-called quadripartite meetings, see Section 3.3.1 which deals exclusively with quadripartite meetings.

3.1.1 Milestones of the interorganizational EU–COE relations

3.1.1.1 1959 Exchange of letters

Within the EU–COE relations, 'exchange of letters' refers to nonbinding letters written between the SG of the COE and the Commission President of the EEC/EC/EU. The first exchange of letters between the COE and the EEC dates back to 18 August 1959. In this letter the then-SG of the COE, Lodovico Benvenuti, expressed the wish of the Committee of Ministers (COM) to establish close relations with the institutions of the EEC and Euratom as soon as they would be set up. This was a wish the Commission President, at that time Walter Hallstein, was happy to meet, given that the treaty establishing the EEC had anticipated that the Community should establish cooperation with the COE. In so doing they agreed that the Commission would forward the annual report on the activities of the Community to the COE. Following this annual report, the COM may invite the Commission to discuss problems of concern to the COE and, more generally, the Community. Conversely, the COE has agreed to send its own activity reports to the Commission and the Commission may invite COE experts to internal meetings concerning problems of interest to the COE (Benvenuti and Hallstein 1961 [1959]).

3.1.1.2 1987 Exchange of letters

The exchange of letters between the COE (SG Marcelino Oreja) and the EC (Commission President Jacques Delors) concerning the consolidation and intensification of cooperation, dated 16 June 1987, resulted in a number of innovations. According to the COE, the EC, represented by the Commission, would be invited to participate in the work of shared interest on various occasions (committees, meetings of the Ministers' Deputies, Conferences of Specialized Ministers). Regarding any new COE convention, the parties should consider whether a clause – allowing for the EC to become a contracting party to a COE convention or an agreement – is appropriate. High-level meetings between staff of the COE Secretariat and the Commission should be carried out periodically to examine questions of joint interest. Moreover, each side should appoint a senior official to follow the progress of cooperation and serve as a contact point. On the EU side, the Commission may invite representatives of the COE Secretariat to participate in its committees and advisory groups (Oreja and Delors 2001 [1987]). The regular political dialogue (through high-level meetings) took the form of the so-called quadripartite meetings that have taken place since 1989. For more information, see Section 3.3.1 dealing exclusively with quadripartite meetings.

3.1.1.3   *1993 Joint programs*

In contrast to the quadripartite meetings, which constitute the high-level political forum for the exchange of views, the joint programs can be regarded as a practical form of cooperation between the two IOs. Since 1993, approximately 180 Commission–COE joint programs have been conducted predominantly in new COE member states, which at that time were not (or not yet) EU member states. The geographical focus lies on Eastern Europe, South Caucasus, South Eastern Europe, and Turkey. The joint programs aim at strengthening democracy, the rule of law, and respect for human rights. As a rule, the joint programs are cofinanced; however, funding is only rarely shared on a 50–50 basis. In most cases, the EU provides the funds (about 80 per cent), whereas the COE – responsible for implementing the project in the specific country – provides the staff. With this monetary contribution through the joint programs, the EU provides up to about 20 per cent of the COE budget (I-14; I-27).

In this big field of activity, there are some displeasures and criticism on both sides. On the COE side, the criticism is the following: resulting from the distribution of money, the COE often only takes up the role of an executive partner, a necessity for the COE given its budgetary restrictions. Therefore, the 'joint programs' are seen as a cheap alternative for the EU because the COE has the unassailable standards and its own staff (I-5). In other words: '[T]he joint activity was hardly joint activity: they gave us the money and we did the job. So in actual fact we were sort of being contracted' (I-6). Conversely, the EU criticizes the lack of visibility of the EU's contribution to the joint programs on site, maintaining that the COE only communicates the COE's contribution and does not mention that 'all this is only possible because of the funding of the Commission' (I-20; I-22; I-23).

3.1.1.4   *1996 Exchange of letters*

On 5 November 1996 a new set of letters supplemented the arrangement concluded on 16 June 1987. According to the former Commission

President, Jacques Santer, the 1987 exchange of letters needed to be revised and aligned according to day-to-day needs:

> In their different ways both organisations work together in providing Europe with an institutional framework. Their activities, which are usually complementary, now require increasing co-ordination in the light of the respective goals of the Union and the Council of Europe's Statute.
>
> (Santer and Tarschys 2001 [1996]: 9)

In this letter, the Commission aims at strengthening its involvement in the work of the COE. At the invitation of competent COE authorities, the meetings and activities of the COM, Ministers' Deputies, rapporteur groups, and any other working party convened by the COE will henceforward be open to the Commission. The Commission will participate as an observer, without voting rights and involvement in the COE's internal decision-making process. In December 1996, the COM carried the exchange of letters forward and agreed to, generally, 'invite the Commission to participate in the meetings of the Ministers' Deputies [...] as well as in all subsidiary groups in which it has an interest' (COM 1996). At the same time the COE 'reaffirms its interest in being invited to participate in those Commission departmental meetings in Brussels which will consider matters of mutual interest' (COM 1996).

3.1.1.5 2001 Joint Declaration

Unlike the previous exchanges of letters, the 'Joint Declaration on Cooperation and Partnership' signed on 3 April 2001 sets out subject-related objectives. The cooperation between the two IOs aims at strengthening democracy, rule of law, and respect for human rights. Apart from that, cooperation shall be extended to social cohesion, research, ethical questions, and the field of education and culture, all objectives on which the COE Secretariat and the relevant Commission units shall consult each other. Moreover, the Joint Declaration introduces an annual meeting, the so-called Senior Officials' meeting, which should give officials of the Commission and the COE the opportunity to decide on objectives, conceive activities, observe joint programs, and evaluate their implementation (Patten and Schwimmer 2001).

Nonetheless, the 2001 Declaration as well as the preceding exchanges of letters 'were restricted in scope and substance' (Polakiewicz 2009: 11). Only the Commission signed and adopted the texts, and consequently the documents did not cover intergovernmental activities of the Council of the EU, albeit working relations and meeting mechanisms did emerge between the Council of the EU and the COE, for example meetings between the Troika of the Article 36 Committee of the EU and the COE (see Section 3.3.3 dealing exclusively with the Article 36 Troika (CATS) meetings).

3.1.1.6   *2006 Juncker report*

The Third Summit of Heads of State and Government of the COE, which took place in Warsaw in May 2005, stipulated the realignment of the principal tasks of the COE for the future (COM 2009b). This reorientation contained the long-term positioning of the COE within the European integration process – and therefore above all its assertiveness toward the EU (Brummer 2008a: 230). The final declaration states on this issue:

> We are resolved to create a new framework for enhanced co-operation and interaction between the Council of Europe and the European Union in areas of common concern, in particular human rights, democracy and the rule of law.
>
> (COM 2005a: article 10)

The Action Plan of the Summit substantiated this general claim. According to the Action Plan, a MOU between the COE and the EU shall be drafted. Following ten guidelines, the MOU shall create a new framework of enhanced cooperation and political dialogue (COM 2005b: Chapter IV.1).

To complete the new foundation of the relations between the COE and the EU, the Heads of State and Government asked Jean-Claude Juncker, Prime Minister of Luxembourg, to prepare, 'in his personal capacity', a report on the COE–EU relationship (COM 2005a: article 10). Juncker submitted the report 'Council of Europe–European Union. A sole ambition for the European continent' less than a year later, in April 2006. Juncker began on the basis of an assumption that both organizations have the same origins. Hence, they should not be considered rivals, but on the contrary complement each other. In practice, however, he found that the relations remain unsatisfactory:

> Although each has enriched the other, the two organisations remain at best a shaky team. Although each has borrowed from the other, they have never been able to make themselves permanently complementary.
>
> (Juncker 2006: 2)

The report itself deals first with the main subject-related issues – human rights, democracy, and rule of law – as well as with the joint programs, the EU's Neighborhood Policy, youth, education, cultural cooperation, and intercultural dialogue. Second, it analyzes the existing consultation and cooperation mechanisms. Third, the report covers the question of the EU's accession to the COE. Finally, Juncker compiles 15 final recommendations for the partnership between these two organizations, among which one can find the claim for the EU's accession to ECHR and the call for EU bodies to recognize the COE as the Europe-wide reference for human rights. Also, Juncker emphasizes the (then future) Fundamental Rights Agency's need to deal exclusively with fundamental rights regarding the implementation of EU law (Juncker 2006).

3.1.1.7   2007 Memorandum of Understanding

As foreseen in the Action Plan of the Warsaw Summit of the COE, an MOU between the COE and the EU was adopted in May 2007. The MOU expresses principles of cooperation before it goes on to mention the focal areas of cooperation (human rights, rule of law, democracy, democratic stability, intercultural dialogue, education, youth, and social cohesion). The last part of the MOU designs the arrangements for cooperation (for example meetings and mechanisms), mentions the joint programs, and discusses the visibility of the partnership and the follow-up (COM 2007a). For an in-depth analysis of the MOU, see Chapter 7.

3.1.1.8   2007 Cooperation Agreement between PACE and EP

The request for interparliamentary cooperation in the Juncker report resulted in a Cooperation Agreement that was signed by the PACE and the EP in November 2007. The Agreement aims at improving the cooperation as well as increasing synergies, and stipulates joint meetings and hearings in order to achieve these goals. Moreover, the Agreement allows for the integration of representatives of one parliament into committee-level work of another parliament through invitations for members and rapporteurs of the corresponding committees and regular contacts between rapporteurs (COE 2007b). Although the former president of the PACE, René van der Linden, evaluates the Cooperation Agreement as a 'milestone' for the PACE–EP relations, it has not met these expectations. Following the negotiations of EU accession to the ECHR, the cooperation between PACE and EP gained new impetus and a PACE–EP Joint Informal Body was established, and it has met twice in 2011 (PACE 2011).

3.2   Actors in the relations between the EU and the COE

Whereas the previous section introduced the general interorganizational milestones in the history of the EU–COE relations, this section focuses and introduces the respective actors involved. First, the perception of EU and COE as international organizations will be discussed (Section 3.2.1). Three subsequent subsections deal with EU actors, namely, the Commission (Section 3.2.2), the Special Representative of the Commission to the COE (Section 3.2.3), and the General Secretariat of the Council of the EU (Section 3.2.4). The last two subsections pay attention to the COE actors, namely, the Secretariat of the COE and the SG (Section 3.2.5), and the Liaison Office of the COE with the EU (Section 3.2.6).

3.2.1   The EU and COE as international organizations

To reach a better understanding, it is necessary to clarify the terms 'international regime', 'international institution', and 'international organization'. International regimes can be described as 'sets of implicit or explicit principles, norms, rules, and decision-making procedures around which actors' expectations converge in a given area of international relations' (Krasner 1983: 2), yet they are not actors. Similarly, international institutions can be defined as 'a set of rules that stipulate the ways in which states should cooperate and compete with each other' (Mearsheimer 1994/95: 8). International organizations, by contrast, are 'material entities possessing physical locations (or seats), offices, personnel, equipment, and budgets' (Young 1989: 32). Hence, IOs can be considered to be autonomous, purposive actors and can be further classified into nongovernmental and intergovernmental organizations.

Nevertheless, in order to meet the needs of this research project, a broader, sociological definition of organizations is required. Hence, from a sociological perspective, an organization can be described as 'a collectivity with relatively identifiable boundary, a normative order, authority ranks, communication systems, and memberships coordinating systems; this collectivity exists on a relatively continuous basis in an environment and engages in activities that are usually related to a goal or a set of goals' (Hall 1972: 9). This definition clearly exceeds the definition of Young (which is in fact concerned only with what organizations possess) and allows the treatment of organizations as social systems that have an environment and interact with other social systems. Hence, organizations are considered to be open social systems, and this definition is to be used in this research.

Before scrutinizing the actors in the IOR, one has to be aware of the fact that the two organizations can vary significantly in their tasks, purpose, and size. Yet, the research at hand considers both as IOs, even though one might characterize the EU as being an 'unusually ambitious intergovernmental organization' (Jönsson and Strömvik 2005: 13). The EU and the COE differ in terms of institutional attributes such as access to membership, policy coverage, institutional apparatus, decision procedures and processes, and mechanisms to ensure output compliance (MacMullen 2004: 409–23). Thus, the EU is, at least partly, a supranational arrangement, whereas the COE is mainly, but not exclusively, an intergovernmental entity.

Moreover, the EU and the COE have highly differing financial resources at their disposal. The COE budget for 2010 amounts to € 211 million (COM 2009e), which means a zero real growth of member states' contributions. Given that the COE has been suffering from zero real growth for many years already (Strasser 2000: 135; Taylor 2008: 1249), this does not come as a surprise. As a result, the COE's budget 'is widely perceived as insufficient to meet its mandate' (De Schutter 2008: 514). On the contrary, the EU experiences increasing budgets, and the adopted 2010 budget will amount to € 141.5 billion (EP 2010). However, while the COE dedicates its entire budget to the subject area of human rights as well as legal and cultural cooperation in the 47 COE member states (COM 2009e), the EU spends only a minimum of the total budget (1.2 per cent), which equals € 1.0 billion, to the subject areas of freedom, security, and justice in the 27 EU member states (Commission 2010b: 7–8). In addition to the discrepancy in their financial resources, the size of bureaucracy, in terms of human resources, also varies significantly: 2000 persons are working for the COE (the ECtHR included), whereas the EU employs 30,000 civil servants (Brummer 2008a: 256; Taylor 2008: 1249). Additionally, the COE lags behind the EU in terms of media attention and political weight. While the COE can gain political support from the EU, the EU does not need political support from the COE (I-5; I-15). Overall, the two IOs are not on an equal footing with regard to their means. This unequal allocation of resources is also reflected in the interorganizational relationship: especially, but not exclusively, from the COE side, the relationship is seen as imbalanced (I-3; I-4; I-5; I-14; I-28; I-31), with the main points of criticism being imbalanced reciprocal representation and access to information. In his report, Juncker (2006: 28) also elaborates on this issue and states: 'Balanced reciprocal representation is not a feature of relations between the EU and the Council of Europe'. While in Strasbourg the EU is allowed to attend any meeting (for example the Minister's Deputies meeting and all kinds of working party meetings) and speaks on behalf of the EU member states, in Brussels the EU does not show the COE the same level of official recognition nor the same systematic access to information. Even though the COE's officials are consulted, consultation is not systematic and it takes place before the EU working groups. The EU working groups and meetings of the COREPER (Committee of Permanent Representatives) are not open to COE's experts. Juncker goes on to criticize the fact that COE officials are consulted on a merely ad hoc basis and on the same footing as NGOs. Hence, the report calls for a systematic cooperation in all areas where the EU and the COE competences coincide:

> This cooperation would be organised beforehand, when legislative initiatives were being taken and co-ordinated, or joint programmes planned, and after the event, when standards were being applied or work done on the ground.
>
> (Juncker 2006: 28)

By contrast, the COE is criticized by the EU for reacting in a rather defensive way each time the EU develops a new file with a fundamental rights dimension (I-10; I-12; I-16; I-18; I-23; I-28). Following this perspective, the COE's behavior makes cooperation difficult. The present research will recall attention to this behavior at a later date, that is Chapters 4–8 dealing with the policy and the institutional cases.

3.2.2   The main EU actors

3.2.2.1   *European Commission*

Prior to the establishment of the European External Action Service (EEAS), the Directorate-General for External Relations (DG RELEX) within the Commission was in charge of relations with the COE. After a reorganization of Directorate B in June 2009, the former unit dealing exclusively with OSCE and COE merged with the unit responsible for the UN. The new unit (B3 'Multilateral relations: UN, OSCE, Council of Europe') at that time covered the multilateral relations with all three IOs (I-17; I-28). Despite the fact that the COE is not a mere 'external affair' – most of the COE member states are EU member states as well – the unit concerned with the COE is part of DG RELEX. However, the relations between the two IOs contain an external (non-EU member states) as well as an internal dimension (EU member states). This decision results in a somewhat peculiar situation in which the staff of the unit dealing with the COE – associated with DG RELEX – oversees only one out of two dimensions, that is the external dimension (I-17). The internal dimension of the relations affects various directorates-general, for example Directorate-General for Employment, Social Affairs and Equal Opportunities (DG EMPL) and the Director-General for Education and Culture, but most importantly the Directorate-General for Justice, Freedom and Security (DG JLS). Most of the directorates within DG JLS deal with subject matters in which the COE is also engaged.

With the José Manuel Barroso Commission II (2010–2014), the structure of the units and services underwent some modifications. In July 2010 the former DG JLS divided into two separate directorates-general: the Directorate-General for Justice (DG JUSTICE) and the Directorate-General for Home Affairs (DG HOME). In simple terms, the new DG JUSTICE deals with fundamental rights (for example data protection), criminal justice, and civil justice, whereas the DG HOME tackles internal security (for example fight against terrorism), immigration/asylum, and migration/borders. Accordingly, new posts were established, that is, the Commissioner for Fundamental Rights. As of January 2011, DG JUSTICE subsumed former tasks of DG EMPL by gaining the new Directorate D dealing with questions of equality, inter alia nondiscrimination policy and the Roma coordination.

Regarding relations with the COE, the staff of B3 in DG RELEX describes itself as the coordinator: in order to know what is happening in other policy fields, the unit responsible for relations with the COE in DG RELEX organizes so-called interservice group meetings, usually attended by about 20 persons working on different subject matters. On a monthly basis, colleagues from various DGs and services who have frequent interactions with the COE are invited to the meeting. Ideally, the various DGs and services have a coordinator themselves, who they send to the interservice group meetings. The DG RELEX' task in this process is threefold: first, to inform the participants about important developments; second, to monitor the relations of the various DGs and services with the COE; and third, to coordinate input from the DGs and services, for example, to the yearly stocktaking document of the COE. When the COE reviews the implementation of the MOU, DG RELEX collects information from the various DGs and services and channels it through their ambassador to the COE to be taken into account (I-17).

3.2.2.2   Special representative of the European Commission to the COE

While the COE established a Liaison Office in Brussels (COM 1974b) as early as the 1970s, the EU took its time opening an office in Strasbourg. In 2005, the Commission President José Manuel Barroso made the first move toward an office and appointed a Representative of the European Commission to the Council of Europe (henceforward, the Representative). This position was itinerant, meaning that the Representative spent only a couple of days on-site in Strasbourg.

In June 2007, the Commission President transformed the position of the Representative (COM 2008a) so that the current Representative has a higher hierarchical position – the incumbent is an ambassador – and additionally spends more time, that is four out of five days, in Strasbourg. In December 2008, the Commission made the decision to open a delegation at the COE. The new office, the Delegation of the EU to the COE, officially opened in January 2011 (Ashton 2011). In terms of staffing, the EU office enlarged: the current Ambassador and Head of Delegation is working together with three (new) Deputies to the Head of Delegation dedicated to different policy issues.

In his report, Juncker welcomed the idea of opening an EU office in Strasbourg at the COE, which at that time was already on the horizon. Moreover, he appreciated the fact that the Representative was to become resident. His only disapproval was of the abstention of the Council of the EU from this activity:

> Less encouraging is the EU Council's decision not to participate in this operation. It would help to strengthen the ties between the two organisations if the EU established an office with resources commensurate with the strategic importance of co-operation with the Council.
>
> (Juncker 2006: 28)

The former Delegation of the Commission to the COE consisted of only one staff member, whose workload was immense (the order does not necessarily mirror the importance of the tasks): first, representing the Commission at COE's activities and meetings (for example working groups of the Ministers' Deputies); second, informing the various units in the Commission about developments in Strasbourg; third, informing the EU member states of developments in Brussels; fourth, assuring that contacts between the organizations ran smoothly ('fire brigade type of job'); fifth, assisting the EU Presidency (for reasons of readability, this research refers to the 'EU Presidency' when in fact it is the Presidency of the Council of the EU). Whereas the first three tasks of the Representative are self-explanatory, the latter two tasks need to be elaborated on. The fourth task entails that the Representative is the contact person in case there are problems, for example, if the EU fails to meet some of the *acquis* of the COE. Should this occur, the Representative acts as the 'fire brigade', that is, making sure that the persons involved start talking to each other and try to understand what the other organization had been doing. By contrast, when the Representative does not hear about certain issues, it implies that IOR are good. Providing the EU Presidency with support for its coordination role is the fifth task: when the COE tackles policies that are of EU competence, the EU Presidency is supposed to coordinate the position of the Union. If so, the EU presidencies, especially the smaller member states, turn to the Commission, the Representative, for advice.

The coordination process is institutionalized: every Monday, the Representative participates in the so-called EU coordination meeting at the COE hosted by the EU Presidency. These meetings, attended by all 27 ambassadors of the EU member states, aim at finding common positions on issues tackled at the weekly COM's Deputies meeting. The EU Presidency, with input from the member states and the Commission, sets the agenda. The issues discussed can be both external relations and internal issues. In these meetings, the Representative also takes the opportunity to inform EU member states of what has happened in Brussels over the course of the past week (I-28).

3.2.2.3 *General Secretariat of the Council of the EU*

Similar to the organization of the Commission, the General Secretariat of the Council of the EU (henceforward, General Secretariat of the Council) consists of directorates-general. Prior to the establishment of the EEAS, one could find the desk-officer for the COE within the DG 'External and Political–Military Affairs' (DG E). The desk-officer for the COE was a staff member of the Directorate 'Western Balkans Region, Eastern Europe and Central Asia' and held the position of a desk-officer for a specific country of the region and for the COE at the same time. One part of the work of the desk-officer for the COE is to host the Council working party on the Organization for Security and Co-operation in Europe and the Council of Europe (COSCE), which takes place on a monthly basis and deals with matters related to the COE (as well as to the OSCE), 'notably those pertaining to the Common Foreign and Security Policy'

(Council 2008a: 116). In order to discuss COE-related matters, the COSCE working party invites members, for example directors-general, from the COE two or three times per EU Presidency (I-21).

As is the case for the Commission, the person dealing with the COE in the General Secretariat of the Council is also attached to the unit responsible for external relations. However, compared with the Commission, the structure differs in the sense that the COE desk-officer is not part of a unit dealing with IOs, but of a geographical unit. Following this structure, one could assume that the COE is exclusively seen as a partner for cooperation in non-EU member states.

Besides DG E, the Directorate-General H 'Justice and Home Affairs' (DG H) is the most involved in relations with the COE. The unit 'coordination team' therein covers the external relations, for example, not only with the United States, but also with the COE, in the Justice and Home Affairs (JHA) field. Therefore, even within the JHA field, the COE is seen as partner for external relations (with non-EU member states) rather than for internal issues. Concerning the COE, the Coordination Team has agreed to distribute information from the COE for the General Secretariat of the Council (for example invitations for working group meetings, documents), and is also involved in the preparation of the meeting between the Troika of the Article 36 Committee of the EU and the COE (I-15), which will be discussed in Section 3.3.3.

3.2.3 The main COE actors

3.2.3.1 *Secretariat of the COE / Secretary General*

Although strictly legally speaking it has only two main organs, the COM and the PACE, the COE rests on four pillars: 'the Committee of Ministers, its decision-making body; the Parliamentary Assembly, its deliberative body; the Congress of Local and Regional Authorities, which speaks for those authorities, and the Secretariat, its executive arm, which is led by the Secretary General' (Petaux 2009: 14). The SG is regarded as the 'natural spokesperson for the Organisation as a whole' (COM 2000), who comments on political events and ongoing developments through press releases in the name of the COE.

Within the COE Secretariat, the directorates and the directorates-general assist and support the development, the implementation, and the monitoring of COE standards. Externally, they establish contacts with relevant institutions in the COE member states as well as non-member states, other IOs, and NGOs (Brummer 2008a: 125–32). Prior to the reform of the COE Secretariat structure, the Directorate for External Relations (DER) was responsible for relations with the EU, as well as other IOs and nonmember states. Similarly to DG RELEX in the Commission, the DER coordinated and monitored the relations of the various DGs with other organizations. For example, for the evaluation of the implementation of the MOU, the DER compiled information on the IOR of other units in the Secretariat of the COE. In addition to the high-level quadripartite meetings, which take place once every Presidency period, the staff of the DER met the staff of DG RELEX at the annual Senior Officials' meeting (I-3; I-28). Unlike the DER, the DGs, for example Directorate-General of Human Rights and Legal Affairs (DGHL) and Directorate-General of Social Cohesion (DG III), are topical units of the COE Secretariat, which ideally are connected with their respective thematic counterparts in the Commission as well as the General Secretariat of the Council.

3.2.3.2   Liaison Office of the COE with the EU

The Liaison Office of the COE with the EU (henceforward, Liaison Office) is part of the DER. As early as 1974, the COM 'favoured the setting up of a Council of Europe office in Brussels for liaison with the [European] Communities in order to facilitate contacts and the exchange of information' (COM 1974b: 1). However, despite its early establishment, interest in the Liaison Office has somewhat cooled in the meantime. After 1989, the COE focused on Central and Eastern Europe, and more or less forgot about the developments in Brussels. Consequently, the first head ran the Liaison Office for 26 years. During this period of time, the Liaison Office achieved only an average performance; relations with the EU remained superficial and were limited to DG RELEX in the Commission. Since 2004, when a new head entered into office, the Liaison Office has widened its relations with the EU. On the Commission side, the Liaison Office established contacts with other DGs of interest to the COE (for example DG JLS, DG EMPL), on director-level as well as desk-officer level. Also, the Liaison Office set up closer relations with the Council of the EU (I-5).

Following the recommendation in the Juncker report, as of 2008, the COE's Brussels Office has been upgraded by a Special Representative of the SG at Ambassador's level. Juncker suggested this upgrade so that, ideally, the relationship would be balanced and, therefore, the head of the Liaison Office would be able to 'enjoy the same level of official recognition or the same systematic access to information as the EU representative in Strasbourg' (Juncker 2006: 28).

3.3   Meeting mechanisms

This section highlights the different kinds of meeting mechanisms, including the high-level quadripartite meetings (3.3.1), the Senior Officials' meeting in the external relations field (3.3.2), and the Article 36 Troika (CATS) meetings in the JHA field (3.3.3).

3.3.1   Quadripartite meetings

The regular political dialogue (through high-level meetings), mentioned in the exchange of letters in 1987, was enforced in 1989 by the meeting of the Council of the European Communities on 20 March 1989 (GS 1989) and the Declaration of the COM on 5 May 1989 (COM 1989). The quadripartite meetings are supposed to bring together the Commission and the Presidency of the Council of the EU with the Presidency of the COM and the SG of the COE on a regular basis. In these meetings, the aim is to 'create reciprocal awareness of programmes, mutual interests and possible joint activities' (COM 1989). While the first documents only stipulate that the quadripartite meetings should be held regularly, the 1996 conclusions of the Council of the EU and the Commission on arrangements for cooperation between the EU and the COE state that the quadripartite meetings 'will as a rule be held every six months' (Commission 1996).

Throughout the years, the presidencies of the COE and the EU have arranged 29 quadripartite meetings, the first of which took place in Paris on 11 July 1989 (COM 2006c). As can be seen in Table 3.2, the quadripartite meetings primarily took place either in Brussels or in Strasbourg, but some, also in other cities like Paris, Luxembourg, and recently in Madrid. The frequency of the meetings differs between three months (November 2006–February 2007) and three and a half years (November 1991–April 1995). In the latter period, no quadripartite meeting was organized because of the repeated difficulty of finding a date that suited everyone's schedule. On the one hand, the EU focused to a greater extent on internal developments, since the negotiations preceding the TEU fell during this time period. On the other hand, the Presidencies of the COM of the COE and the Council of the EU partly overlapped, that is, UK (November–December 1992) and Belgium (November–December 1993) (COM 2006c, 2009f).

When looking at the participants quoted in Table 3.2, one can see that, on the COE side, the SG attended all quadripartite meetings, except for one in 2008. On the EU side, however, the Commission President – as originally desired by the COE (COM 1989) – participated in only four quadripartite meetings. The Commissioner for External Relations and

Table 3.2 Participation at quadripartite meetings between the COE and the EU

		Quadripartite meetings			
		COE		**EU**	
	Date and place	**Presidency**	**SG**	**Presidency**	**Commission**
1.	11.07.1989 Paris	Norway	SG	France	President
2.	25.03.1990 Lisbon	Portugal	SG	Ireland	"
3.	07.10.1990 Venice	San Marino	SG	Italy	"
4.	15.05.1991 Strasbourg	Sweden	SG	Luxembourg	SG
5.	20.11.1991 Strasbourg	Sweden and Switzerland	SG	Netherlands	"
6.	07.04. 1995 Paris	Cyprus	SG	France	Member
7.	06.11.1995 Madrid	Czech Republic	SG	Spain	"
8.	23.10.1996 Strasbourg	Estonia	SG	Ireland	"
9.	28.04.1997 Luxembourg	Finland	SG	Netherlands	President and Member
10.	15.09.1997 Brussels	France	SG	Luxembourg	Member
11.	01.04.1998 Strasbourg	Germany	SG	UK	"
12.	07.10.1998 Strasbourg	Greece	SG	Austria	"
13.	10.02.1999 Strasbourg	Hungary	SG	Germany	"
14.	06.10.1999 Strasbourg	Iceland	SG	Finland	"
15.	14.03.2000 Strasbourg	Ireland	SG	Portugal	"
16.	03.04.2001 Strasbourg	Latvia	SG	Sweden	"
17.	20.11.2001 Brussels	Lithuania	SG	Belgium	"
18.	25.09.2002 Strasbourg	Luxembourg	SG	Denmark	"
19.	17.06.2003 Luxembourg	Moldova	SG	Greece	Director-General of Enlargement
20.	23.03.2004 Brussels	Netherlands	SG	Ireland	Member

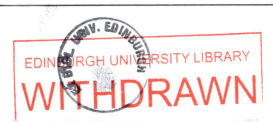

52

Table 3.2 (Continued)

Quadripartite meetings				
	COE		EU	
Date and place	Presidency	SG	Presidency	Commission
21. 16.03.2005 Brussels	Poland	SG	Luxembourg	Member
22. 15.03.2006 Strasbourg	Romania	SG	Austria	Commissioner for External Relations and European Neighborhood Policy
23. 03.11.2006 Brussels	Russian Federation	SG	Finland	Director for Multilateral Relations and Human Rights
24. 13.02.2007 Brussels	San Marino	SG	Germany	Deputy Director-General, DG RELEX
25. 23.10.2007 Strasbourg	Serbia	SG	Portugal	Commissioner for External Relations and European Neighborhood Policy
26. 10.03.2008 Brussels	Slovakia	SG	Slovenia	Deputy Director-General, DG RELEX
27. 10.11.2008 Brussels	Sweden	DSG	France	Deputy Director-General, DG RELEX
28. 11.05.2009 Madrid	Spain	SG	Czech Republic	Commissioner for External Relations and European Neighborhood Policy
29. 27.10.2009 Luxembourg	Slovenia	SG	Sweden	Acting Director-General, DG RELEX

Source: COM (2006c); COM (2006b); COM (2007b); COM (2007c); COM (2008c); COM (2008d), COM (2009c); COM (2009d); COM (2009f).

External Neighborhood Policy was present only three times. In 15 out of 29 meetings, a 'simple' member represented the Commission.

Although the quadripartite meetings are the only high-level political rendezvous between the two IOs, they usually tend to be rather short, at maximum one hour, and formal; that is discussions often remain superficial (I-14; I-20; I-31). The agenda of the quadripartite meetings can be roughly subdivided into two categories: issues concerning the relations between the EU and the COE (internal issues), those concerning current political questions (external issues). The first category contains the MOU as well as previous agreements, such as the Joint Declaration, the Juncker report, and the ongoing issue of the EU's accession to ECHR. Moreover, talks have revolved around the EU FRA and the European Court for Human Rights. In addition, the joint programs and internal developments (for example the Third Summit of Heads of State and Government of the COE) are also subjects of recurring discussions.

The second category, current political questions, primarily touches on developments in countries in South Eastern and Eastern Europe and countries of the South Caucasus. So far, Belarus, Georgia, and Serbia and Montenegro have been most often on the agenda. Other reviewed countries are Moldova, Russian Federation, Turkey, and Ukraine. Besides the above-mentioned countries, other thematic issues are discussed, such as the fight against terrorism after the 2004 bomb attacks in Madrid (COM 2006b, 2007b, 2007c, 2008c, 2008d, 2009c, 2009d).

The quadripartite meetings usually result in a concluding statement in which the EU and the COE take up joint stances on the treated issues; however, in November 2006 the 23rd Quadripartite Meeting broke this rule. Since it was not possible to settle differences, the Finish Presidency of the EU preferred not to adopt joint conclusions, and the Russian Presidency of the COM confined itself to draw up a report of the meeting. The 23rd Quadripartite Meeting was also noticeable insofar as external issues – contrary to most quadripartite meetings – were at the bottom of the agenda. Controversial issues were mainly internal issues affecting the relations between the EU and the COE, namely the MOU and the EU FRA (COM 2006b).

The 23rd Quadripartite Meeting has shown that high-level contacts between the EU and the COE are not necessarily courtesy exchanges. In fact, this meeting has revealed considerable clashes of interest between the two IOs. Questions of assertiveness and the protection as well as the extension of their own interests and spheres of influence guide the reasoning of the participants. Yet, it should be highlighted that some of the disagreements, for example, on Belarus, result from individual political preferences of the officiating presidencies (Brummer 2008a: 235).

Despite the fact that the 23rd Quadripartite Meeting brought up an intense discussion between the two IOs, the quadripartite meetings generally face two kinds of problems: first, they are not high-level meetings, and second, they lack substantial outcomes. On the COE side, there is disappointment about the fact that top EU persons are missing. This, however, may be linked to the fact that the meetings often remain superficial and do not have a great political impact. So what are the reasons? On the one hand – and here one goes around in circles – this problem is connected to the participants, their availability, and their decisiveness, especially in political questions. On the other hand, sometimes the lack of outcomes results from the lack of issues to be discussed; especially if both Presidencies are EU member states, it can be difficult to have political points on the agenda every six months. Lastly, there is no specific follow-up mechanism that assures the implementation of the joint conclusions in order to avoid continuously repeating the same statements (I-5; I-14; I-20; I-28; I-31).

Thus far one can understand Juncker (2006: 25) when he states that, over the years, 'the formula has lost some of its substance' and that the 'meetings need to be up-graded, and more effective interinstitutional relations developed in general'. His words are becoming even more important given that there has been no quadripartite meeting since October 2009 (March 2011). The adoption of the Lisbon Treaty brought forth ambiguity concerning the question of who should represent the EU in quadripartite meetings, whether it is the new High Representative for Foreign Affairs and Security Policy or someone else. Additionally, there is an EU internal reflection process on the question of whether the quadripartite meeting should turn into a 'tripartite meeting', in which case the High Representative for Foreign Affairs and Security Policy would be the only high-ranking EU participant, also compensating for the EU Presidency. The question, however, is whether member states would accept this format, for example, when the 'tripartite meeting' would tackle issues not of exclusive EU competence but sensitive issues of shared competence (I-20; I-38). It remains to be seen how this reflection process will resolve in the future.

3.3.2   Senior Officials' meetings

Since the Joint Declaration in 2001, the so-called Senior Officials' meetings have taken place annually in either Brussels or Strasbourg, and brought together the director of DER (COE Secretariat) and the director for multilateral relations and human rights of DG RELEX (Commission) with their respective teams. The Senior Officials' meetings usually take place in December in order to review the cooperation between both organizations during the past year and reflect on current developments (I-20). The last senior officials' meeting took place on 8 December 2010 in Strasbourg (COE 2011a).

Officially, the Senior Officials' meetings are 'designed for planning and co-ordinating co-operation at a technical level' (COM 2009b). Given that it is mostly external relations staff who are meeting, issues concerning non-EU member states, that is the implementation of different activities in specific countries, are high on the agenda. Also, the meetings provide an opportunity to discuss and exchange views on political developments, for example, in Moldova or in Belarus. In some cases, members from other operational DGs of the Commission and the Secretariat of the COE join the meetings (I-17). However, even though the Senior Officials' meetings have an agenda that is agreed on beforehand, in the past no information, neither the agenda nor the minutes of the meetings, were made available to the public.

Contrary to past meetings, the reports of the last two senior official meetings in 2009 and 2010 are publicly available. From the last report, one can tell that the meeting had not only an external dimension (for example discussion on countries like Russia and Georgia) but also an internal dimension (for example presentation of structural changes in each organization). The internal issues tackled the creation of the EEAS, start of negotiations with a view to accession of the EU to the ECHR, and the COE reform (COE 2011a). One could argue that the growing importance of internal issues on the agenda of the Senior Officials' meetings mirrors the current developments in the relations between the EU and the COE (I-20).

Besides the external relations staff, who come together to meet at senior-official level, the personnel of the legal units also have joint meetings. In 2010, the COE suggested setting up a new consultation mechanism. The adopted mechanism, named 'mutual informal information mechanism' (MIM), foresees an informal consultation process at the desk-officer level. For the EU, it was important that MIM was an informal mechanism that was not institutionalized. Since 2011, three meetings have taken place with external (for example Neighborhood Policy) as well as internal issues (for example new EU initiatives such as the detention green paper) on the agenda.

3.3.3   Article 36 Troika (CATS) meetings

The Article 36 Troika (CATS) meeting is a personal initiative of a former civil servant of the COE who started working for the EU during the 1990s. The idea of this meeting was to set up a direct contact mechanism between the COE and the Council of the EU, since contact had previously occurred exclusively with the Commission on the EU side (I-12; I-15). Hence, since March 1997, the Troika of the Article 36 Committee of the EU – consisting of the Presidency, the incoming Presidency, the General Secretariat of the Council and the Commission – has met with representatives of the COE Secretariat once every Presidency period, with the meetings taking place either in Brussels or in Strasbourg (Council 2001a: 22).

It was necessary to set up a meeting mechanism between the COE and the Council of the EU and the presidencies, because the Commission in the former third-pillar area did not and still does not enjoy as much power as in the former first pillar (I-12). Table 3.3 lists the dates of the meetings between the Troika of the Article 36 Committee and the COE, the so-called CATS meetings, and sets out the main items on the agenda. In addition to the presidencies, who mostly send members

Table 3.3   Meetings between the Troika of the Article 36 Committee and the COE

Meeting between the Troika of the Article 36 Committee and the Council of Europe (CATS)

Date	Place	Items on the agenda Three out of the first five items on the agenda (less 'opening of the meeting' and 'adoption of the agenda')
09.11.1999	Brussels	Cyber crime, mutual assistance in criminal matters, sexual exploitation in criminal matters
26.05.2000	Strasbourg	Mutual assistance in criminal matters, cyber crime, sexual exploitation of children
13.11.2000	Brussels	Financial crime and cooperation, cooperation in the field of criminal justice, police cooperation
22.03.2001	Brussels	Financial crime and cooperation, cooperation in the field of criminal justice, police cooperation
22.10.2002	Strasbourg	Terrorism, cyber crime, assistance programs in Russia and Ukraine

24.03.2003	Brussels	Terrorism, European arrest warrant, cyber crime
27.05.2004	Brussels	Terrorism, European arrest warrant, trafficking in human beings
19.04.2005	Strasbourg	COE developments in the legal field, framework decision on combating racism and xenophobia, accession of the EU to the ECHR
04.12.2006	Brussels	Terrorism, state of play with respect to the signature and ratification of COE conventions, sexual exploitation of children
21.05.2007	Brussels	Framework decision on combating racism and xenophobia, terrorism, state of play with respect to the signature and ratification of COE conventions
24.06.2008	Brussels	Framework decision on terrorism, COE convention on mutual legal assistance, COE conventions in criminal matters
08.12.2008	Strasbourg	Framework decision on terrorism, cooperation in criminal matters, rights of the child and trafficking in human beings
19.05.2009	Brussels	COE conventions in the criminal field, terrorism, EU developments in the criminal field
08.10.2009	Brussels	Cooperation in the preparation of legal instruments, preparation of the Stockholm Program, framework decision on trafficking in human beings
21.06.2010	Strasbourg	Accession of the EU to the ECHR, procedural rights, implementation of the Stockholm Program
06.12.2010	Brussels	Cyber crime, data protection, information on current legislative initiatives at the level of EU/COE
15.06.2011	Strasbourg	Information on current legislative initiatives at the level of EU/COE, EU support for COE conventions, cyber crime
16.12.2011	Brussels	Information on current legislative initiatives at the level of EU/COE, EU support for COE conventions, data protection

Source: Council (1999); Council (2000a); Council (2000b); Council (2001b); Council (2002); Council (2003); COE (2004a); Council (2005); COE (2006a); Council (2007); Council (2008b); Council (2008c); Council (2009b); Council (2009d); Council (2010a); Council (2010b); (Council 2011b); (Council 2011a).

of their ministries of justice (or interior), the General Secretariat of the Council is mostly represented by the Director-General or the Director for Justice and Home Affairs (DG H) and their team. From the Commission, the meetings are usually attended by staff from the former DG JLS as well as occasionally by the Representative of the European Commission. On the COE Secretariat side, the Director-General of Human Rights and Legal Affairs or one of the directors of DGHL and their staff as well as the Director or the Deputy Director of the Liaison Office participate in the meetings (Council 2008b, 2008c).

In total, there are about 20 participants in each meeting, most of whom tend to know each other as many of them have either worked in the COE themselves or have been invited to Strasbourg on a regular basis. Accordingly, the meetings' atmosphere is usually friendly and personal. However, regarding the content, there is not always consensus, since, to some extent, the COE doubts the loyalty of the EU to its *acquis* (I-15).

One aim of the CATS meetings is to inform the other organization about one's own ongoing activities (for example legislative initiatives). Whereas the COE benefits from learning about what is happening in the EU, particularly about former third-pillar questions, the EU can benefit from the COE's spreading of information to all its 47 member states, even to those that are not EU member states.

A second aim of the CATS meetings is to enhance the cooperation between the two IOs. The issues touched upon in the CATS meetings revolve around new legislative initiatives, own activities of both organizations (for example conferences, programs, reports), and cooperation between the two IOs in general (for example working methods) or between specific institutions of the two IOs. Another issue complex is the cooperation with countries like Russia in the JHA field (Council 2008b, 2008c). The following quotation from 2008 tackles the question of working methods:

> [B]oth sides agreed on the importance of informing each other, as early as possible, of new policy developments that might affect the developing acquis of both the EU and the CoE. [...] Parties undertook to actively pursue these contacts and as well as *to avoid slowing down and negative interference in the effectiveness of their mutual activities*. The EU underlined nevertheless that the level of cooperation existing between the EU MS couldn't be developed at the same extent as with member of CoE/non EU MS.
>
> (Council 2008c: 5, emphasis added)

Here one can see two recurring points of contestation between the EU and the COE. Although they highlight the importance of informing one another as early as possible, the quotation speaks about the slowing down of and negative interference in the effectiveness of their respective activities. This is based on the fact that, when the EU puts forward its own policy instruments, EU member states tend to defer or even suspend the ratification process of the COE conventions. The encouragement of EU member states to ratify COE conventions to which they have acceded has to be seen in this context. By contrast, the EU retains that cooperation between the EU member states, by definition, goes beyond cooperation between COE member states, which must be seen in connection to the 'Disconnection Clause' (see Chapter 5) on the one hand, and attempts of the COE to lift EU initiatives to the COE level on the other hand (I-16; I-23; I-31). Yet, the EU agreed to publicly call upon member states to sign, ratify, and implement COE conventions, which it did in February 2009 (Council 2009f).

For the past several years, the CATS meetings have struggled with the prevailing opinion that they are a rather formalistic forum for the exchange of views, which, according to critics, has been primarily comparing notes instead of real cooperation. The timing of the meetings, usually starting at 5 pm at the earliest after a long Article 36 session, might add to the fact that there has been less of a substantial dialogue. In recent years, however, meetings have tended to become more substantial and provide an arena for real discussion. It goes without saying that the quality of these meetings also largely depends on the willingness of the EU Presidency to talk about substance and its opinion toward the COE (I-14; I.23; I-30; I-31). Currently, there are ongoing discussions as to how the CATS meetings need to be restructured following the adoption of the Lisbon Treaty.

Part II
Policy Cases

The case studies examined in this part of the book – data protection (Chapter 4), the fight against terrorism (Chapter 5), and the fight against the Roma discrimination (Chapter 6) – begin by providing the reader with an introduction to the respective issue area. As the relations analyzed tackle practical policy issues, they are expected to be rather operational and low level (compared with relations dealing with institutional issues). The chapters highlight the COE's role in the respective issue area by going through its legislative instruments and concerned bodies, for example the expert committees. Subsequently, the chapters turn to the EU's role in the respective issue area, and correspondingly scrutinize its legislative instruments and concerned bodies, for example the working groups. Then, the chapters examine the interorganizational contacts between the EU and the COE in their respective issue areas. At the core of these chapters is the subsequent analysis of the interorganizational relations between the EU and the COE in the respective issue area. The empirical cases conclude by analyzing the results against the background of the theoretical framework.

4
Data Protection

This chapter scrutinizes the IOR between the EU and the COE concerning data protection. Within this issue area, one can observe – over the time frame of 30 years – a powerful EU interested in data protection, pressuring the COE, the previous undisputed standard-setter, and heavily impacting decisions made in Strasbourg. The originally envisaged EU accession to the COE Convention 108 on data protection has never materialized. In the wake of a competitive EU directive on data protection, the COE – fearing marginalization – took a critical stance toward the EU's newfound interest. However, the EU, to an ever-increasing degree, has been pushing back the leadership role of the COE. Before tackling these issues in depth, this chapter starts out by highlighting the beginnings of data protection law at the member state level and by tackling both the COE's and the EU's roles concerning data protection.

4.1 Thirty years of data protection law

In Europe, the data protection legislation has mainly developed over the past 30 years. At the European level, one can trace the legal sources of the data protection back to the ECHR, which opened for signature in 1950 and entered into force three years later. Two articles therein are worth highlighting: Article 8 (the right to respect of private and family life, home, and correspondence) and Article 10 (the right to freedom of expression) (COE 1950). Data protection legislation balances these two fundamental rights. At the member state level, among the first data protection laws were the federal Hesse Act (1970) of Germany, the *Datalagen* in Sweden (1973), and the *Bundesdatenschutzgesetz* of Germany (1977). Toward the end of the 1970s, other countries such as France, Denmark, and Luxembourg also introduced data protection laws (Simitis 2001: 101; Cannataci and Mifsud-Bonnici 2005: 6).

4.2 The Council of Europe's role in the data protection field

4.2.1   The COE European Data Protection Convention

From the beginning of the 1970s, the COE carried out studies on the protection of individuals with regard to automatic processing of personal data. In 1973/74, the COM, the decision-making organ of the COE, was the first to adopt resolutions on data protection. Though these resolutions were not binding, they urged member states to set up data protection legislation in both the private and the public sector (COM 1973, 1974c). A number of member states enacted data protection laws within a few years of the passing of the second resolution, and others incorporated data protection as a fundamental right into their constitutions (Spain, Portugal, and Austria). However, given that the data flow went beyond national borders, and thus exceeded the capability of national laws, additional protection for individuals was required. The COE realized the need to harmonize this question at an international level, and therefore adopted the Convention for the Protection of Individuals with regard to Automatic Processing of Personal Data (ETS Nr. 108, hereafter, 'Convention 108') in 1981, after three years of preparatory work (Csonka 1996: 197). Convention 108 entered into force in 1985 and has been ratified by 43 member states so far (June 2012) (COE 2012m), and until today continues to be the only Legally binding international treaty dealing with privacy and data protection (COE 1981), setting out the principles within which a person may enjoy the right to protection of his/her personal data with regard to the free flow of information across borders. One of the Convention's basic purposes is to reconcile the two aforementioned rights of the ECHR: respect for privacy (Article 8), and the free flow of information (Article 10).

> To this end, it defines a 'common core' of basic requirements which ought to be implemented in the legislation of these contracting parties [...] with a view to providing, the obligation to take appropriate security measures for the protection of personal data stored in automated data files against accidental or unauthorized destruction or accidental loss, as well as against unauthorized access, alteration or dissemination.
>
> (Csonka 1996: 197)

Moreover, the parties to Convention 108 need to establish sanctions and remedies for the misuse of data protected by the Convention. Also, the Convention entails the set up of a consultative committee targeted at monitoring the implementation of the Convention principles in the domestic law of the contracting parties. Finally, the Convention puts forward the free flow of information principle in order to prevent 'data protectionism' (Csonka 1996: 198).

According to the COE, Convention 108's strengths are:

- its legally binding force;
- its cross-cutting scope of application. Convention 108 protects against privacy intrusions by public and private authorities;
- a comprehensive legal framework for the transfer of personal data among countries that have ratified Convention 108;
- a platform for multilateral cooperation through a Consultative Committee, where all states parties are working together on an equal footing, exchanging ideas and best practices, as well as developing new standards.

(COE 2010b: 1)

The impact of Convention 108 can be seen on various levels. First, at least 43 member states have enacted data protection legislation. In addition many member states now share similar provisions in data protection laws given the regular monitoring consultations of the committee. Second, it has provided the underlying legal framework for another regional regulation on data protection, that is, the EU Directive 95/46/EC on the protection of individuals with regard to the processing of personal data and the free movement of such data (Csonka 1996: 198; Cannataci and Mifsud-Bonnici 2005: 6).

From 1981 to 2002, the COE developed 13 sectorial recommendations (COE 2010c: 35–78) – in addition to Convention 108 that defined the rules according to each area within which personal data are processed: 'The recommendations can be considered models of how the general principles can be integrated and contextualized in the different sectors using personal data (for example in the medical and insurance sectors, and by the police)' (Cannataci and Mifsud-Bonnici 2005: 7). Though these recommendations are not binding, various member states have integrated them into their national legislative framework.

Since 2002, the legislative initiative of the COE in the field of data protection has come to a temporary halt. In May 2010, right before the Convention's 30th anniversary in 2011, the COM commissioned the

Consultative Committee to modernize Convention 108 (COE 2010b: 2), a process that will likely take several years. As a basis for discussion, a group of experts carried out a legal study on the lacunae of Convention 108 resulting from technological developments (Dinant 2010), and a public consultation process was launched in 2011. According to the road map, draft proposals should be finalized by June 2012 (COE 2012k, 2012l).

4.2.2 The COE committees of experts – CJ-PD and T-PD

Originally, the COE set up two different committees of experts in the field of data protection. To draw up the sectorial recommendations, the COE established a committee of experts on data protection in 1976, which subsequently became the *Project Group on Data Protection (CJ-PD)* in 1978. This committee was composed of experts from each member state (COE 2012g). Apart from drawing up and monitoring the recommendations, the CJ-PD also drafted guiding principles for the protection of personal data, for example, with regard to smart cards (COE 2012h).

Articles 18–20 of the Convention 108 cover and outline the set up of another consultative committee, the *Consultative Committee of the Convention for the Protection of Individuals with regard to Automatic Processing of Personal Data (T-PD)*, to which each party of the Convention appoints a representative; nonmembers have the right to be represented by an observer. The T-PD is responsible for interpreting the provisions of the Convention and improving its application. It is also concerned with the amendment of the Convention (COE 1981).

Due to financial reasons (worded 'in the concern of rationalization of resources'), the COE merged the two committees in 2003. Now both members who are parties to the Convention 108 and members who are not sit in the new enlarged T-PD, also known as T-PD+, whose tasks comprise the amendment of the Convention as well as the drafting of reports, guidelines, and guiding principles on various topics (I-10; I-32, I-33).

4.3 The European Union's role in the data protection field

4.3.1 The EU's attitude toward data protection until the end of the 1980s

Even though the EP advised the Commission as early as 1975 on the need for rules defining the conditions under which personal data may be processed, 'for more than a decade, the Commission adopted a hesitant, if not hostile, attitude' (Simitis 2001: 101). The Commission stuck to its position despite the growing number of data protection legislation in the member states or the Convention on Data Protection of the COE. The Commission at that time understood itself primarily as an economic unit that was interested in the functioning of a free and unhindered exchange of goods and services. Personal data, in this reasoning, was not considered something to be protected as an individual's fundamental right but as a simple good to be circulated.

However, the ongoing discussions at the national level as well as in the EP forced the Commission to slightly attenuate its negative attitude toward common rules (Simitis 2001: 101–2). In March 1981, the Commission recommended its member states to sign and ratify the COE Convention 108 (81/679/EEC). Even though one might think that the Commission backed down, exactly the opposite was true. The Commission exercised pressure on the COE to renounce Convention 108. To avoid endangering its adoption, the compromise was to include Article 12 paragraph 2, which states:

> A Party shall not, for the sole purpose of the protection of privacy, prohibit or subject to special authorisation transborder flows of personal data going to the territory of another Party.
>
> (COE 1981)

As far as transborder flows of personal data are concerned, this particular provision could possibly limit the protection of data substantially. It goes without saying that such an article, promoting the proliferation of data, is clearly out of place in a Convention that aims to establish barriers hindering access to personal data (Simitis 2001: 102–3). Those who were of the view that the Commission should not come up with a proposal for common rules were especially satisfied with this amendment, and they supported the idea of the EU joining Convention 108 (I-35). However, as the Convention did not allow for the EU to accede, this plan was not realized. Therefore, it was necessary to adopt an amendment to the Convention, but this did not take place until 1999 (COM 1999).

4.3.2 EU Data Protection Directive 95/46/EC

Given its attitude toward the quest for common rules described in the previous section, the Commission's 'Communication on the protection of individuals in relation to the processing of personal data in the Community and information security' of September 1990 (Commission 1990) came as a surprise. Observers could not explain the radical shift of opinion, as it appeared to them that nothing had changed since the Commission had last rejected the idea of a directive. One explanation suggests that the communication was due to the sudden pivotal function of fundamental rights at the EU level from the 1990s, which beforehand was overshadowed by the Common Market logic of free movement of goods. The Commission turned its priorities upside down (from unhindered exchange of personal data to the limits of their use), as can be seen from paragraph 10 of the Commission's Communication below:

> Since the object of national laws in this field is to protect the fundamental rights of individuals, and in particular the right to privacy, and since the Community has itself stressed the importance it attaches to fundamental rights [...] the action taken by the Community must not have the effect of reducing the level of protection, but, on the contrary, of ensuring a high level of protection throughout the Community.
>
> (Commission 1990: 5)

According to Simitis (2001: 104–5), this development is not an arbitrary change of policy, but instead reveals the EU's slow, but clear, shift from an economic to a political union. Consequently, the Commission had to reconsider its policies in order to comply with the EU's new obligation to respect fundamental rights.

In October 1995, the EP and the Council adopted the Directive 95/46/EC on the protection of individuals with regard to the processing of personal data and on the free movement of such data. When looking at this Directive, it is particularly striking how much it resembles the COE's Convention 108. Scholars' comments on this distinctive feature range from such cautious evaluations as '[the Directive] uses Convention 108 as its point of departure' (Cannataci and Mifsud-Bonnici 2005: 7) or as 'underlying legal framework', to the more straightforward assessment '[the Directive] almost entirely replicates the content of the 1981 Council of Europe Convention on Data Protection' (Juncker 2006: 13).

> Recital paragraph 11 of the Directive 95/46/EC itself states that the protection of individual's rights and freedoms contained in the Directive 'give substance to and amplify those contained in the Council of Europe Convention of 28 January 1981 for the Protection of Individuals with regard to Automatic Processing of Personal Data'.

Consequently, the Directive adds to the first generation of data protection laws whose common characteristic is the 'omnibus' approach

(Simitis 2001: 106; Cannataci and Mifsud-Bonnici 2005: 7). The 'omnibus' approach formulates very general, abstract rules, which treat different sectors all in the same way (for example hospitals, statistical offices, and police authorities). However, although the Commission already had experience in the previous legislative approaches at hand and knew of the importance of distinctly sectoral rules, it chose a strategy similar to those launched in the late 1960s and early 1970s: '[T]he opportunity to abandon the old schemes and to opt for a new type of regulation combining a few general principles with sectoral provisions specifying and detailing these principles was missed' (Simitis 2001: 108).

Subsequent to the 'omnibus' approach-directive, the EU issued sectoral data protection directives and framework decisions, as the COE had done previously with the sectoral recommendations following Convention 108. These sectoral data protection directives were Directive 97/66/EC and Directive 2002/58/EC dealing with data protection in the telecommunication and the electronic communication sectors, respectively. In 2008, the Council of the EU adopted the Framework Decision 2008/977/JHA on the protection of personal data processed in the framework of police and judicial cooperation in criminal matters, thus covered data protection in yet another sector. With this Framework Decision, the EU tried to strengthen data protection in the former third-pillar area, in which firstly Directive 95/46/EC does not apply, and in which secondly, respect for fundamental rights was previously questioned and to a large extent abandoned (Simitis 2001: 116–8; Cannataci and Mifsud-Bonnici 2005: 12). Also in the case of this Framework Decision, the COE sees the link to its *acquis*, in particular the 1981 Convention 108 as well as the 1987 Recommendation on the use of personal data in the police sector, to which, however, the Framework Decision does not explicitly refer (Council 2008c: 3).

Returning to the Directive 95/46/EC, member states were obliged to implement it within a three-year time span, as laid out in Article 32(1) of the Directive. Therefore, one of the Directive's merits is the introduction of the very first data protection laws in two EU member states, Greece and Italy. Although Greece and Italy participated in the discussions on Convention 108 and the ensuing recommendations, both countries had previously failed to adopt data protection legislation. Above all, the Directive aimed at establishing common union-wide rules for the (at that time 15) member states of the EU. Scholars, however, state that the Directive did not live up to its expectations and failed to subject the processing of personal data to rules common to all member states. This is due to the fact that the common rules are not precisely defined but only indicate the direction to be taken, a vagueness that finds its roots in the complicated history of the Directive and the many compromises that had to be found. In Simitis' view (2001: 110–5), this vagueness, which is widespread in case of conventions, is not advisable in regulations such as EU directives.

In the subsequent years, one can see the growing importance attached to data protection at the EU level: the EU Charter of Fundamental Rights (2000) prominently lists the right to protection of personal data. Besides the aforementioned sectoral directives and the framework decision, the EP and the Council adopted Regulation (EC) Nr. 45/2001 on the protection of individuals with regard to the processing of personal data by Community institutions and bodies, and on the free movement of such data. They also decided (2004/55/EC) upon the establishment of a European Data Protection Supervisor in December 2003. In addition, the FRA is interested in the impact of data protection measures (FRA 2008).

Concerning the Data Protection Directive itself, things have since calmed down. During the next 15 years, none really considered the possibility of modifying the Directive, although the time has been ripe. However, in 2009, the Commission initiated the process of reviewing the general EU legal framework on the protection of personal data, and the COE ushered in the process of modernizing Convention 108 soon thereafter. On the EU side, the aim is to modernize the Directive and integrate it with other existing EU data protection instrument. Currently, the Commission is proposing a framework consisting of a regulation (replacing the Directive) and a directive (replacing Framework Decision 2008/977/JHA) (Commission 2010a: 3, 2010d: 5, 2012a: 4). Although it remains to be seen how the different modernization processes in the EU and in the COE develop further, it deserves notice that – after 15 years in case of the EU and almost 20 years in case of the COE – both organizations have decided to review their instruments almost at the same time.

4.3.3   The EU Working Party Article 29 and Committee Article 31

Article 28 of Directive 95/46/EC stipulates the set up of independent control authorities in the member states. Article 29 complements the supervisory authorities of the member states with a supranational working party, the Working Party on the Protection of Individuals with regard to the Processing of Personal Data, also known as the *Article 29 Working Party*. The Article 29 Working Party consists of representatives of national authorities, a representative of the control authority monitoring EU institutions and bodies, and a representative of the Commission. This working party's tasks involve ensuring the uniform application of the Directive (for example by drawing up recommendations), providing expert opinions, and advising on possible changes to data protection law.

The Article 29 Working Party is not the sole commission established by the Directive. Article 31 sets up a committee that is entrusted with ensuring as well as promoting a common regulation. As opposed to the Article 29 Working Party, the so-called *Article 31 Committee* is a comitology committee assisting the Commission in implementing the Data Protection Directive. In contrast to the Working Party, the Committee consists of representatives of member states. It must be highlighted, though, that the Article 31 Committee tackles only one specific point of the Directive: its major and only role is to deal with proposals from the Commission on adequacy findings in third countries. In other words, whenever the Commission wants to declare that a specific country has an adequate level of protection, this Commission's proposal has to go through the eyes of the Committee (I-10). Having seen the tasks of the Article 29 Working Party and the Article 31 Committee, it is safe to say that only the Article 29 Working Party is potentially in contact with the COE, whereas there is almost no link between the Article 31 committee and the COE, which will be seen in the next section.

4.4 Interorganizational contacts in the data protection field

4.4.1 Reciprocal representation: T-PD Committee and Article 29 Working Party

The Commission is an observer to the COE data protection expert committee meetings, the meetings of the T-PD, which normally take place in Strasbourg. In total, there are four meetings per year: the plenary meeting of the T-PD takes place annually, and the meetings of the bureau of the committee take place three times per year (COE 2012f). The Commission has been systematically invited to these meetings since the adoption of the EU Data Protection Directive in 1995, but whether the Commission, in terms of the secretariat of the Article 29 Working Party (DG JUSTICE, Directorate C), attends the meetings regularly depends on the importance assigned to the COE by the head of the data protection unit. In some cases, the head of unit attends the meetings him/herself; in other cases he/she sends a representative, and again in other cases it is not possible for the Commission to attend due to time constraints (I-2; I-10; I-19).

The general *setting of the COE data protection meetings* is the following: normally, the T-PD bureau meetings are two to three days long, whereas the T-PD plenary meeting takes three to four days. The bureau functions as a kind of management board that prepares the agenda for the T-PD plenary, and hence their meetings are smaller, consisting of the chairs of the T-PD, a few other member states, staff from the COE Secretariat (for example T-PD secretary), scientific experts, and the observer of the Commission. In contrast, besides the aforementioned members of the bureau meetings, also one or two representatives from almost every member state sit in the plenary meetings (COE 2010d: App. 1; 2010f: App. 2). The atmosphere in the meetings is pleasant and cooperative, which is also the case in the plenary meetings. In contrast to Brussels, where the climate is tense when binding instruments are being negotiated, the atmosphere in Strasbourg is generally more relaxed (I-33). A facility – common to COE committee meetings in general – that probably adds to the pleasant atmosphere is the joint dinner that occurs once during the meeting. This tradition allows participants to discuss among themselves in an informal context, for example, the topics tackled earlier in the meetings (I-2; I-19; I-33). It goes without saying that this sociability facilitates the establishment of trust between participants.

While the previous paragraph discussed the settings of the meetings, the following three paragraphs set out the usefulness of the Commission's attendance in these meetings. The Commission's main interest in participating in these meetings is threefold:

- while participating, the Commission is able to intervene whenever a COE proposal contradicts the EU Data Protection Directive,
- attending the meetings helps the Commission to make sure that the EU member states 'behave well', that is to say they do not take a position in the COE setting not compatible to EU law,
- and finally, the Commission benefits from the COE expert studies and the ensuing discussions that tackle issues parallel to those approached in Brussels. (I-19)

The aforementioned first interest refers to the informally called *external competence* of the Commission. Since member states agreed to common rules in the EU context in Directive 95/46/EC, they are not allowed to negotiate international treaties or take international commitments alone, given that these commitments could potentially contradict the Directive. This also applies to measures taken in Strasbourg that belong to the scope of the Directive. In these cases, the Commission asks the

Council of the EU to negotiate the content of a specific COE recommendation on behalf of the EU. In a second step, the Commission goes to Strasbourg (together with the member states) in order to assert that – if necessary – a certain provision of the recommendation needs to be modified in order to comply with the Directive (I-10).

The second interest highlights a phenomenon one could call *schizophrenia at the member state level*. Whether the schizophrenia results from a lack of knowledge and/or coordination or is a deliberate decision due to political reasons, EU member states do not always position themselves in the same way in different settings (for example EU versus COE setting or EU versus OECD (Organization for Economic Co-operation and Development) setting) (I-2; I-5; I-11; I-12; I-14; I-19; I-24). The lack of knowledge and/or coordination arises when, at the member state level, different units or even ministries are responsible for relations with the EU and the COE (Konrad Adenauer Stiftung 2006: 7). Following this division, member states use different channels for communicating with Brussels and Strasbourg, which can result in different positions of member states in the EU and the COE setting on the same issues.

The EU's third interest in participating in the data protection expert meetings reflects the *strength of the COE* in retrieving expertise. On the one hand, the personnel within the COE Secretariat generally grow to be experts over time: since officials often stay in a dossier for a long time and perhaps have chemistry for the dossier they are dealing with, the COE staff become experts in their very own field of activity. Therefore, there is a great deal of accumulated expertise to be found within the COE Secretariat. On the other hand, the COE has a certain capacity in retaining experts and receiving excellent expert studies. Given that the COE cannot afford higher payment for the experts (as, for example, the EU does), experts who are working for the COE really believe in the work and the importance of the COE, which most likely explains the high quality of their studies (I-5; I-12; I-15; I-16; I-19; I-23; I-39).

By contrast the COE Secretariat is not invited on a regular basis to the meetings of the Article 29 Working Party in Brussels (I-2; I-19). The fact that the EU is able to attend COE meetings without problems whereas this is not true the opposite way, that is, of COE attending EU meetings, is a feature common to all policy issues. Hence, the unbalanced reciprocal representation is one of the points Juncker (2006: 28) criticizes in his report on the relations between the EU and the COE.

Besides the interorganizational contacts in the COE setting, COE Secretariat staff and their counterparts in the Commission also meet in other contexts, for example, in OECD settings in Paris or at meetings of the FRA in Vienna. In addition, there are two data protection conferences, one European and one worldwide, in which EU and COE staff might also participate. Therefore, the contacts in various data protection contexts are frequent and one could speak of 'one big data protection family' (I-13; I-19).

4.5 IOR in the field of data protection

This section reviews the issues of interest in the relations between the EU and the COE in the data protection field. Accordingly, this section touches upon the EU's accession to the COE Convention 108 and the EU Data Protection Directive, brings up the question whether the EU dictates the data protection policy in Strasbourg (with the example of Personal Name Records (PNR)), and explores the possibilities of cooperation between the two players in the data protection field.

The idea of *EU accession to the COE Convention 108* dates back well into the 1980s. However, in the beginning, this discussion had not (yet) been as outspoken as in the 1990s; there were no documents referring to either the work of the Commission in the field of data protection or the potential accession of the EU to the Convention. As mentioned, the supporters of the EU acceding to the Convention were especially those who did not want the Commission to tackle data protection and who preferred data protection to be dealt within the COE framework (I-35). However, this plan was not realized during the 1980s, given that the original version of the Convention 108 did not provide for EU accession (COE 1981).

In the 1990s, accession had taken a back seat, given the fact that the EU was busy with drafting its own directive (I-35). After the adoption of the EU Data Protection Directive, there was another attempt, which canalized in an additional amendment to Convention 108 allowing the EU to accede in June 1999 (COM 1999). Toward the end of the 1990s, there was willingness both in Strasbourg and in Brussels, and accordingly meetings always tackled the question of *when* the EU was to accede to the Convention (I-10). However, this willingness disappeared: although more than 10 years have passed since the adoption of the amendments, not all COE member states have already accepted it. It should be added, though, that not even all EU member states have ratified the amendments (COE 2012m). So one might ask why this is the case, and why the ratification process is still ongoing. While officially both the EU and the COE support the idea of EU accession to the

COE Convention, reasons and motivations for why the EU is not (yet) a party to the Convention 108 can be found on both sides.

On the EU side, one finds two different, informal, lines of argumentation. The first relates to the issue of data protection itself: the Commission questions whether all parties of Convention 108 can show a level of adequate data protection. If the EU were to accede to Convention 108, it would obligate itself to exchange data with all the 43 parties of the Convention, even with COE member states that the EU qualifies as third countries. In case of third countries, the EU usually enforces a specific procedure that recognizes the adequacy of the level of protection provided by this country. With the EU as a party to the Convention it would have to give up these adequacy procedures, as Article 12 foresees the (unhindered) exchange of personal data between all parties of the Convention. The second line of argument concerns, more broadly, the relationship between the COE and the Commission in this standard-setting task: some EU member states are concerned that the EU's official accession to Convention 108 would restart discussions on how the Commission's work relates to the COE's work or, in other words, on the role of the Commission vis-à-vis the COE. The member states fear that this undesired discussion would further complicate matters. Therefore, they opt for leaving it the way it already is (I-19; I-33; I-35).

On the COE side, there is another line of argumentation, mostly borne by COE member states that are not members of the EU. Those member states do not accept the amendments because they fear that, if the EU accedes to the Convention, the EU will set the standards while the others are obliged to align themselves with them. According to their view, data protection decisions would then be taken in Brussels, and no longer in Strasbourg. Whether the COE Secretariat shares that opinion and therefore opposes the EU accession, informally of course, is up in the air. However, one can assert that during the past few years, the COE did not prioritize the EU's accession; otherwise the COE Secretariat would have put pressure on its member states to reconsider their opinion and to accept the amendments (I-2; I-10; I-19).

Having briefly reviewed the considerations and fears of both the EU and the COE concerning this issue, it does not come as a surprise that the accession of the EU to Convention 108 is still outstanding (June 2012). It remains to be seen whether there will be another attempt in the future and, if so, when the accession will finally take place.

The fear of the COE that the EU would outstrip it in the data protection field can be observed not only in the discussion on the EU's accession to the COE Convention but also in the *establishment of the EU*

Data Protection Directive. At the end of the 1980s, when the Commission began developing the idea of its own directive in data protection, the COE reacted by reluctantly questioning why the EU needed to have its own legislation in this field when the 'marvelous Convention 108' was already in existence in Strasbourg. Following the COE's reasoning, instead of adopting its own initiative, the EU would only have to accede or ask its member states to accede to the COE Convention. However, the EU nearly initiated the Maastricht Treaty and wanted to highlight its respect for and the promotion of human rights, and accordingly it was simply not enough to only refer to the Data Protection Convention of the COE. Moreover, the line of argumentation was that the EU needed a stronger, more precise piece of legislation in data protection. Following the EU attitude, the Directive 95/46/EC was based on Convention 108, which also states Recital Paragraph 11 of the Directive, but surpasses the Convention by introducing more precision (I-10).

In conclusion, one could say that the EU succeeded in having its own legal instrument in data protection and the big fight between the COE and the EU on this issue never materialized. The COE, in the end, simply registered the adoption of the Directive 95/46/EC (I-33). Whether the EU Directive was indeed successful in achieving 'more precision' is another question, since its vagueness is exactly one point of criticism from legal scholars. Having said that, one might understandably wonder whether the EU's 'need for more precision' was indeed the crucial factor in this case or whether organizational self-interest played a role.

The previous sections mentioned that some of the COE member states fear a bone-crushing role of the EU in data protection following EU accession to Convention 108. However, even without acceding, the 27 EU member states form the majority within the COE (47 member states), and, therefore, the *EU strongly affects the agenda and the decisions taken in the COE setting.* This section outlines two ways of how this is happening: first, it sets out how the EU impacts decisions taken in the COE setting; second, it describes how the EU's work in data protection affects what comes up on the Strasbourg agenda.

First, the EU, more specifically the Commission, 'interferes' in the COE data protection work, given that the 27 EU member states form the majority within the 47 COE members. After the adoption of Directive 95/46/EC, there is no way around the Commission in negotiating and drafting a new recommendation or convention in the COE, since the Commission launches a coordination process of all the 27 EU member states in order to ensure that the new initiative does not contradict the Directive. Of course, the Commission is keen on highlighting that,

despite the coordination process, the EU does not prevail over the COE
in data protection, as can be seen from the following quotation:

> But because it is in a good relationship with the COE and the EU we
> do this exercise in a rather flexible way, meaning that we don't appear
> as the European Community from the very beginning of the work
> in Strasbourg. For example they have decided [some] years ago to
> prepare this draft recommendation on profiling. We, us Commission
> with member states (our own member states), we participate to the
> T-PD, and we leave the project to develop itself in a free way, up to a
> certain point, then we intervene as European Community to ensure
> compatibility. *We don't want of course to dictate the law in Strasbourg,
> no of course not.*
>
> (I-10, emphasis added)

Despite the Commission's emphasis on how flexibly it exercises its
'external competence', the COE's point of view, understandably, is
different, and holds that the EU carries out a 'coordination communautaire' whenever the COE is drafting a legal instrument, a coordination
process that ultimately impacts the COE product. This is already the
case in data protection, even though the EU is not a party to Convention 108. However, if the EU were to be a member of the Convention,
as one already can experience in other policy issues, the Commission
would define a 'position communautaire' on all texts and then – according to this reasoning – all the other non-EU member states would have
to follow (I-2; I-19; I-33). In sum, one could say that the EU impacts the
decisions taken in the COE setting via the majority of EU member states
and the 'external competence' of the Commission.

Second, this paragraph at hand outlines how the data protection
work of the EU affects the Strasbourg agenda. In general, EU member states have less room to maneuver in topics that are related to the
EU; therefore, whenever parallel processes on the same issues are occur-
ring in both Strasbourg and in Brussels, EU member states are reserved
toward the Strasbourg process. This reservation might stem from the
fact that, on a general level, member states do not want to derogate
the process in Brussels and, more specifically, representatives of member
states in Strasbourg might not always know what their colleagues from
the same member states will be saying in Brussels on a specific issue.
Hence, in some cases, EU member states believe that a specific issue is
too sensitive and therefore would rather tackle it in Brussels than in
Strasbourg (I-2).

Not only is this reflection theoretical but also applies to the data protection field in practice. One case is the politically sensitive issue of PNR, which is more specifically the exchange of passenger data, for example, between the EU and the United States, in order to prevent terrorist attacks. Following the argument between the EU and the United States on the conditions under which passenger data should be handed over, and the adoption of two EU instruments and their subsequent annulment by the ECJ in 2006 (Article 29 2007a: 3), the COE T-PD wanted to itself adopt a position paper on PNR to join the discussion from a clearly data protection side. However, the COE was not successful in achieving this initiative, since the EU, more specifically the Commission, raised a plea. After the Commission objected, EU member states backed off 'because when Brussels is upset then some member states say "ooh ah Brussels is upset, we should not be going ahead with that"' (I-2). Instead of the COE T-PD, the EU Article 29 Working Party adopted an opinion on the issue of PNR in February 2007 (Article 29 2007a).

It is clear so far that the IOR aforementioned in data protection are rather conflictive: the EU did not accede to the COE Convention 108, the COE disapproved of the EU Directive 95/46/EC, and there are some examples of how the EU affects and limits the work of the COE in data protection. But despite being rather conflictive, the big fight, for example, a turf battle, has been missing. As conflicts are mostly dormant in the data protection relations, their intensity has been low. Generally, when looking at the above-named issues of interest in data protection relations, it becomes evident that most of them can be framed as one specific type of conflict, namely the COE's fear of being marginalized. Throughout the 1970s and 1980s, the COE held the undisputed standard-setting role and leadership in data protection. However, the picture has blurred since the mid-1990s, and, particularly with the implementation of the EU Directive and the various other sectorial directives, the EU challenges the COE's leading role in setting data protection standards. The COE looks at the growing leverage of the EU with skepticism and rejection, which, for example, became visible during the stories of the suggested EU accession to Convention 108 or the reaction of the COE to Directive 95/46/EC. However, there is not much the COE can do given its budget limitations. Another one of the EU's advantages is the direct policy impact of its directives that member states are forced to comply, whereas the often-operose ratification and implementation process of COE conventions leaves much to be desired. Since the end of the 1990s and to an ever-increasing degree, the EU has been pushing back the role of the COE to promoting and extending the idea of data protection in COE member states that are not (yet) members of the EU. In doing so, the COE fulfills the role that can be subsumed under the keyword 'antechamber function'.

When exploring the question of how the leadership role worked out in the hands of the EU three peculiarities stand out: *first*, in the past decade, the Commission, more specifically the DG JUSTICE, lacked a person who was fighting for data protection and the further development of the existing data protection legislation, for example, in terms of clear priorities. The Council of the EU, in part, was even more supportive of data protection in negotiations preceding the legal initiatives than the Commission. Following this behavior of the DG JUSTICE, it does not come as a surprise that for 15 years there were no major legal developments in the data protection field. The related sectorial directives and the framework decision adopted within this period were often tackled within different units in the Commission (for example DG Information Society and Media) or immediately prepared within the Council of the EU. Accordingly, the coordination and cooperation that is sometimes missing among the different EU units (be it inside the Commission or the Council of the EU) dealing with data protection can be, provocatively, described as the *second* feature of the EU's data protection leadership. *Third,* data protection cannot be seen as detached from other political developments at the EU level: against the background of 9/11 and the fight against terrorism, data protection has a difficult time. With the help of the magic word 'counterterrorism' it has often become possible to undermine the protection of personal data. The second and third features reinforce each other, as can be seen from the following example: the Proposal for a Council Framework Decision on the use of PNR for law enforcement purposes, first initiated in 2007, was tackled within the Council of the EU by the Multidisciplinary Group on Organized Crime (Council 2009a). To that effect, this group decides on sensitive data protection issues without even involving the Council Working Party on Data Protection. This is a situation that is not at all uncommon, and is reflected in the small number of meetings of the Council Working Party on Data Protection in the past few years. The EU 2009 Stockholm Program has brought about the rebound of the issue of data protection by helping to put it back on the EU agenda (Council 2009e: 18–9). Time will tell if and how the Stockholm Program and the modernization process of the EU data protection instruments will further advance the level of protection of personal data in the EU.

The conclusion will look at the question of cooperation. Can examples of cooperation in data protection be found, and if so, what do they look like? *Cooperation in data protection between the EU and the COE* is very little developed; some would even say that cooperation in data protection is almost nonexistent. Fittingly, matters of coordination are seen as cooperation: the contact between the EU and the COE is seen as important because it helps them to coordinate their own meetings with the public. Given that EU and COE events are sometimes targeted at the same public, the interorganizational contact is seen as important in order to prevent events from being set on the same date (I-2; I-40). In effect, this is a question of coordination, letting the other organization know what one is doing oneself, rather than cooperation (joint action for mutual benefit).

Still, there are two (minor) examples of cooperation, including, first, cooperation when new initiatives are underway. In the COE setting, this cooperation takes the form of joint discussions and contributions from the Commission. In the EU setting, cooperation – at its best – means giving the COE access to restricted documents and the COE Secretariat providing input. This brings us to the next general imbalance in the interorganizational relationship between the EU and the COE, not limited to data protection: while the COE has a very open policy with regard to access to documents, the EU does not. The COE has to request documents and often does not get access. Whether the Commission personnel provide the staff of the COE Secretariat with the restricted documents in these cases highly depends on the chemistry between the involved counterparts and whether there is trust between them (I-2). One can see from this example that there is no formal, institutionalized process of informing each other on new initiatives. In contrast, cooperation depends on how well the counterparts get along with each other; it depends on the individual persons involved in the IOR in the data protection field.

The second example involves cooperation between the EU and the COE regarding the European Data Protection Day, which was introduced through the launching of a new initiative by the COE in 2007. Taking place annually on 28th January, the day was chosen because it marks the beginning of the signing of the COE Convention 108. The initiative aims at increasing European citizens' awareness of data protection and their right to privacy (Article 29 2007b: 2). The EU highly welcomed the idea of a European Data Protection Day and supported the initiative. However, there are no joint activities: the EU has its own activities, whereas the COE has no budget and urges member states to finance

activities through their own budgets. Also, there is no formal coordination process; instead, the counterparts simply inform one another about
initiatives when they meet in other contexts, for example, when they
participate in other conferences or seminars (I-10). Summing up, one
can say that the EU, more specifically the Commission, politically sup-
ports the COE initiative in terms of availing oneself of the opportunity
of raising data protection awareness, but they only – if at all – manage to
coordinate the timetables of their activities and do not engage in joint
activities.

The fact that interorganizational cooperation in data protection is
somewhat sparse might result from two *aggravating circumstances*. On the
one hand, the COE budget limitations clearly impacted its data protection activities. Due to staff shortages, the data protection unit, in
essence, was a one-person unit for most of the past years. To make things
worse, the civil servant therein was not only tackling data protection,
but also handling another thematic issue unrelated to data protection.
Likewise, the T-PD bureau and plenary meetings were cut in both dura-
tion and frequency (I-2; I-10; I-33). Given that the budgetary resources
are lacking, the COE official must prioritize and probably does not
always have enough time for engaging in IOR (for example, coming to
Brussels on a regular basis). This can be seen as an example of how the
physical opportunity (in terms of slack intraorganizational resources)
impacts the relations between the EU and the COE.

On the other hand, the personnel fluctuation in data protection was
rather high on the COE side (compared with 'normal' COE standards),
and also on the EU side there has not always been continuity since
the mid-1990s. This fluctuation complicated the establishment of trust
between the counterparts, and the relations between the specific counterparts were not always easy. Indeed, the partial lack of getting along
with each other at an individual level was reflected in declining IOR
for that specific period. Accordingly, one can see that in some cases
the relations between organizations simply depend on the relations
between individual counterparts. It goes without saying that this is particularly true for relations that are not (yet) institutionalized. In 2009
there was another change and the counterparts abandoned their posts
on both sides (I-2; I-10; I-19; I-33), leaving the IOR entirely to their
successors.

Since the interorganizational cooperation is somewhat sparse in data
protection, there is much to work on. The section at hand lists *three
possibilities of how to improve the practical cooperation*, besides the possible
accession of the EU to Convention 108.

First, since there is a lot of ambiguity about how the other organization works, one could organize joint meetings in Brussels and Strasbourg in order to increase the mutual knowledge. Presentations therein could tackle the question of why there are different committees and what their task is; or, more generally, of how the COE convention system works as compared to the EU system with directives and framework decisions.

Second, in order to prevent duplication and unnecessary parallel developments, one could bring the T-PD Committee and the Article 29 Working Party closer together and improve the communication by nominating contact persons of each body and harmonizing the working plan. So far, both expert groups have not been able to harmonize their working plan, nor do they have an institutionalized procedure of informing one another on debated issues and adopted solutions.

Third, given the asymmetry in reciprocal representation and access to information, one could balance reciprocal representation from the Commission and the COE Secretariat and facilitate access to restricted documents of the other organization. In cases in which it is impossible or unnecessary to increase reciprocal representation, one could provide a summary of the expert meeting. Accompanying this is the institutionalization of the relations in data protection. If there were institutionalized practices of inviting each other to meetings, discussing the legislative initiatives of the other organization in joint meetings or by providing input, and sharing and exchanging information, relations would not depend to such a large extent on the individual relations between the involved counterparts in Brussels and Strasbourg.

Summing up, one can state that, given the rather poor interorganizational cooperation in data protection, there is a lot that can be advanced. Concluding this empirical part, the subsequent section goes on to analyze the data protection case against the background of the theoretical framework.

4.6 IOR in data protection – analysis and explanatory factors

As can be seen from the previous section, the IOR between the EU and the COE in the data protection field, range from rather conflictive to slightly cooperative. So what does this mean in terms of IOR theory? To answer this question, this section aims at linking the empirical results to the factors facilitating (hindering) interorganizational cooperation established in the theoretical framework. For the sake of completeness, it should be added that not all factors are equally important to all cases.

The data protection case omits one of the factors, the organizational characteristics factor.

4.6.1 Interest (policy and organizational)

In general, both IOs share the interest of protecting human rights within Europe. However, it is worth highlighting that while the COE – most importantly through the ECHR – has promoted human rights since the early 1950s, for most of the last decades the EU was neutral in regard to the respect of human rights (Greer and Williams 2009: 464,71). Greer and Williams (2009: 471) elaborate on this note: 'The subsequent gradual construction of a discourse that human rights were fundamental in the creation of the European Project [...] is a myth.' The following paragraph will examine whether this observation has had any contemporary impact on the way the two IOs approach human rights.

In the data protection case one can see policy congruence. In addition, both IOs have the same angle since the COE Data Protection Convention has inspired EU legislation. Conflicts have resulted from organizational self-interests: first, the EU accused the COE of acting in a defensive way when the EU developed the first directive dealing with data protection in the mid-1990s. Second, the plan that the EU would become a member of the COE convention did not materialize due to the fact that non-EU member states (and implicitly also the COE Secretariat) feared that the EU would then 'dictate' data protection policy in Strasbourg.

4.6.2 Socialization

This section mainly considers one of the two aspects of the socialization factor: trust (at the individual level between persons involved in the IOR). The first aspect of the factor at hand, the organizational culture, is difficult to analyze on a one-to-one basis. Rather, it seems reasonable to scrutinize this aspect from a cross-case perspective (see Chapter 8). In general, the fact stands out that a lack of clarity prevails in both IOs about the working methods and tasks of the other organization.

Regarding the second aspect, the data protection case is a clear example of the importance of the individual level: the officials involved in the IOR. When there is 'good chemistry' between the counterparts, relations run smoothly (for example regular reciprocal representation, exchange of restricted documents), whereas when this chemistry between counterparts is lacking, the IOR tends to lapse (for example the EU, feeling superior, does not see the need to participate in the COE meetings or follow COE developments, while at the same time the COE cannot access

EU meetings or documents). From this, one can infer that relations are not institutionalized and are dependent – to a great extent – on the personal will of the counterparts. In sum, one can say that, particularly for the operational relations (relations dealing with policy issues), the data show the importance of the socialization factor. In these cases, cooperative relations largely depend on the existence of knowledge and trust at the individual level.

4.6.3 Physical opportunity

To recall Section 2.2 of Chapter 2 on the theoretical framework, the physical opportunity factor looks at the existing infrastructure in the external environment (transport system) as well as the intraorganizational resources available for IOR.

Strasbourg suffers from a *transport system* in need of improvement in terms of flight and train connections from/to Brussels. The transport system handicaps the possibility of short-notice meetings: staffs really need to be convinced of the need of attending despite the costly and time-consuming journey. Against this background, it goes without saying that informal social interactions such as luncheons or drinks after the meetings are of lesser importance. Liaison Offices on site in Brussels and Strasbourg compensate for these difficulties. However, due to staff shortages, officials have to concentrate on conflictive relations while ignoring other ones. Hence, data protection has not attracted much attention.

Moving on to the second aspect, the *intraorganizational resources*, the EU and the COE have highly differing financial resources at their disposal. One joke circulating at the COE is as follows: 'What's the difference between the COE and the EU? In the COE there is one person working on 20 dossiers and in the EU there are 20 persons working on one dossier.' Although this is an overstatement, the COE budget limitations also pose limits to the IOR: in a one-person unit, like in the data protection case, there is not much time left for IOR, for example, for attending meetings in Brussels.

4.7 IOR in data protection – conclusions

The preceding sections set out to scrutinize the relations between the EU and the COE by going deep into a specific policy issue, namely data protection. When data protection first became a legislative issue about 30 years ago, it was apparent that – shortly after the first data protection laws at the member state level – the COE was among the first to tackle data protection in the beginning of the 1970s. The COE Convention 108, the only legally binding international treaty dealing with privacy and data protection, followed in 1981. In contrast, the EU understood itself primarily as an economic unit and adopted a hesitant attitude toward data protection well into the 1980s. The Commission left personal data to be protected at the national level by the laws in its member states, and at the supranational level by the COE Convention 108, whose ratification it recommended to its member states. When the Commission then proclaimed its interest in adopting its own data protection instrument, it left its observers wondering why it had turned its priorities upside down. Essentially, the new interest in data protection was due to the – suddenly pivotal – function of fundamental rights at the EU level from the 1990s. Once the EU Directive 95/46/EC on data protection was adopted, it was astonishing to see how much it resembled the COE Convention 108. It became evident that the Commission followed the 'omnibus' approach of the first generation of data protection laws instead of opting for a new type of regulation combining a few general principles with detailed sectoral provisions. Although both organizations issued sectoral rules in the form of recommendations and directives ensuing the adoption of Convention 108 and Directive 95/46/EC, neither considered the possibility of reviewing the very two data protection instruments until 2009. The particularly interesting point of the modernization processes that started soon thereafter is that they are ongoing in both Brussels and Strasbourg.

Having discussed the data protection instruments and the expert committees of the EU and the COE, these sections have demonstrated the interorganizational contacts in the data protection field. It turns out that the Commission is regularly invited to the expert committees of the COE and has three main interests in participating in these meetings, namely, assuring the compliance of new COE proposals with the Data Protection Directive, assuring the proper behavior of its own member states, and benefiting from COE expertise. In contrast, the COE is invited to the EU expert committees quite rarely.

Analyzing the EU–COE relationship in data protection, these sections have touched upon the unsuccessful EU accession to Convention 108, have described how the COE first reacted reluctantly to the EU Data Protection Directive, and have discussed how the EU strongly affects the agenda and the decisions taken in the COE setting. The fact that these conflicts seethed under the surface but never ascended might result from the diminished political weight of the COE in data protection as well as their lacking financial and human resources. The COE's fear of becoming marginalized plays a role, as the EU took over the COE's leading role in setting data protection standards. However, there is not much the COE can do given its budget limitations. Another advantage of the EU is the direct policy impact of its directives, since member states are forced to comply, while the often-operose ratification and implementation process of COE conventions leaves much to be desired. Since the end of the 1990s and to an ever-increasing degree, the EU has been pushing back the role of the COE to the mere promotion and extension of the idea of data protection in COE member states that are not (yet) members of the EU. In doing so, the COE fulfills the role that can be subsumed under the keyword 'antechamber function'.

Section 2.2 of Chapter 2 hypothesized that the following four, in part mutually dependent, factors impact on the nature of the relationship between IOs: the interest (policy and organizational self-interest), the organizational characteristics, the socialization, and the physical opportunity factors. In terms of IOR theory, the data protection case has shown that the interest factor (in particular the organizational self-interest) plays a major role in the EU–COE relations. To put it in a nutshell, whenever organizational self-interests are at stake, they override the shared policy interest, similar to some kind of priority rule. Accordingly, one can conclude that if the organizational self-interest is high in one of the IOs, the IOR are most probably conflictive. The socialization factor is reinforcing the direction predetermined by the interest factor while, at the same time, is unable to override it and reverse the trend. The data protection case is a clear example of the importance of the individual level, namely, the officials involved in the IOR. Cooperative relations, to a considerable degree, depend on the existence of knowledge and trust at the individual level. The physical opportunity factor, the environmental features, and the intraorganizational resources do not have a direct impact on whether the relations are cooperative or conflictive. The staff involved in IOR cannot control these conditions, but they still have to cope with these challenges (for example lacking resources) and that is how this factor indirectly exerts influence on the extent of the IOR.

5
Fight against Terrorism

This chapter scrutinizes the suspense-packed IOR between the EU and the COE in the fight against terrorism, which, as one can see in the following text, is the case with the second-highest level of conflict, only seconded by the controversies over the EU FRA. The conflict arises from the competitive situation of the two IOs in combating terrorism in the aftermath of 9/11. This chapter traces the origins of the COE Convention on the Prevention of Terrorism, shows how the EU limited the COE's role by supporting the UN approach, and tackles the controverssial inclusion of the 'Disconnection Clause' into the Convention. After the successful adoption of the Convention, the EU's decision to launch its own initiative by copying the COE consensus into a framework decision caused major ill humor in Strasbourg. Prior to analyzing in depth the contentious matters and the defensive behavior of the COE, the following sections tackle the issue of terrorism in Europe prior to 9/11(5.1) and the roles of the COE (5.2) and the EU in this issue area (5.3).

5.1 Terrorism in Europe until 9/11

Terrorism in Europe is not a new phenomenon. Well before the terrorist attacks in the United States on 11 September 2001, Europe had to deal with terrorism. However, in contrast to the United States, Europe, more specifically Western Europe, was mostly concerned with one category of terrorism, the so-called domestic or indigenous terrorism. Beginning primarily in the 1970s, this form of terrorism aggravated the threat in Western Europe in general and some nation states in particular: to name only a few, Italy experienced the escalating violence from the indigenous revolutionary organization Red Brigades, West Germany engaged in a vicious battle against the domestic radical Baader-Meinhof gang, and Spain was preoccupied with a spiral of violence induced by the separatist Basque group ETA.

This being said, the United States' pleas to take action against international terrorism fell on deaf ears of the Europeans. The problems with internal terrorist movements, the Cold War, and the resulting diverging geopolitical interests hampered the attempt to find a common ground in the fight against terrorism (Cardona 1992: 247-50; Hoffman 1999: 63–5). Despite some earlier initiatives, the attacks of 9/11, in this regard, can be seen as a trend reversal, increasing exponentially the adopted instruments against international terrorism in Europe. This also becomes evident in the following section on the role of the COE and those of the EU in the so-called fight against terrorism.

5.2 The Council of Europe's role in the fight against terrorism

The COE has pioneered the fight against terrorism in Europe. As early as 1974, the COM adopted its first resolution on international terrorism (COM 1974a), with other declarations (COM 1978) and recommendations (for example COM 1982) following thereafter. In 1977, the European Convention for the Suppression of Terrorism (ETS Nr. 90) opened for signature and entered into force in 1978 (COE 1977). This Convention aims at ensuring that alleged 'terrorists are not able to evade punishment by unduly exploiting national extradition laws and international extradition treaties' (Cardona 1992: 250). Those legal instruments usually contain one important exception to extradition: the political offense exception. Accordingly, many member states invoked this exception in extraditing alleged terrorists because of their disagreement over what constitutes a 'terrorist' as opposed to, for example, a 'freedom fighter' (Lagodny 1989: 583). In an effort to address this problem, Article 1 of the Convention for the Suppression of Terrorism narrows the scope of the political offense exception, as it forbids considering certain offenses as political or politically motivated. However, Article 5 and Article 13 are working in the opposite direction, as they offer member states a possibility to reject a request for extradition under specific circumstances (COE 1977). The Convention has been heavily criticized because of this weakness, but observers stress that this is 'no more than an attempt to accommodate political and even constitutional problems that would have otherwise prevented some states from ratifying it' (Cardona 1992: 251).

About 25 years passed before the responsible Multidisciplinary Group on International Action against Terrorism (GMT) finally considered the possibility of updating the Convention on the Suppression of Terrorism. The Protocol amending the Convention entered into force in 2003 (COE 2003), which means that it was the first treaty to emerge from the period after the attacks of 9/11 (Hunt 2006: 604). The aim of the Protocol was, inter alia, to extend and mainstream the list of offenses to be considerably 'depoliticized', with all the offenses described in the relevant UN antiterrorist instruments adopted in the aftermath of the terrorist attacks.

However, this was only the COE's first step in the fight against terrorism post-9/11: the COE almost immediately set out to draft a new convention dealing with terrorism; the resulting European Convention on the Prevention of Terrorism is the object of the following section.

5.2.1 The COE Convention on the Prevention of Terrorism

The European Convention on the Prevention of Terrorism (ETS Nr. 196; hereafter, 'Convention 196') opened for signature in May 2005 and entered into force in June 2007. It has been ratified by 29 member states, and a further 14 member states have signed but not (yet) ratified the Convention (June 2012) (COE 2012d). Convention 196 was the third counterterrorism instrument of the COE to emerge from a period of intensive policy development following the terrorist attacks in 2001 (Hunt 2006: 603–4).

Convention 196 is not an overarching framework for the prevention of terrorism, but rather has a limited scope 'dealing with the prevention of terrorism and covering existing lacunae in international law or action' (CODEXTER 2004). Nonetheless, Convention 196 is particularly noteworthy because it was the first international treaty that addressed the terrorism phenomenon from a preventive side rather than a suppression side (I-5). Therefore, Articles 5–7 of Convention 196 criminalize activities that are thought to facilitate and perhaps provoke terrorist offenses, that is, public provocation to commit terrorist offenses and the recruitment and training for the purposes of terrorism (COE 2005b), whereas previous binding law commitments in this field traditionally dealt with activities such as hijacking and bombing.

The fact that Convention 196 did not, as contemplated, became a comprehensive European counterterrorism convention with an agreed generic definition of terrorism therein resulted from the EU intervention. In 2004, at a meeting of the COE's Committee of Experts on

Terrorism (hereafter, 'CODEXTER'), the initiative was dealt a fatal blow when the Presidency of the EU declared that it would not support the COE's comprehensive convention on terrorism. Instead, the EU opted for supporting the UN strategy, as evident from the following statement:

> In the light of the Declaration of the European Council of Combating Terrorism of 25 March 2004, the key role of the UN in elaborating a comprehensive convention against terrorism should be supported. Taking into account the ongoing efforts of the UN, it was not, at present, advisable to start negotiating a comprehensive convention against terrorism in the Council of Europe.
>
> (CODEXTER 2004)

'[I]n order to avoid duplications of efforts' (Council 2004: 1), the EU advised the COE to stick to a limited approach, tackling certain aspects of terrorism that had been overlooked by previous instruments. Delegations of non-EU member states criticized the EU approach as an 'expression of a political position'. Moreover, they argued that these political considerations, at that point in time, should remain outside the debate, so that CODEXTER could propose possible technical solutions to identified problems. At the close of the meeting, the members of CODEXTER were not able to reach a consensus on whether or not the COE should elaborate on a comprehensive counterterrorism convention. Therefore, it was agreed instead to undertake the work toward a limited-scope instrument concentrating on prevention.

To recall, this work resulted in Convention 196, and its most important achievement is the criminalization of three offenses; or, to say it in the words of Hunt (2006: 609): 'It is not a huge exaggeration to say that the [Convention 196] is really all about the three offences it sets out to create'. Article 5 defines public provocation to commit a terrorist offense as 'the distribution, or otherwise making available, of a message to the public, with the intent to incite the commission of a terrorist offence'. Under the provision addressing the recruitment for terrorism offense, Article 6 conceives 'solicit[ing] another person to commit or participate in the commission of a terrorist offence'. The training for terrorism offense (Article 7) includes inter alia providing 'instruction [...] for the purpose of carrying out or contributing to the commission of a terrorist offence' (COE 2005b: 4). What is noticeable is that all these provisions employ the term terrorist offence as the core element in their definitions. According to the Explanatory Report (Article 1 Paragraph 48), this term was chosen because other suggestions, for example, to actually define 'terrorism', were rejected with reference to the limited scope of the Convention. Scholars, however, criticize that, on the contrary, it would have been possible to emboss a 'mini-definition' of terrorism (Hunt 2006: 612).

In conclusion, despite the criticism and weaknesses, this section should have made clear that Convention 196 was a significant step forward in the development of the international regime for countering terrorism. It also demonstrated the impact of the EU on the development and embodiment of Convention 196, most noticeably the deviation from the original COE idea of developing a comprehensive convention on its own. Correspondingly, we will see in the following Section 5.5 that the interorganizational relationship between the EU and the COE in the field of counterterrorism is, above all, rather conflictive.

5.2.2 The COE committees of experts – GMT and CODEXTER

Following 9/11, the COM aimed at strengthening international action against terrorism, and decided upon the setting up of a Multidisciplinary Group on International Action against Terrorism in order to improve the effectiveness of the existing COE instruments (COM 2001). Only a few months after 9/11, in December 2001, the GMT had its first meeting. The GMT focused on two tasks: first, revising the 1977 European Convention on the Suppression of Terrorism and, second, identifying the priorities for future action by the COE. Subsequently, the GMT met six times and finally submitted the result of its work at the COM session only 11 months later, in November 2002. With regard to the first task, the work of the GMT resulted in the adoption of the Protocol amending the Convention on the Suppression of Terrorism (COE 2003). With regard to the second task, the GMT identified a number of priority areas to be worked on accordingly, which were endorsed by the COM (2002a). Finally, the GMT proposed the setting up of a committee of experts on terrorism 'responsible for coordinating and following up the counterterrorist activities of the Council of Europe in the legal field' (COE 2012b).

As it had itself suggested, the GMT was replaced by CODEXTER in 2003. The new Committee, consisting of representatives of the governments of the COE member states, is instructed to:

- – coordinate the work on terrorism within the COE committees,
- – identify possible additional priority activities against terrorism and to make appropriate proposals to the COM,

- draw up country profiles on counterterrorism capacity and promote the exchanges of best practice, for example on the protection
  and compensation of victims of terrorism, and
- promote the effective implementation of the COE's action against
  terrorism, in particular Convention 196.

(CODEXTER 2008: 3)

CODEXTER had its first meeting in October 2003 and since then has
met regularly. As will be seen in Section 5.4, it was also the forum in
which Convention 196 was negotiated.

5.3   The EU's role in the fight against terrorism

5.3.1   EU's counterterrorism activities until 9/11

Similarly to the COE, there was some pre-9/11 work on terrorism at the
EU level, as terrorism slowly entered its realm during the 1970s (Coolsaet
2010: 875). In 1979, EU member states tentatively developed principles
for counterterrorism, a forum for exchange, and a legal instrument, the
so-called Dublin Agreement. In 1979, the EU member states first raised
the idea of defining terrorism. Though they did not quite arrive at a specific definition, they developed two principles that gained widespread
support and defined EU-counterterrorism policy:

- Terrorism is a collective threat that requires a collective response;
- Terrorism is a threat to democratic values that requires a democratic response.

(Cardona 1992: 250)

These principles highlight the respectfulness of the rule of law in the
fight against terrorism. This approach is consistent with the diagnosis
of Wilkinson (1986), who pointed out that liberal democracies have to
balance military–security counterterrorism activities with judicial and
political control. The second step, the legal instrument called the Dublin
Agreement, was the effort to ensure the uniform application of the
COE Convention of the Suppression of Terrorism between EU member
states. According to the Dublin Agreement, the extradition proceedings
between EU member states should work without qualification and reser-
vations. Nevertheless, the 'political offence' reservation was maintained
(Cardona 1992: 251–2).

At the operational level, the Terrorism, Radicalism, Extremism, and
political Violence (TREVI) Group was established in 1976 as a forum

for discussion and cooperation on counterterrorism and policing. The TREVI arrangement has since been superseded by the third pillar of the 1992 Maastricht Treaty, formally the Treaty on the European Union, pertaining specifically to immigration and asylum, policing, customs, and legal cooperation and including the mandate to create the European Police Office (Europol) (Hoffman 1999: 71–2; Coolsaet 2010).

In sum, it's clear that there were some rather minor activities on terrorism at the EU level before the attacks of 9/11, with the activities in the 1970s – principles on counterterrorism upholding the rule of law and the Dublin Agreement on the uniform application of COE Convention 90 – particularly worth highlighting. In the 1990s, the Maastricht Treaty brought important alterations due to the creation of the third pillar, which provided a legal basis for the fight against terrorism. However, it was the emergence of Al Qaeda (and with it global terrorism) that turned terrorism into a major preoccupation for the international community. However, the attacks in European cities, Madrid (2004) and London (2005), were what particularly revived and boosted counterterrorism decision making at the EU level. Therefore, one could speak of an 'event-driven elaboration of an EU counterterrorism strategy' (Coolsaet 2010: 858), which resulted in a patchwork of different measures without an overall, coherent design in mind.

The following section reviews specific EU counterterrorism measures since 9/11. It does not list all the adopted measures and activities, but instead concentrates on those that are of concern to the IOR between the EU and the COE in the fight against terrorism.

5.3.2   Framework Decision 2008/919/JHA amending the Framework Decision 2002/475/JHA on combating terrorism

Immediately after the attacks in 2001, the Commission (2001b) drafted a Proposal for a Council Framework Decision on combating terrorism. The adopted Council Framework Decision 2002/475/JHA is clearly innovative, as it provides EU-wide definitions of terrorism and criminal sanctions. The concept of terrorism has two dimensions. On the one hand Article 1 refers to a list of obvious criminal acts such as kidnapping or seizure of public transports, and on the other hand it reports on acts that are aimed at 'seriously intimidating a population, or unduly compelling a Government or international organisation to perform or abstain from performing any act, or seriously destabilising or destroying the fundamental political, constitutional, economic or social structures of a country or an international organization'.

This definition is not only innovative, but also heavily contested: scholars note that this rush to action of the EU 'resulted in the adoption of its own highly controversial definition of terrorism that went significantly beyond any other binding definition previously agreed in an international forum or context' (Hunt 2006: 607). As a result, this 'over-broad definition' could potentially criminalize protests at meetings such as the G-8, and these people would subsequently become 'terrorists' (Bunyan 2002, 2010).

In 2006, the Commission started examining and amending the Council Framework Decision of 2002, and the amendment process took two years altogether. In November 2008, the Council of the EU adopted the Framework Decision 2008/919/JHA amending Framework Decision 2002/475/JHA on combating terrorism. When looking at the document, it is particularly striking how much the Framework Decision 2008/919/JHA resembles the COE Convention 196. As a matter of fact, the Commission essentially copied and pasted the Convention on the Prevention of Terrorism and from it made an own legal instrument. The explanatory memorandum states that, because of the COE efforts in the field, the EU needed to catch up:

> This proposal updates the Framework Decision on combating terrorism [2002/475/JHA] and aligns it with the Council of Europe Convention on the prevention of terrorism, through including public provocation to commit terrorist offences, recruitment for terrorism and training for terrorism in its concept of terrorism.
>
> (Commission 2007)

As exemplified, the Framework Decision 2008/919/JHA involves the essence of Convention 196, along with the three new provisions: public provocation to commit a terrorist offense, recruitment for terrorism, and training for terrorism. Given the fact that the new EU document adopts previously agreed-upon COE provisions, and given that all EU member states are members of the COE, the Commission concluded that EU member states would support the amendment. The explanatory memorandum 'confirmed that there is sufficient support for the amendment of the Framework Decision on combating terrorism [...] insofar as the criminalisation does not go further than the balance achieved in the Council of Europe' (Commission 2007: 5).

Despite the incorporation of Articles 5–7 into the EU document, what was not absorbed was Article 12 on conditions and safeguards ensuring that Articles 5–7 are carried out while respecting human rights obligations and the principle of proportionality. 'The original version introduced by the Commission had no protections and the EU was generally resistant to recognize any problems' (Banisar 2008). As a matter of fact, the amendment has been strongly criticized for the lack of human rights protection equivalent to those incorporated in Article 12 by NGOs like Amnesty International (2008), and also the EP (2008c) and the PACE (2008).

In the end, the criticism, including the large outcry of the COE, led to the adoption of a new section on freedom of expression. Article 2 underlines that the Framework Decision shall not lead member states to take measures in contradiction of fundamental principles relating to freedom of expression. Nevertheless, this concession does not satisfy all critics: according to Statewatch, this solution still raises problems as many of the protections are only nonbinding declarations (Banisar 2008: 10).

As one can tell from this section, in the fight against terrorism case, the EU has clearly drawn inspiration from the COE. Whether and how this decision of the EU to adopt COE provisions impacts the interorganizational relationship in counterterrorism is tackled in detail later.

Before continuing to Section 5.3.3 dealing with the EU working group on terrorism, another EU action underlining the importance of the issue of terrorism on the EU's agenda is worth highlighting: the creation of an EU Counterterrorism Coordinator in March 2004. The EU Counterterrorism Coordinator, who is located in the General Secretariat of the Council of the EU, has the task of coordinating the work of the Council of the EU in the fight against terrorism and of maintaining an overview of the EU's instruments (European Council 2004b: 13). In his position, the EU Counterterrorism Coordinator has some contacts with the COE, for example, in the settings of the CODEXTER meeting, but his rather busy agenda often prevents him from attending the meetings (I-23).

5.3.3   The EU Terrorism Working Group and the Article 36 Committee (CATS)

The EU has two Council working groups entirely devoted to the issue of counterterrorism: the *Terrorism Working Group* and the *Working Party on Terrorism* (COTER). The former, previously located in the third pillar, is responsible for internal threat assessments, practical cooperation, and coordination among EU bodies. The latter, previously a second-pillar group, handles current issues in the area of international cooperation against terrorism (Lugna 2006: 109–10; Coolsaet 2010: 861–2). COTER is, so to speak, a second-pillar advisory group on counterterrorism and political issues. Among other tasks, COTER is also working to implement the EU counterterrorism strategy. Both working groups also held joint meetings in order to integrate the internal and the external dimensions. As COTER is primarily dealing with international cooperation in counterterrorism, this is the working group with potential interorganizational contacts with the COE.

Another committee in the JHA field with which the COE has contacts is the *Article 36 Committee*, also known as CATS, which was set up by Article 36 of the Maastricht Treaty. Its role is to coordinate criminal matters and judicial cooperation. Following Article 36 TEU, CATS gives opinions for the attention of the Council of the EU, be it on request or on its own initiative, and contributes to the preparation of discussions of the Council of the EU in the JHA area. The members of the Coordination Committee, which meets monthly, are senior officials from the member states' interior and/or justice ministries. As the name 'Coordination Committee' suggests, CATS coordinates the work of the competent third-pillar working groups dealing with police cooperation and judicial cooperation in criminal matters. It also oversees the Schengen Information System as well as the work of the EU agencies, and the various bodies in the field of police and judicial cooperation (Europol, Eurojust, Cepol, and so on) (Lugna 2006: 109). In the framework of the interorganizational coordination meetings, the Troika of the Article 36 Committee meets with the COE (ideally) once every Presidency period. In this setting, representatives of the current and the incoming Presidency, as well as the General Secretariat of the Council and the Commission, come together with representatives of the COE Secretariat. Terrorism is recurrent on the agenda of these meetings, as seen in Section 5.4.

5.4 Interorganizational contacts in the fight against terrorism

5.4.1 Reciprocal representation: CODEXTER and CATS

As is the case in data protection, the Commission is entitled to participate in the meetings of *CODEXTER*. The CODEXTER meetings normally take place in Strasbourg, with the exception of one meeting in Madrid in 2009. Since its establishment in 2003, there have been 21 meetings of CODEXTER, the frequency ranged from one meeting in 2003 to five meetings in 2004. It was the negotiation phase of COE Convention 196 that made the five meetings necessary in 2004 and the two meetings in the first half of 2005. Since 2006, CODEXTER has met two times per year (COE 2012a).

The Commission has been systematically invited to these meetings since the creation of the predecessor of CODEXTER, the GMT, in 2001. Indeed, the Commission has participated in the committee meetings since the very beginning, and with CODEXTER starting to negotiate a new treaty, the Commission has become even more interested. Only for a short period from 2006 to 2007 during which a reorganization of the terrorism file within the Commission took place, the Commission did not attend the Strasbourg meetings. Besides the Commission, the General Secretariat of the Council of the EU can also send representatives to the meetings (CODEXTER 2008: 4). Therefore, alongside with the Commission, the General Secretariat of the Council of the EU has also participated in past meetings. The interorganizational contact between the COE and the General Secretariat of the Council of the EU had been particularly strong at the time of the preparation of COE Convention 196. This was due to the fact that the Council of the EU coordinated the position of the EU member states, given the primarily national competence in the field of counterterrorism (I-4; I-18; I-23; I-25; I-29).

The *general setting of the COE counterterrorism meetings* is the following: the six GMT meetings, which took place between 2001 and 2002, lasted for one to three days, and the meetings of the successor CODEXTER also range between one and three days. There are about 100 participants in the meetings of CODEXTER. Compared with the COE data protection T-PD Committee meeting (see Section 4.4.1 of Chapter 4), there is no formally organized joint dinner. However, since the meetings last for more than one day, there are always informal dinners, during which members of the Committee as well as the observers, representatives of the Commission, and the General Secretariat of the Council of the EU come together. Similar to the data protection case, the atmosphere in CODEXTER meetings is more relaxed than in meetings in Brussels. On the one hand, this might be explained by the tradition of joint lunches or dinners, which is part of the COE 'working philosophy'. In doing so, members get to know each other and they develop a fruitful working relationship. On the other hand, this might be explained by the member states thinking of the COE as being less powerful. Therefore, member states feel like they are in charge and can control the outcome, and even if the outcome does not please them, they are not obliged to implement the decision but can rather choose not to ratify the treaty (I-4; I-16; I-23; I-18). While the previous paragraph briefly outlined the setting of the CODEXTER meetings, the ensuing paragraph sets out the interests of the EU representatives toward participating in the meetings.

Regarding the EU representatives' interests in participating in CODEXTER meetings, one has to distinguish two time frames:

- *First*, in the pre-Convention 196 time frame, the EU's interest in participating is obvious: the EU cannot ignore the establishment of a new international treaty in an area that concerns EU member states and is of utmost importance to the EU itself. When EU member states are party to an international treaty, the EU often claims the inclusion of a so-called 'Disconnection Clause'. Therefore, it is very important for the EU to closely follow the negotiations for an international treaty in an environment like the COE. Also, during the negotiation phase of the COE Terrorism Convention, the EU urged the inclusion of a 'Disconnection Clause', which inter alia led to conflictive IOR between the EU and the COE.
- *Second*, in the post-Convention 196 time frame, the EU's interest in participating is less pronounced. Since the CODEXTER meetings tackle policy issues and problems with which the EU is also involved, it is good and useful for EU personnel to be informed of the developments within the COE setting. However, it is not of highest priority for them to attend the meetings themselves; in fact, the EU representatives have not always managed to attend the past few meetings. In their view, a good summary of the meetings would be sufficient in order to gain the relevant information (I-4; I-18; I-23).

Concluding this section, the following three paragraphs focus on the reciprocal COE's involvement and representation in the EU meetings. By contrast the COE Secretariat is not systematically invited to the meetings of *COTER*, the Working Party on Terrorism. The fact that EU working group meetings are closed to COE staff does not only apply to the issue of counterterrorism, but is also feature common to all policy issues and is criticized as unbalanced reciprocal representation by Juncker (2006: 28) in his report on the IOR between the EU and the COE. Returning to the meetings in the field of counterterrorism, the COE Secretariat asked on a number of occasions to be invited systematically as an observer to the meetings of COTER. However, the EU did not give in to these requests, instead stated that this was not provided for in the EU framework. Although the COE has no observer status as the Commission has in the COE setting, the COE Secretariat is occasionally invited to COTER meetings. These meetings, however, do not qualify as 'regular' Council working group meetings, but instead are informal meetings between COTER and the COE Secretariat, or, in the words of the COE Secretariat staff, they rather have the format of auditions (I-4, I-16; I-29).

Beside the (irregular) interorganizational contacts in the meeting of COTER, there are coordination meetings in the realm of JHA, in which COE Secretariat staff and personnel of the General Secretariat of the Council of the EU and the Commission dealing with this issue get together. The *meetings of the Troika of the Article 36 Committee with the COE Secretariat* take place one to two times per year. Since the issue of terrorism has regularly been on the agenda of this meeting, this section goes on to review the Article 36 Committee meetings with the COE.

Terrorism was on the agenda in all of the nine meetings that took place between October 2002 and May 2009. Therefore, one can assume that terrorism was of high priority in the IOR for that period, whereas previous and later meetings were not concerned with terrorism. In the first meeting tackling (inter alia) terrorism, the COE informed the EU participants of the work accomplished in the GMT (Council 2002: 4–7). This meeting in 2002 still falls within the immediate aftermath of the 9/11 attacks, when IOs began their work on counterterrorism. Subsequent meetings informed EU participants of the adoption of the Protocol amending the 1977 Convention on the Suppression of Terrorism (Council 2003: 1), and the adopted EU measures following the Madrid attacks in March 2004 (for example the Counterterrorism Coordinator) as well as the task of CODEXTER to elaborate a new convention for fighting terrorism (COE 2004a: 3–4). In the April 2005 meeting, the COE introduced two new instruments in the realm of counterterrorism: the COE Convention on the Prevention of Terrorism and the COE Convention on Laundering, Search, Seizure and Confiscation of the Proceeds from Crime and on the Financing of Terrorism. Furthermore, the COE called upon the EU to consider adopting a 'position communautaire' for the member states to sign and ratify these instruments as well as the Protocol amending the 1977 Convention on the Suppression of Terrorism (Council 2005: 2). Further meetings included a presentation of COE work followed by the presentation of EU work (COE 2006a: 3–5) as well as state of play with respect to the signature and ratification of the COE Terrorism Conventions (Council 2007). The last three out of the nine meetings dealing with terrorism focused on one specific EU instrument: the EU Framework Decision 2008/919/JHA amending the Framework Decision 2002/475/JHA on combating terrorism. Within the three meetings that took place in 2008 and the first half of 2009, the EU and the COE discussed the new instrument and potential problems that may thus arise (Council 2008b, 2008c, 2009c). As the following section inter alia deals extensively with the issue of the EU Framework Decision 2008/919/JHA, this section will leave the matter at that.

5.5   Interorganizational relations in the fight against terrorism

This section reviews the issues of interest in the relations between the EU and the COE in the field of fighting terrorism. Accordingly, this section touches upon the question of the 'Disconnection Clause' in the COE Convention on the Prevention of Terrorism, brings up the history of origin of the EU Framework Decision 2008/919/JHA amending the Framework Decision 2002/475/JHA on combating terrorism and the reaction of the COE to this development, and explores the possibilities of cooperation between the two players in the fight against terrorism.

At the time when the COE Convention on the Prevention of Terrorism was negotiated, there were sometimes sharp debates on the inclusion of the so-called Disconnection Clause. In addition to Convention 196, the 'Disconnection Clause' was also disputed in the COE Convention against Trafficking in Human Beings (ETS Nr. 197) and the COE Convention on Laundering, Search, Seizure and Confiscation of the Proceeds from Crime and on the Financing of Terrorism (ETS Nr. 198) (Juncker 2006: 15).

The first use of the 'Disconnection Clause' dates back to the end of the 1980s. The standard formula of the clause can be found in the 1989 European Convention on Transfrontier Television (ETS Nr. 132, hereafter, 'Convention 132'), in which Article 27 (1) states:

> In their mutual relations, Parties which are members of the European Economic Community shall apply Community rules and *shall therefore not apply the rules arising from this Convention* except in so far as there is no Community rule governing the particular subject concerned.
>
> (Emphasis added)

'Disconnection Clauses' such as the one laid out in the example of Convention 132 have the purpose to 'safeguard the application of Community law between EU member states against potentially diverging provisions of an international treaty' (Polakiewicz 2009: 8). Through the use of the 'Disconnection Clause', EU members ensure that – if necessary – the rules of the multilateral convention would not apply to their relations inter se; instead, EU members may apply specific rules agreed among themselves. From a legal point of view, these agreements on special relations are valid, given that they are freely negotiated and accepted by the parties to a specific convention. From the EU's point of view, these clauses are necessary to avoid endangering the ongoing integration process. Therefore, the EU specifically requested these special relations provisions at least in 17 international treaties (Koskenniemi 2006: 147). It is worth highlighting that the practice of including 'Disconnection Clauses' is particularly frequent in COE conventions (Polakiewicz 1999: 69; Smrkolj 2008: 1–3; Dawar 2010: 4–5).

In contrast to the EU, the COE is skeptical toward the use of the 'Disconnection Clause' in COE treaties: The COE fears that the EU 'might, in applying its conventions, fall short of the minimum standards accepted' (Juncker 2006: 15). In other words, the COE considers its use as a weakening and watering down of their standards, which can be deduced from the following statement taken from the Committee of Legal Advisers on Public International Law CAHDI report on the consequences of the so-called Disconnection Clause within international law in general and within COE conventions in particular.

> [The] indiscriminate and frequent use of such clauses may inadvertently lead to the erosion of the object and purpose of important standard-setting treaties, or inspire similar practices with regard to the relations inter se between states engaged in integration processes in other regions.
>
> (COM 2008b: 2)

Given the diverging views of the EU and the COE, the question of the 'Disconnection Clause' was highly debated in the case of Convention 196. This example reveals conflictive IOR and is not a paradigm for good cooperation between the two IOs in the preparation phase of this Convention (I-4; I-18; I-23; I-29). The COE did not understand the need for this specific 'Disconnection Clause', as can be seen from the following quotation:

> [T]he Disconnection Clause was an unfortunate example, because it appears more as an imposition from the EU side than as part of an exchange of information or trying to make the other ones understand why that clause was necessary so that was a very unfortunate example because it took even some EU member states by surprise and it really appears as an imposition. And when the Secretariat of the Council

[of Europe] approached the Commission and the Council [of the EU] and told them that they ought to produce an explanation they felt that they did not need to explain it there was that understanding that the members of the EU have the majority in the COE – 47 countries – so they would not have to explain it, but the problem here is that even within the their [the EU's] own member states there was no understanding of why that clause was necessary. (I-4)

In the opinion of the EU, the use of 'Disconnection Clauses' is unavoidable, as it preserves the autonomy of EU law. For EU staff, it is not understandable why the 'Disconnection Clause' is subject of recurring discussions, as for example in the CATS meetings, and why the COE insists that the EU should end this practice. In their view, it is obvious that the EU needs the 'Disconnection Clause' in case EU standards are different, for example, due to deepened integration among the 27 member states (I-16; I-18; I-23).

Eventually, the 'Disconnection Clause' dispute challenged the adoption of Convention 196, which depended on the successful agreement between the EU and the COE on this issue (Council 2005: 3). In May 2005, after lengthy discussions, the EU accommodated the COE with a Declaration clarifying the need for and the scope of the 'Disconnection Clause' in the COE treaties. The most important statements of this Declaration are the following:

> [The] European Community/European Union and its Member States reaffirm that their objective in requesting the inclusion of a 'Disconnection Clause' is to take account of the institutional structure of the Union when acceding to international conventions, in particular in case of transfer of sovereign powers from the Member States to the Community. *This clause is not aimed at reducing the rights* or increasing the obligations of a non-EU party vis-à-vis the European Community/European Union and its Member States, inasmuch as the latter are also parties to this Convention.
>
> (COE 2005b: Explanatory Report, emphasis added)

In the end, the following clause was introduced in Article 26 of Convention 196:

> Parties which are members of the European Union shall, in their mutual relations, apply Community and European Union rules in so far as there are Community or European Union rules governing the

particular subject concerned and applicable to the specific case, without prejudice to the object and purpose of the present Convention and without prejudice to its full application with other Parties.

(COE 2005b)

It goes without saying that after this contradictory debate, not everybody was pleased with this decision. Especially some non-EU member states, among them Russia, were very unhappy with the inclusion of the 'Disconnection Clause' and the format that it took (I-23; I-29). However, it is noteworthy that, in contrast to the formula used in previous conventions such as Convention 132, the clause at hand in Convention 196 meets the concerns expressed in the literature (Hummer and Schmid 2008: 314).

In conclusion, it is important to allude to the fact that – as a matter of course – there are also de-escalating voices in this issue. In his report, Juncker (2006: 16) admits that the EU will probably be unable to dispense with 'Disconnection Clauses'. Therefore, he simply sees them as EU clauses and opts for also calling them that what they actually are. In addition, within the two IOs, there are de-escalating voices that on the one hand understand the COE's uneasiness with this matter and on the other hand make implausible claims that the EU, using these 'Disconnection Clauses', will adopt lower human rights norms (I-16; I-32).

Having reviewed the matter of the disputed 'Disconnection Clause', the next step is to scrutinize the relationship at the time of drafting of the EU Framework Decision 2008/919/JHA amending the Framework Decision 2002/475/JHA on combating terrorism, which is equally conflictive. This is reflected in the fact that the issue of the EU Framework Decision was brought up in all the meetings between the Troika of the Article 36 Committee and the COE during that time (Council 2008b, 2008c, 2009c).

As set out in Section 5.2.3, the EU Framework Decision 2008/919/JHA strongly resembles COE Convention 196, as it absorbs the new offenses of Articles 5–7. The COE disapproved of the new EU initiative. The COE SG Terry Davis clearly expressed his reservation toward the EU Framework Decision, which, in his view, was unnecessary, by stating:

Key parts of the EU Commission's anti-terrorist package duplicate the 2005 Council of Europe Convention on the Prevention of Terrorism. [...] The European Union can and should make a substantial contribution to the fight against terrorism by acting within its powers and building on existing national laws and international instruments. On the other hand, it should avoid duplication, which not only wastes resources but may also create confusion and double standards and ultimately undermine our collective response to the threat of terrorism.

(COE 2007a)

The COE SG also aired his displeasure over the fact that, up until that point, only very few of the EU member states had ratified the COE Convention 196. As in other cases, EU member states have a tendency to 'forget' about the ratification of COE instruments the moment the EU puts forward an initiative, which is a big concern for the COE. This occurs whenever EU member states are waiting for the EU outcome (of a specific legal initiative) and – for that period and/or beyond – stop the COE ratification process (of the equivalent convention) at the national level. However, in the case of the Framework Decision 2008/919/JHA, the EU staff highlights that negotiations inside the EU were very fast and took less than six months and therefore did not so much hamper the ratification process of the COE Convention 196 (I-12; I-15; I-16). This issue was on the agenda of the meeting of the Troika of the Article 36 Committee with the COE in December 2008:

> Another of the CoE's concerns had to do with a possible slowing down of the pace of ratifications by the EU Member States, precisely because of the entry into force of the FD [Framework Decision]. This point was generally reiterated by the CoE side throughout the meeting. It would be unfortunate if EU legislative action in areas covered by the CoE Conventions would result in a disincentive for EU Member States to ratify and implement those important instruments.
> (Council 2008c: 2)

The COE was especially disappointed in the EU decision to draft its own initiative because it had hoped that the EU would support the COE conventions on counterterrorism instead of making its own legislation. For the COE it was tough to swallow the fact that, although the Commission and the General Secretariat of the Council of the EU were actively involved in the drafting of this instrument, the EU did not bring itself to urge its member states to ratify these instruments but rather chose to present its own targets in November 2007 (Taylor 2008: 1255). Instead of officially supporting the COE conventions, the

Commission pressed ahead by accentuating the amenities of the EU legislation in the explanatory memorandum, dealing a heavy blow to the COE:

> [The Framework Decision] entails the advantage of the more integrated institutional framework of the European Union (in particular: no lengthy procedures of signature and ratification like for the Council of Europe Conventions, application of proper follow up mechanisms, common interpretation by the Court of Justice).
>
> (Commission 2007: 2)

On this note, the EU holds that the COE has only benefited from the EU's putting forward of the initiative because the EU is more visible and has more political weight. Moreover, the COE should appreciate the EU initiative in the area of follow-up and monitoring. When thinking it out, the Framework Decision would 'ultimately ensure [...] the support of 27 Member States for the objectives of the CoE Convention' (Council 2008c: 2). Staff members who share this view within the COE are the minority. Besides this argumentation, one can find the perception within the EU that the two initiatives are complementary, as the COE focused somewhat more on prevention while the EU somewhat more on repression (I-14; I-15; I-18).

The fact that the EU had a rather different focus recalls the heavily criticized decision to leave out the safeguard provision. What has incensed critics, like NGOs in the field of human rights, is the line of argumentation that the EU used to explain itself, as in the following quotation:

> And then when I said, if you are copying it why not copy it altogether, they [the Commission staff] said, well we don't need to because this is obvious and we have all the safeguards [...]. And I said well if all this is obvious and this is already all in the COE why do you need to take another text, and the answer was quite clear [...]. They told me, well if we have a framework decision it's in EU law, it's much more binding, it's much more precise. [...] So when it serves the logic [...] to extend the acts that can be criminalized under terrorism, they are happy to take the COE Convention and to make an argument by this to give more weight to the instruments but when it doesn't serve their purpose [...] they explain to you that it is very difficult, that it poses a lot of obstacles, that you risk creating double standards, that you risk having conflicting laws and so on (I-11)

One can see that the line of argumentation of the EU, in part, was controversial. The COE tried to counterbalance by stating that 'it regretted the lack of clear reference to the CoE acquis and also the lack of reference to conditions and safeguards in preventing terrorism, as set forth in Art. 11 of the CoE Convention' (Council 2008c: 2). The big outcry of the COE and the ensuing discussions ensured that the EU reviewed the text of the Framework Decision and recycled the provision on the safeguards (I-16). Furthermore, the EU agreed to reaffirm the importance of the ratification process. To this end, the EU publicly called upon member states to sign, ratify, and implement the COE conventions, especially in the area of criminal justice, in February 2009. The COE Convention on the Prevention of Terrorism is counted among these. The COE welcomed the special mention of the EU's support of the legislative work of the COE (Council 2009c, 2009f), but was astonished by the fact that it took the EU three years to publicly ask its member states to become party to Convention 196 – even though the Commission and the General Secretariat of the Council of the EU had a very active role in the negotiation process. Therefore, one might suggest that, for the EU, it was more important to successfully conclude its own initiative before supporting the Convention (I-4). An accession of the EU itself to the COE Convention is still (June 2012) pending.

The somewhat hostile opinion of the COE toward the EU Framework Decision is not only due to the content question of safeguards, but is also due to the *competitive situation of the EU and the COE*, as well as the asymmetry of political weight and resources at the COE's expense. In Strasbourg, there is, at least partly, the prevailing perception that the relationship between the EU and the COE is imperfect and imbalanced. Given the asymmetry of resources, the COE does not receive kindly the 'tendency' of the Commission to use its initiative power by relying on a consensus that results from the COE. Following this view, it is unjust that the COE, having only few resources at hand, accomplishes a convention and that subsequently the EU, with many slack resources, adopts the text one to one and turns it into a framework decision. This situation gets even more difficult as the EU often does not refer explicitly to the COE *acquis*, which is frustrating to the COE and nourishes the doubts of the COE toward the loyalty of the EU to its *acquis* (I-4; I-15; I-26). Within the EU personnel, some understand the fear of the COE:

> But we need to make sure that we do not step on to the toes of the COE. And they fear rightly that the EU often repeats with bigger boots – that is bit more resources and political power – what the COE does at technical level. And this technical work should not be destroyed by our big political boots. (I-16)

Furthermore, the COE does not understand why the EU member states work out normative standards only to negotiate a slightly different text in the same field in Brussels soon thereafter. This was the case when the Commission slightly changed the terminology of the COE Convention 196 before transferring it in the Framework Decision, affronting the COE drafters who had been involved with this issue for years. On this note, there was a rather old saying within the COE that one gets something fast in Brussels, but right in Strasbourg (I-14; I-16). Finally, the COE has to face the fact that, without the consent of the Commission, the 27 EU member states and the long list of states subscribing to the EU coordinated view, there is no agreement on new human rights standards in Strasbourg (Taylor 2008: 1256). All this, of course, adds up to the Strasbourg perception that the relationship is imbalanced and in need of improvement.

Contrary to the experiences in Strasbourg, the EU has some difficulty in understanding the fear of the COE and all the problems connected to the Framework Decision. Obviously, the EU has a different point of view. Following the EU's reasoning, it is because of two factors that texts deviate when adopted in Brussels. First, following their opinion, the COE sometimes goes too far with the consensus reached in specific conventions, and member states – although previously in agreement – do not fully bear the decision (for example the extent of criminalization), which is reflected in subsequent absent ratifications when member states return home. In the EU setting, however, there is nothing comparable member states can do, given that legislation is binding. Therefore, negotiations in the EU are serious and agreements far more difficult to reach, and even when the same person attends the meetings in Strasbourg and in Brussels, he/she might behave completely differently (I-12; I-18). Second, another reason is the visibility in Brussels: the public, the media, and a variety of observers are looking at what is happening in Brussels, and at the same time do not care about the COE although it may be as sensitive:

> Just take the example of the prevention of terrorism for instance, there the COE did their convention and it took them two years to negotiate it, it was not at all sensitive, immediately when the EU took it up then it became extremely sensitive, national parliaments came in on the file, EP came in on the file and it was exactly the same offences that we basically incorporated into the EU law. (I-12)

Finally, another *aggravating factor* is worth highlighting: the IOR were also particularly difficult in this issue area due to the fact that the responsible counterparts did not get along well on a personal level. The COE alluded to the high turnover of staff in the Commission (DG JLS) and the resulting difficulty in building good communication channels. The EU agent accused the COE counterpart of being dishonest, saying that everything was okay to her face, but complained about the EU behind her back. After the press release of the COE SG in which Terry Davis said that the EU did not cooperate (see above), the EU agent thought that – to put it bluntly – no matter what the EU does, if the EU consults, asks, and informs the COE or not, in the end the COE 'will be angry anyway'. Meanwhile, the COE personnel have changed, and there is a new willingness to cooperate and work together on both sides (I-4; I-18; I-25).

In conclusion, the last part of this section reviews the possibilities of cooperation and ways of further improving the working relationship. First, in contrast to the data protection field, there is an institutionalized forum for interorganizational contacts between the involved counterparts: the CATS meeting. However, in any event, the CATS meetings did not prevent conflict with regard to the EU Framework Decision, and most staff within both organizations agree that there were probably not enough talks. However, the conflict mainly arose between the Commission and the COE Secretariat, and CATS meetings bring together first and foremost the General Secretariat of the Council and the COE Secretariat (with the Commission attending only to a certain extent). Not to decrease the importance of the CATS meetings, the talks resulted in the modification of the proposal for the Framework Decision and a statement of support from the EU for the COE Convention.

The last part of this section deals with two examples of *cooperation in the fight against terrorism between the EU and the COE* and possible ways of improving the practical cooperation.

First under examination is cooperation when new initiatives are underway, that is, the COE and the EU informing each other of their respective new initiatives in the field of counterterrorism. This exchange of views also resulted, for example, in the modification of the safeguard provisions in the EU Framework Decision. However, this cooperation is rather asymmetric: while the COE involves the EU whenever new instruments are prepared, the EU does not systematically integrate the COE. Even though the COE may be approached in the drafting phase of an instrument (Commission), the COE is left out in the negotiations of the Council of the EU at the latest (I-4; I-11; I-12; I-14). Also, in his report on the IOR between the EU and the COE, Juncker (2006: 28) criticizes that COE officials are merely consulted on an ad hoc basis and on the same footing as NGOs. Moreover, the EU should not be deprived of the COE's expertise.

Supporting Juncker's claim, the COE, of course, is eager to bring in its own *acquis*:

> The same is when we are now developing cooperation, common work on a new EU legislation. In many cases the new legislation of the EU is developing in fields where the COE already has its own acquis and its own ... So *instead of reinventing the wheel* we are saying 'listen, here is the COE and before you start drafting your own let's have a look and we are giving you at a disposal what is already done in the COE in this field'.
>
> (I-3, emphasis added)

Therefore, in order to improve cooperation, mechanisms are needed through which the COE can be systematically involved and it cannot be the last one on the list to be contacted. Furthermore, one could think of possible ways to enable the participation of the COE Secretariat staff in EU working groups. Concluding this example, it is noteworthy that enabling the COE to participate would be a difficult undertaking due to the transfer of sovereignty in the EU framework. Moreover, even the COE staff itself forms two camps on whether it would be necessary and useful to be invited to and participate in the EU working groups (I-29; I-32).

The *second* example involves cooperation that takes the form of political support for each other's legal initiatives. The above example of the EU calling upon its member states to ratify the COE Convention has been made clear; however, the support was subject to restrictions, namely the prior successful adoption of the EU's own legal instrument, which means that organizational self-interest sometimes stands in the way of cooperation. Furthermore, the COE is very interested in garnering EU, whereas the EU does not care so much about political support from the COE. This results from the fact that the COE lags behind the EU in terms of political weight, visibility, and resources. Therefore, the EU would not gain much from a statement of support from the COE (I-4; I-12; I-29). Possible ways of changing this situation would mean developing the resources and visibility of the COE, which is in the hands of the member states of the COE, the media, and, finally, the COE itself in terms of repositioning its tasks and priorities. The latter is part of the new reform of the COE SG Thorbjørn Jagland (see Chapter 9). Concluding this empirical part, the subsequent section goes on to review and analyze the fight against terrorism case against the background of the theoretical framework.

5.6   IOR in fight against terrorism – analysis and explanatory factors

As discussed in Section 5.5, the IOR between the EU and the COE in the fight against terrorism case vary widely in terms of conflict and cooperation. To examine what this means in terms of IOR theory, this section aims at linking the empirical results to the factors facilitating (hindering) interorganizational cooperation established in the theoretical framework.

5.6.1   Interest (policy and organizational)

In general, both IOs generally share the interest of protecting human rights within Europe, though the COE – most importantly through the ECHR – has promoted human rights since the early 1950s, and the EU was neutral with regard to the respect of human rights for most of the last decades (Greer and Williams 2009: 464,71). It will be shown whether this observation has had any contemporary impact on the way the two IOs approach human rights.

In the fight against terrorism case, one might specifically ask if we can observe law enforcement versus human rights approach; however, the data show that this is not the case. The COE Convention, in fact, goes very far in terms of criminalization compared with other (previous) antiterrorism treaties. What are found, however, are differences of opinion on how to achieve the best human rights protection in Europe, for example, whether the inclusion of a 'Disconnection Clause' or the EU Framework Decision is needed. While emphasizing policy interest, the line of argument of both IOs actually reflects underlying organizational self-interest.

5.6.2   Organizational characteristics

These interests represent a very simplified unitary view of the actors, which needs to be complemented. Since this project treats IOs as multiple actors, one must also consider the possibility of different actors pursuing diverging or even conflicting goals (complexity). Additionally, and leaving aside the interest aspect, as the sheer number of actors increases, the more difficult the IOR gets. In the fight against terrorism case, the then COE SG issued hostile press releases hindering the establishment of a trustful cooperation. One could infer from this observation that, besides the involved counterparts at the operational level, one must consider the behavior of leaders and notabilities in order to fully grasp the IOR.

5.6.3 Socialization

One of the two aspects of the socialization factor is considered here: trust (at the individual level between persons involved in the IOR). In the fight against terrorism case (in the JLS area), the so-called CATS meetings bring together the General Secretariat of the Council with the COE Secretariat. The Commission attended to some extent. Although the issue of the Terrorism Framework Decision was often on the agenda in the meetings, the conflict did not hold off. However, the conflict mainly arose between the Commission and the COE Secretariat. While the official dealing with terrorism in the COE Secretariat was the same for several years, the high staff turnover in the responsible Commission unit impeded the establishment of trust. Also, due to the principle of rotation, staff may deal with very different topics during their career in the Commission, while staff in the COE Secretariat often grows to be experts in a specific issue area. This may lead to diverging assessments, especially during drafting processes.

5.6.4 Physical opportunity

The physical opportunity factor examines the existing infrastructure in the external environment (transport system) as well as the intraorganizational resources available for IOR.

Due to the practice of institutionalized meetings, staff is already convinced of the need of attending, despite the costly and time-consuming journey caused by Strasbourg's lacking transport system and needs for improvement in terms of flight and train connections from/to Brussels. Liaison Offices on site in Brussels and Strasbourg further compensate for the inconvenient transport system. The fact that officials are not able to follow all the IOR (in the different subject areas), but have to concentrate on a few, does not run contrary to the fight against terrorism case. Due to staff shortages, officials often concentrate on conflictive relations while ignoring others; accordingly, terrorism gained much attention and was high on the agenda of the Liaison Offices. Moving on to the second aspect, the intraorganizational resources, the EU and the COE have highly differing financial resources at their disposal. The COE budget limitations sometimes pose limits to the IOR: however, the COE unit in the fight against terrorism case is not as much affected by budget limitations as other units.

5.7   IOR in fight against terrorism – conclusions

The preceding sections set out to shed light on the IOR between the EU and the COE with regard to combating terrorism, the second policy issue to be analyzed after data protection. Although Europe had to deal with – mostly domestic – terrorism well before the attacks of 9/11, the attacks were a trend reversal in the sense that they increased exponentially the instruments adopted against international terrorism in Europe. It has been shown that the COE pioneered the fight against terrorism in the 1970s, inter alia with Convention 90, which entered into force in 1978. Afterwards, interests in this issue area were quieted. It was not until 2001 that the COE undertook major efforts in updating Convention 90 and drafted a new counterterrorism convention. Convention 196 opened for signature in 2005 after swift negotiations. Convention 196's rather limited scope resulted from the EU's declaration that it would not support a COE comprehensive convention on terrorism, but would rather stick to the UN strategy. Similar to at the COE level, there had been some minor activities on terrorism at the EU level since the mid-1970s. But besides 9/11, particularly the attacks in European cities had revived and boosted EU counterterrorism decision making. A major issue in the relations between the EU and the COE in this field is the Framework Decision 2008/919/JHA amending the Framework Decision 2002/475/JHA on combating terrorism: in 2006, the Commission started examining and amending the 2002 Framework Decision. When the Commission issued the proposal in 2007 it was astonishing how much the new document resembled the COE Convention 196, in that it copied the three main provisions therein.

Having discussed the counterterrorism instruments and the expert committees of the EU and the COE, the preceding sections have drawn attention to the forums for interorganizational contacts in the field of fighting terrorism. In the framework of the CODEXTER meetings, the Commission and the General Secretariat of the Council of the EU were actively involved in the negotiation of the COE Convention 196. In contrast, the COE is not regularly invited to the EU working group meetings in the realm of counterterrorism. In addition to the COE counterterrorism expert meetings, there are coordination meetings in the realm of JHA between the General Secretariat of the Council of the EU and the Commission on the one hand, and the COE Secretariat on the other, and these ideally take place two times per year.

Analyzing the EU–COE relationship in the fight against terrorism, it turned out that the relations were primarily conflictive. Three particular incidents, to be specific, several actions of the EU that cause the COE concern, explain the conflictive relations between the EU and the COE. First, the fact that Convention 196 has a rather limited scope resulted from the EU declaration that it would not support a comprehensive COE convention on terrorism but would rather stick to the UN strategy. Second, the EU's demand to include the 'Disconnection Clause' in the COE Convention on the Prevention of Terrorism did not ease the relation ship. Third, the COE was not pleased to see the extent to which the new EU Framework Decision resembled COE Convention 196, copying the three main provisions therein. The COE's hostile reaction to this development can be explained by the competitive situation of EU and COE in this issue area as well as the Strasbourg perception of imbalanced relations at the expense of the COE.

Section 2.2 of Chapter 2 hypothesized that the following four, in part mutually dependent, factors impact on the nature of the relationship between IOs: the interest (policy and organizational self-interest), the organizational characteristics, the socialization, and the physical opportunity factors. In terms of IOR theory, the fight against terrorism case has again shown that the interest factor (in particular the organizational self-interest) plays a major role in the EU–COE relations. Again, one can conclude that, if the organizational self-interest is high in one of the IOs, the IOR are most probably conflictive. Two factors, complexity and socialization, reinforce the direction predetermined by the interest factor; at the same time, these factors are unable to override the interest factor and reverse the trend. In the fight against terrorism case, the fact that the responsible counterparts did not get along well on a personal level complicated the relationship between the EU and the COE even further, which shows the importance of the socialization factor. The physical opportunity factor, the environmental features, and the intraorganizational resources do not have a direct impact on whether the relations are cooperative or conflictive. The staff involved in IOR cannot control these conditions, but they still have to cope with these challenges (for example lacking resources) and that is how this factor indirectly exerts influence on the extent of the IOR.

6
Fight against Roma Discrimination

This chapter scrutinizes the IOR between the EU and the COE in combating Roma discrimination. Europe's biggest ethnic minority is worth examining, since it shows how the EU has expanded its interest in human rights issues since 2000. While the COE had been one of the first and preeminent European organizations addressing Roma since the early 1990s, the issues surrounding Roma only became internally important for the EU in 2004. This chapter sheds light on the questions of how the COE reacted to the new EU activities (fear of duplication) and whether the EU is reinventing the wheel or if the EU incorporates what is already in existence in Strasbourg. Before looking into these issues in depth, the subsequent section starts out by introducing Europe's biggest ethnic minority and tackling the COE's and the EU's role in fighting Roma discrimination.

6.1   The Roma, the biggest ethnic minority in Europe

Currently, there are between 10 and 12 million Roma ('Roma' is to be understood as a comprehensive term including Roma, Sinti, Kale, Travelers, and related groups in Europe) living throughout Europe (COE 2012j). There are doubts as to the disaggregated data on the Roma population, which have always been quite unreliable. As, not always, there is agreement on which (sub-)groups to be included into the label 'Roma' due to nation states using different methods, and Roma choosing not to self-identify as such, estimates vary between 8 and 15 million. With a population of this size, the Roma form the biggest European minority, outnumbering the population of several European countries. The European Roma are spread across practically all European nation states, with the largest percentage found in Central and Eastern Europe and the

Balkans, namely the former Communist-ruled countries (COE 2006b: 3; Liégeois 2007: 27–34; Commission 2010c: 8–11).

The Roma have had a long history of being socially, politically, and economically marginalized in countries where they have lived. Yet, before the fall of Communism, there was hardly any interest in the substandard living conditions of the Romani minority, neither in the East nor in the West. It was only around the early-to-mid 1990s that the situation of the Roma gained attraction at national and international levels: 'Roma rather suddenly became the subject of frequent news, headlines, numerous international conferences, hundreds of programs and projects (usually funded by intergovernmental organizations [...] and international NGOs), and new legislation and institutions in almost every Central and Eastern European [...] country where they live' (Ram 2010: 198).

Scholars explain this sudden interest of European organizations as 'an open concern with the potentially destabilizing effects of westward migration' (Guglielmo and Waters 2005: 763) as a result of the fall of Communism and ethnic conflicts within the countries concerned. They further argue that the initial concerns about migration, security, and integration later gave way to a rights-based approach, in which the minority status of the Roma along with their need for protection gained wider recognition. This policy shift from migration toward minority has been traced by the scholars in the OSCE as well as in the context of the EU. Yet, critics point out that there has not been a unique and one-sided approach, but rather various approaches by the OSCE, the COE, and the EU, and that the policy shift fits best only in the EU context (MG-S-ROM 2008a: 10).

Whether there are different policy approaches from the EU and the COE to the question of fighting Roma discrimination and, if so, what do they look like and how this will be reflected in the IOR in the field of Roma will be analyzed in the ensuing sections.

6.2 The Council of Europe's role in the fight against Roma discrimination

Along with the OSCE, the COE is one of the first and the preeminent European organizations addressing minority issues. As far back as the 1960s, the COM as well as the PACE of the COE adopted resolutions and recommendations attempting to bring attention to the problems faced by Roma; however, their texts did not draw much consequences (Vermeersch 2002: 85; Xanthaki 2004: 170–1; Sasse 2005: 681; Ram

2010: 200). It was only from the beginning of the 1990s that the COE intensified its activities on the Roma, and its action became more coherent and organized. The PACE Recommendation 1203 (1993) on Gypsies in Europe marked the beginning of the COE's substantial work on Roma issues, reflecting a stronger commitment toward Roma protection, as can be seen in the general observations set out in paragraph two of the Recommendation:

> A special place among the minorities is reserved for Gypsies. Living scattered all over Europe, not having a country to call their own, they are a true European minority, but one that does not fit into the definitions of national or linguistic minorities.
>
> (PACE 1993)

Moreover, paragraph nine of the Recommendation underlined that texts concerning minorities in general 'are important to Gypsies, but as one of the very few nonterritorial minorities in Europe Gypsies need special protection' (PACE 1993).

Among the instruments the COE adopted with regard to the rights of the Roma during the 1990s was the European Charter for Regional or Minority Languages (ETS Nr. 148, hereafter, 'Convention 148'), which entered into force in 1998. Convention 148 contains specific provisions stipulating the Romani language as nonterritorial (COE 1992). Three years later, in 1995, the first international treaty on ethnic minorities, the Framework Convention for the Protection of National Minorities (ETS Nr. 157), opened for signature. Also, the COE set up a Coordinator of Activities concerning Roma and Travelers in 1994 and a Committee of Experts on Roma and Travelers in 1995. Besides these two Conventions, there are another two legally binding instruments relevant to Roma that are even older: first, the 1950 Convention for the Protection of Human Rights and Fundamental Freedoms (ETS Nr: 5, hereafter, 'ECHR') and, second, the 1961 European Social Charter (ETS Nr. 35).

The subsequent sections, describing the COE instruments and activities aimed at improving the situation for Roma, focus on the developments since the mid-1990s, when the numbers of Roma within the COE member states increased considerably due the accession of Central and Eastern European countries.

6.2.1 The COE instruments in the fight against Roma discrimination

This section deals with the instruments and activities deployed by the COE to improve Roma protection within its member states since the mid-1990s. Most importantly, this section tackles the Framework Convention for the Protection of National Minorities and the Coordinator of Activities concerning the Roma and Travelers, both of 1994. Subsequently, it briefly addresses the developments at and since the turn of the millennium, in particular, specific policy recommendations with regard to the Roma of the COM, Roma campaigns, and, more generally, other bodies within the COE dealing with specific aspects of the Roma.

The *Framework Convention for the Protection of National Minorities* (ETS Nr. 157, hereafter, 'Framework Convention') opened for signature in February 1995 and entered into force three years later in February 1998 (COE 1995). It has since been ratified by 39 member states and a further four member states have signed – but not (yet) ratified the Framework Convention (June 2012). The Framework Convention was the first international treaty on ethnic minorities and 'is the most comprehensive legally binding multilateral instrument yet designed to protect the rights of persons belonging to national minorities' (Hofmann and Friberg 2004: 130). The Framework Convention entails state obligations rather than setting out individual or collective rights. It has been argued that some of these provisions fall short when compared with international standards, namely UN standards; however, others are considered to exceed existing minority rights standards. The central tool of the Framework Convention, however, is the monitoring mechanism in order to ensure its implementation: member states are obliged to write reports and to stay in contact with the concerned advisory committee. Therefore, the Framework Convention qualifies as a living instrument, developing new standards through its interpretation on the basis of opinions and resolutions, similarly to the ECHR.

Another milestone event occurred in 1994 when the COE established the position of a *Coordinator for Roma and Travelers issues* (hereafter, 'Coordinator'). Besides coordinating the activities on Roma within the COE, the Coordinator ensures cooperation with other relevant IOs working on Roma, in particular the OSCE and the EU, and establishes working relations with Romani NGOs. Furthermore, the Coordinator advises the COE SG on policies and problems regarding Roma (Liégeois 2007: 241).

From 2000 onwards, the COM adopted five *specific policy recommendations* – Rec(2000)4, Rec(2000)17, Rec(2004)14, Rec(2005)4, and Rec(2006)10 – with regard to improving education, the economic and employment situation, housing conditions, and health of the Roma, drafted by the Committee of Experts on Roma and Travelers.

Finally, *other COE bodies* have also been involved in specific aspects of the Roma, including the European Commission against Racism and

Intolerance (ECRI), an independent human rights monitoring body within the COE that has been active since 1997. ECRI meets the request of the COM to pay attention to discrimination, prejudice, and violence against Roma by consistently following the situation of Roma and referring to it in most of its reports (Xanthaki 2004: 183). The Commissioner for Human Rights, in place since 1999, is also an independent institution within the COE, mandated to promote the awareness of and respect for human rights in the 47 COE member states (Brummer 2008a: 193–5). As such the Commissioner for Human Rights is increasingly concerned with the situation of the Roma. With the *Dosta! Campaign* launched in 2006, the COE aims at breaking down Roma prejudices and stereotypes. The 'Equal Rights and Treatment for Roma in South Eastern Europe' campaign started out as part of a joint program between the COE and the Commission. In addition to that region, it has been implemented in various member states of the COE, including EU member states such as Italy, Romania, Slovenia, Latvia, Bulgaria, France, and Greece (COE 2012i).

Following concerns about the Roma rights during the summer, the COE SG Thorbjørn Jagland called for a *High-Level Meeting on Roma*, which took place in October 2010. Representatives of the 47 COE countries, the EU and Roma NGOs gathered in Strasbourg to condemn widespread discrimination against the Roma and their social and economic marginalization. In the so-called Strasbourg Declaration, participants established guiding principles and priorities in the fight against Roma discrimination and marginalization (COM 2010b). As a result of the Strasbourg Declaration, a Special Representative of the COE SG on Roma Issues was appointed in November 2010 and an Ad Hoc Committee of Experts on Roma Issues was created in February 2011 (SG 2011).

Having reviewed some of the COE activities and instruments in improving the situation of the Roma, the next section focuses on the establishment and tasks of the Committee of Experts on Roma and Travelers.

6.2.2 Committee of Experts on Roma and Travelers (MG-S-ROM) and the Coordinator for Roma and Travelers Issues

As an effective measure consequent to the PACE Recommendation 1203 (1993) on Gypsies in Europe, the COM decided to set up a COE body responsible for reviewing the Roma situation on a regular basis, the Committee of Experts on Roma and Travelers (MG-S-ROM). MG-S-ROM, having many tasks, is instructed to:

(i)   study, analyse and evaluate the implementation of policies [...] and practices of member states concerning Roma and Travellers and act as a forum for the exchange of information, views and experience on policies, good practice and issues relating to Roma and Travellers at domestic level and in the context of relevant international instruments [...].

(ii)   draw up guidelines for the development and/or implementation of policies which promote the rights of the Roma and Traveller populations taking into account the findings of the monitoring mechanisms of the relevant legal instruments of the Council of Europe.

(iii)   keep under review the situation of Roma and Travellers in member states in compliance with relevant legal instruments of the Council of Europe.

(MG-S-ROM 2008b: 1-2)

The Committee is composed of representatives (governmental or nongovernmental experts) qualified in the field of Roma, appointed by the member states' governments (MG-S-ROM 2008b: 2). The MG-S-ROM meetings normally take place either in Strasbourg or within the country holding the Presidency of the COE (for example 2009 Seville, 2006 Bucharest). Usually, there are two MG-S-ROM meetings per year, one taking place between March and May and the other in November. It will become clear in the subsequent sections that the MG-S-ROM meetings provide a place for interorganizational contact between the EU and the COE representatives.

Before concluding and moving on to the EU's role in the fight against Roma discrimination, the internal coordination mechanism for activities on Roma within the COE is briefly mentioned Since the establishment of the position in 1994, the Coordinator, in order to exchange information and coordinate activities on Roma throughout the COE Secretariat, organizes quarterly meetings, which are attended by about 15–20 participants from different DGs and bodies within the COE (I-27).

6.3   The EU's role in the fight against Roma discrimination

6.3.1   EU's activities on the Roma in the context of accession until 2000

At the outset of enlargement in the early 1990s, the EU did not have a minority policy of its own, and left the field to the discretion of the COE and the OSCE, which 'engaged in a flurry of standard-setting on minority rights immediately following the fall of the Berlin Wall' (Guglielmo and Waters 2005: 766). Prior to the 1990s, the EU had directly omitted addressing the rights of ethnic minorities, be it in member states or in applicant countries, and there were even fewer EU documents mentioning the Roma.

Against the background of the upcoming EU enlargement on the one hand, and the fear of a dramatic increase in refugees and asylum-seekers in the EU coming from the Yugoslavia and the post-Communist countries due to ethno-national conflicts on the other hand, the EU increased its attention to Roma in the beginning of the 1990s (Kovats 2001: 93-5; Sasse 2005: 685; Rechel 2008: 182). However, the EU has paid attention to Roma issues only in the context of accession negotiations with candidate countries, while neglecting the topic of minority protection in EU internal affairs (Vermeersch 2002: 85). With EU member states treating their own Roma populations poorly, some scholars allege that '[i]mproving the situation of the Roma *per se* was not a concern of the governments or citizens (that is voters) of the [then] EU-15' (Ram 2010: 200). However, according to other scholars, the EU needed to aim for a minority policy for applicant countries that would not affect the member states' policies, given that it lacked a legal and policy framework with which to address these issues. Due to the lack of experience in this field, it does not come as a surprise that the Commission relied heavily on the COE and the OSCE in developing its policy (Guglielmo and Waters 2005: 766).

In this spirit, one can examine the *Copenhagen criteria* established in June 1993, which specify the political preconditions for the accession of Central and Eastern European countries to the EU. The political Copenhagen condition, inter alia, emphasizing the importance of the protection of ethnic and national minorities, is set out in the following:

> Membership requires that the candidate country has achieved stability of institutions guaranteeing democracy, the rule of law, human rights *and respect for and protection of minorities*.
> (European Council 1993: Sec. 7.A.iii, emphasis added)

When looking at the Copenhagen criteria, one can assess their close resemblance to the criteria for membership of the COE (COE 1949: Chapter 2), which shows one of the ways in which the EU relied on COE standards referred to earlier. Subsequently, the Commission elaborated and followed up on these conditions in the annual reports on the preparedness of candidate countries for membership (Rechel 2008: 174; Ram 2010: 198–9), known as 'progress reports'.

Apart from the accession negotiations with prospective new members, the EU has become involved in Roma-related initiatives in countries of Central and Eastern Europe through the so-called *Phare program* (Kovats 2001: 95). The Phare program is a pre-accession support instrument through which the EU has financed projects in the former candidate countries.

Specific *documents on the Roma* were rather rare during the 1990s; one of them is the document of the Council Working Party on Central Europe (COCEN) adopted at the Tampere Summit in 1999 entitled 'Situation of Roma in the Candidate Countries' (EU COCEN 1999).

In conclusion, it should be added that the 1997 Treaty of Amsterdam strengthened the respect for human rights and fundamental freedoms by enshrining human rights as a fundamental principle of the EU. The EU legislation relevant to minority rights followed thereafter in 2000, though it remained confined to nondiscrimination (Rechel 2008: 180; Ram 2010: 208). The subsequent section reviews EU measures aimed at combating discrimination in general and those concerning Roma in particular. However, the list does not claim to be exhaustive but rather concentrates on those policies that are of concern to the Roma-related IOR between the EU and the COE.

6.3.2 EU antidiscrimination law and Roma-related activities after accession

As suggested earlier the legislative basis for tackling Roma discrimination from 2000 onwards has been the *EU antidiscrimination law*. To combat discrimination, the EU has drawn up two directives: the Council Directive 2000/43/EC of 29 June 2000 implementing the principle of equal treatment between persons irrespective of racial or ethnic origin, and the Council Directive 2000/78/EC of 27 November 2000 establishing a general framework for equal treatment in employment and occupation. Moreover, with the Council Decision 2000/750/EC of 27 November 2000, the EU launched a Community Action Program to combat discrimination. The two Directives prohibit direct and indirect discrimination on the grounds of racial or ethnic origin, religion or belief, disability, age, and sexual orientation, while the Action Program aims at encouraging member states to take concrete measures supplementing the legal initiatives in order to combat discrimination. In the same year, the EU adopted the Charter of Fundamental Rights, which included a provision on nondiscrimination.

As antidiscrimination became the EU policy and accession negotiations expanded to ten Central and Eastern Europe countries, EU attention toward the Roma has increased even further since 2000 (Ram

2010: 199). However, the perspective of the EU Roma policy only changed when 'with accession, the social, rights, and security issues surrounding Roma became *internal* issues' (Guglielmo and Waters 2005: 776–7, emphasis in the original). EU documents highlighting this policy shift are the EP Resolutions of 2005 and 2006 on the situation of the Roma in the EU and on the situation of Roma women in the EU (EP 2005; 2006). Further legislative instruments relevant to Roma were adopted thereafter.

Since 2008, one has been able to witness yet another development in the EU engagement in Roma issues, namely, the occurrence of new high-level political events such as the *European Roma Summit*. Following the decision of the European Council in December 2007, the Commission drew up the first official report on Roma, which evaluated existing policies and instruments of the EU aimed at improving the inclusion of the Roma (Commission 2008). The report was followed by a Summit Meeting on 16 September 2008 in Brussels, with a second Summit taking place on 8-9 April 2010 in Córdoba. The effort to mainstream the Roma into the EU's political agenda is mirrored in the increase in documents and initiatives specifically on Roma: they include a number of EP resolutions (for example the resolution of January 2008 in which the EP urged the Commission to develop a European strategy on Roma (EP 2008b)), a new report of the Commission on Roma social inclusion (Commission 2010c), and Presidency and Council Conclusions from 2007–2010 (Council 2010c).

Having reviewed the legal basis and (some) of the Roma-related activities of the EU, the ensuing chapter deals with the established EU institutions dealing with the Roma, that is, the Inter-Service Group on Roma, the Informal Contact Group, and the Platform for Roma Inclusion.

6.3.3   Informal Contact Group, Inter-Service Group on Roma, and European Roma Platform

To provide an informal framework for exchanging information and coordinating activities with regard to Roma across different IOs, the Informal Contact Group of International Organizations and Institutions dealing with Roma, Sinti, and Traveler (henceforward, 'Informal Contact Group') was set up by the Finnish Presidency of the EU in 1999 as a follow-up to the Tampere Summit. The *Informal Contact Group* ideally brings together representatives of the COE, EU, OSCE, United Nations High Commissioner for Refugees (UNHCR), and the World Bank. The Informal Contact Group meets every six months in Brussels and is chaired by the respective EU Presidency (PR Slovenia 2008: 1). Since the following section, dealing with the IOR between the EU and the COE in the fight against Roma discrimination, elaborates further on the contact within the framework of the Informal Contact Group, this section goes on to discuss the Inter-Service Group on Roma.

Given that a number of different DGs within the Commission (previously mainly DG EMPL and DG ELARG) were dealing with the Roma at this point, an Inter-Service Group was established in November 2004. The purposes of the *Inter-Service Group* meetings are to discuss and coordinate Roma activities within the Commission. It is, so to speak, an internal coordination mechanism. Formerly, the Unit G4 of DG EMPL, Action against Discrimination, Civil Society, chaired the quarterly meeting in which representatives of about 15 other DGs participated (PR Netherlands 2004: 2–3; PR Portugal 2007: 3). As of January 2011, the new DG JUST (created in July 2010) absorbed former tasks of DG EMPL by gaining the new Directorate D dealing inter alia with nondiscrimination policy and Roma coordination. Supposedly, the new directorate within DG JUSTICE will inherit the task of chairing the Inter-Service Group meetings.

As a result of the first EU Summit on Roma, the Council of the EU instructed the Commission to establish a new *Platform for Roma Inclusion* (European Roma Platform) aimed at facilitating exchange of policies and practices between the EU member states, providing analytical support, and stimulating cooperation between all parties concerned (Council 2008d: 2). The platform meetings are decided upon and chaired by the respective EU Presidency. So far six meetings have taken place between 2009 and 2011, bringing together national governments, the EU, IOs, and Romani organizations.

From the above description, the overlap between the European Roma Platform and the Informal Contact Group – in terms of targets and, in principle, also participants – becomes obvious. Accordingly, the European Roma Platform as well as the Informal Contact Group had to consider and discuss the (mid-term) possibility of a merger between the two structures (PR Sweden 2009). Section 6.5 tackling the Roma-related IOR between the EU and the COE will pick up on the issue of the European Roma Platform.

6.4 Interorganizational contacts in the fight against Roma discrimination

6.4.1 Reciprocal representation: MG-S-ROM and Informal Contact Group / Platform

A number of EU bodies are entitled to participate in the COE Roma expert meetings, the meetings of MG-S-ROM: namely the Commission, the Council of the EU, the EP and FRA may send representatives to these meetings (MG-S-ROM 2008b: 4). The MG-S-ROM meetings normally take place two times per year, primarily in Strasbourg. The earlier EUMC and now the FRA participate regularly in the meetings of MG-S-ROM and are very active in terms of commenting on the COE documents. Until 2000, the Commission was not much interested in attending the MG-S-ROM meetings: DG RELEX did not attend despite being invited. Since then, aside from DG ELARG, DG EMPL has shown interest in participating, whereas the Council of the EU has not. However, from a point of view on the interorganizational contact between the EU and the COE, the meetings of the Informal Contact Group are more interesting than the MG-S-ROM meetings. Hence, this section focuses primarily on the latter meeting mechanism.

As previously mentioned, the biannual Informal Contact Group meetings have the purpose of bringing together representatives of different IOs dealing with Roma and providing a framework for the exchange of information. Table 6.1 lists the dates of the meetings of the Informal Contact Group (2004–2010) and sets out the main items on the agenda.

This section goes on to describe the *general setting of the Informal Contact Group meetings*. Table 6.1 shows that, in the past, the meetings did not take place quite as regularly as envisaged: in some years there was only one meeting instead of two, and between 2003 and the first half of 2004 there were no meetings at all. The one-day meetings consist of a morning session and, occasionally, such as in April 2008, an additional afternoon session. In theory, the morning session is limited to governmental IOs whereas the afternoon session is open to NGOs as well (PR Slovenia 2008). However, the aim has proven ineffective in practice, as both sessions have overlapped, and subsequently the IOs and the NGOs have met in one single session (I-27). Concerning the participants, one can observe that, in recent years, participation of OSCE, UNHCR, and the World Bank has declined, while the Informal Contact Group meetings have been transformed into some kind of exclusive EU–COE format. Taking the meeting of April 2008 as an example, one can see that only the EU and the COE representatives have attended. Compared with past meetings, there is a tendency to inviting more and more EU representatives from various bodies other than the Commission and FRA (for example EP, European Economic and Social Committee) (PR Netherlands 2004; PR Portugal 2007; PR Slovenia 2008). Additionally and most recently, the participation of the EU Presidencies increased: in December 2008 the Informal Contact Group established that the 'trio presidency of the European Union [should] be simultaneously associated to the organisation of future meetings' (PR France 2008: 12).

Table 6.1   Meetings of the Informal Contact Group

Informal Contact Group (ICG) Meetings		
Date	**Place**	**Items on the agenda** First three items on the agenda (less 'opening of the meeting')
18.11.2004	Brussels	Exchange of information, monitoring and evaluating activities on Roma issues
09.11.2005	Brussels	Exchange of information, Joint International Conference on the Implementation of Policies/Action Plans for Roma 2006, coordination
03.04.2006	Brussels	Exchange of information, fact-finding mission of the situation of IDPs in Kosovo, combating anti-Gypsyism in Europe
19.12.2006	Brussels	Exchange of information, drawing-up common guidelines on policies for Roma, organization of task forces
11.06.2007	Brussels	Exchange of information, European Roma Strategy process
17.12.2007	Brussels	Impact of current policies and the implementation of recommendations in the member states, fixing priorities, problem of Roma refugees
22.04.2008	Brussels	Development of a European strategy
05.12.2008	Brussels	Recommendations on the effective functioning of the ICG, European Roma Summit, projects, and priorities
28.09.2009	Brussels	ICG and European Roma Platform, extreme forms of discrimination, promotion of wider political representation
10.02.2010	Brussels	Objectives of the Spanish Presidency in relation to the Roma, European Roma Summit, ICG, and the European Roma Platform

Source: PR Netherlands (2004); PR UK (2005); PR Austria (2006); PR Finland (2006); PR Germany (2007); PR Portugal (2007); PR Slovenia (2008); PR France (2008); PR Sweden (2009); PR Spain (2010).

Altogether, there are about 30 participants attending the meetings, but the final number depends on the respective EU Presidency, which can freely decide on whom to invite.

The most important part of the Informal Contact Group meeting is the *le tour de table*, in which the different representatives inform one another of what their organizations have been doing in terms of activities on the Roma in the last six months along with the scope of their future plans. Beyond that, the content of these meetings depends on the priorities of the respective EU Presidency: some of the most recent EU

Presidencies, for example the Swedish, tried to exceed the mere information exchange format by introducing a substantial discussion on thematic issues. However, it remains to be seen whether successive EU Presidencies choose to pursue the new thematic format or return to the format of information exchange. With regard to a joint dinner or lunch after the Informal Contact Group meeting, it also depends on whether the chairing EU Presidency chooses to invite the participants, which is quite common. If nothing has been organized, some members of the Informal Contact Group go out with their colleagues on their own (I-6; I-27; I-36).

In addition to the Informal Contact Group meetings, six meetings of the European Roma Platform have taken place since April 2009. Given the major overlap in participants, the tendency is to organize the meetings of the Informal Contact Group and the European Roma Platform on the same date, for example, the two meetings that took place in Brussels on 28 September 2009. As the European Roma Platform will be one of the issues analyzed in Section 6.5 on the IOR between the EU and the COE in the fight against Roma discrimination, this section does not explain this issue further.

In conclusion, this section focuses on the COE's involvement with and representation in EU meetings. Confronted with the COE Roma expert meetings, in which the EU staff is entitled to participate, the COE Secretariat is not invited to the meetings on Roma of the Inter-Service Group within the Commission. Originally, the COE Secretariat asked to be invited, but there has not been the option to attend, and the COE staff has not insisted. The reason why it is not uttermost importance for the COE to attend these EU meetings lies in the fact that, besides within the COE and the EU framework, there are meetings on Roma in many other contexts. As a matter of fact, the number of conferences, seminars, and events on the Roma have currently increased exponentially. As a result, staffs from the Commission and the COE Secretariat meet nearly every two weeks and at least once every month. Against this background of frequent meetings and the existing informal channels of communication, both sides agree that the need for more formal meetings is not at all pressing (I-6; I-27; I-36).

6.5   IOR in the fight against Roma discrimination

This section reviews the issues of interests in the relations between the EU and the COE in fighting Roma discrimination. Accordingly, this section touches upon specific policy and institutional questions such as the EU Summit on Roma and the new Platform, the possibility of joint activities in terms of statements, projects, and so on, and more generally the EU's interest in owning the leadership in Roma, along with the COE's fear of the EU reinventing the wheel. Moreover, it deals with the joint programs of the two IOs in this issue area. First, the section reviews the new European Roma Summits set up by the EU.

Even though Section 6.4 showed that mechanisms for reciprocal representation are in place, the relations between the COE and the EU, in particular the Roma and Travelers Unit (COE Secretariat) and the unit dealing with Roma in DG EMPL (Commission), were not always straightforward. As an example, the COE was not involved in Commission activities throughout 2008 (drafting of the report on Roma), neither in the development of the strategy nor in the preparatory phase of the *European Roma Summit*. In particular, the Roma and Travelers Unit attempted to get involved through meetings and by mentioning the existing COE documents (I-9; I-27). However, the efforts were not successful as the following citation from a member of an NGO shows:

> In my opinion there was a problem, because the European Commission wanted to have, how to say, to be the owner of the whole process without really letting the COE to be part of the whole process. [The] European Commission would like to be the leaders and to have the leadership in this issue, because they feel they are stronger, they have more resources and possible ideas and they would like to deal with this issue. It is a very important topic, I am not going to say that it is sexy to deal with Roma issues but in a way it is fashionable to deal because you have many possibilities to for different projects, programs. And therefore I think they want to be the leaders on the whole issue. (I-9)

The Head of the COE Roma and Travelers Unit was invited to the European Roma Summit, but space was not granted to COE activities, since he was only invited as rapporteur of a policy panel. Afterwards, the COE complained to the Commission that the SG of the COE was not invited despite the COE's long experience in this field. The COE is concerned that the Commission has begun reinventing the wheel without taking into account the existing work done by the COE. In contrast, the EU argues that it is quite natural for someone to be unhappy about the design of such a Summit, given that there are many different participants with varying expectations (I-9; I-27; I-36).

At the second European Roma Summit on 8 April 2010 in Spain, the COE was also not represented by the SG, but the Director General of Social Cohesion attended the Summit, which, for once, entailed the attendance of a higher political level compared with attendance in the first Summit. Whether caused by the complaints or not, the COE representative also had time to explain some of the recent COE initiatives in this field, which is another improvement from the COE's point of view. Quite self-critically, the Summit participants address the interaction between the different IOs and their initiatives by stating that '[d]espite increased co-ordination, co-operation between the different institutions and international processes (European Union, Decade, OSCE, Council of Europe, etc.) continues to be insufficient' (Spanish Presidency 2010: 16). This issue will be addressed more in depth later in this section.

Somewhat similar to the question of the European Roma Summit is the *European Roma Platform*. The new European Roma Platform also raises the concern from the COE that the EU is trying to reinvent the wheel without taking into account the work done by other actors in this field, for example, work done by the COE. As is clear from the following quote, which sets out the intended aim of the European Roma Platform, it overlaps with the Informal Contact Group in terms of participants, and its tasks resemble those of the COE Roma expert meetings.

> [The aim of the European Roma Platform is to provide for] an exchange of good practice and experience between the Member States in the sphere of inclusion of the Roma, provide analytical support and stimulate cooperation between all parties concerned by Roma issues, including the organisations representing Roma.
>
> (Council 2008d)

As laid out above, MG-S-ROM, the COE Committee on Roma and Travelers, inter alia is instructed to act as a forum for exchange of information and good practice. Therefore, the COE Coordinator for Roma and Travelers Issues repeatedly pointed out this duplication.

> [T]he sharing of information and best practices is already done within the Council of Europe Committee of Experts on Roma and Travellers which, apart from having all EU member states as participants, includes representatives of the European Commission, the OSCE, the UNHCR and several internationl [sic!] Roma NGOs. (PR Spain 2010: 5) [T]he Platform needed to go beyond the traditional exchange of information and provide a veritable issue to the problems facing Roma.
>
> (PR Sweden 2009: 2)

The representative from DG Employment dealing with the Roma held the view that the Informal Contact Group and the European Roma Platform were politically of a different nature and that it was useful for the European Roma Platform to concentrate on a particular theme during each meeting, as was the case with the meeting of September 2009 dedicated to education (PR Spain 2010: 5). Other participants took a more critical stance toward the EU initiative and questioned the added value of the European Roma Platform, or stated that the nature and purpose of the Platform needed to be clarified. One participant accurately stated the problem behind the accumulation of bodies by stating 'that the number of meetings was constantly on the increase and left no time to work' (PR Sweden 2009: 2). This statement, as well as the one above highlighting the insufficient cooperation between IOs and their initiatives, suggests that the increased interest in the Roma (of the EU) has also led to new bodies and meetings dealing with this issue. What appears to be – at least partly – missing is a coherent plan of how the new bodies and meetings fit into the preexisting framework and in what ways they could complement it.

In the meeting of the Informal Contact Group in February 2011, the participants decided to revisit the idea of restricting the Informal Contact Group meeting to only IOs in order to avoid duplication with the European Roma Platform. Henceforward, the European Roma Platform would be the forum in which to exchange information and activities open to IOs and NGOs, while the restricted Informal Contact Group meeting, held immediately after the meeting of the Platform, would provide a forum in which to discuss cooperation and coordination between IOs (I-27).

Apart from this example of disputed institutional issues, one can also find instances of *substantive policy disagreement*. In June 2008, the EU and the COE took up differing positions on the Italian Roma policy, in which the EU, at first, claimed that Italy did not violate the EU antidiscrimination law and fundamental rights of Roma, whereas the COE loudly protested against it (COE 2008; Commissioner 2008, 2009). However, in this case the COE's main counterpart was not the unit dealing with Roma in DG EMPL but a DG JLS unit. The issue in question was the following: from June to October 2008, Italy began a first-round census of the Roma population living in regular and irregular settlements. According to the Italian government, the plan for fingerprinting all Roma residents in camps would curb inadequate housing problems and rising crime rates (ERRC et al. 2009: 3–6). Many observers claimed that the action of the Italian government violated EU law and fundamental rights. More specifically, it would contradict EU data protection law (Directive 95/46/EC), the EU antidiscrimination law (Directive 2000/43/EC), and various fundamental rights protected by the ECHR (ERRC et al. 2009: 19–36). One can derive from this example that the COE, in particular the Commissioner for Human Rights, acted very quickly and loudly, taking a human rights point of view on this issue. In contrast, the EU, more specifically the Commission, changed its position only after the popular outrage demanding an explanation from the competent Italian minister later on in the process. Subsequently, the Italian government amended the law in question. Another example was the question of the return of the Roma originating from Kosovo back to Kosovo and to neighboring countries in the region, to which the EU agreed while the COE did not (I-27; I-36). From this paragraph, it appears that the EU does not find it easy to take a human rights point of view, at least not initially.

Having reviewed instances of conflictive relations, the following two paragraphs shed light on how the *cooperation between the EU and the COE in fighting Roma discrimination* works. With regard to joint activities, one has to mention the general *joint programs* between the Commission and the COE (see Section 3.1.3 of Chapter 3), some of which deal with discrimination against the Roma, either exclusively or within a broader framework. Although it is a so-called joint program, in most cases the EU finances the bigger part, while the COE provides the know-how and the staff. In some cases the EU has provided all the funds, while the COE has carried out the project on its own. Hence, one could speak of the COE being subcontracted in those cases. Returning to joint programs on the Roma, while the EU became (more) interested in the Roma issue after the enlargement of the EU in 2004, the area of application of joint programs and therefore the availability of EU funds have shrunk contemporaneously. This is due to the fact that joint programs – in this format – are invariably targeted toward EU *candidate* countries. Since many of the former COE member states in Central and Eastern Europe became EU member states, there is now no longer the possibility of including them in joint programs (I-6; I-16; I-27). Nevertheless, the Roma issue is still of concern in some of these (now) EU member states. As an alternative, the Roma and Travelers Unit (COE Secretariat), together with the FRA, aims at carrying out joint programs that would focus on EU member states. So far, however, only one Roma-related joint program on the Roma women and health care (2002) has taken place. In 2009, another FRA project formally involved the COE Commissioner for Human Rights (FRA 2009) and informal participation of the Roma and Travelers Unit

(I-1; I-27). Therefore, the COE's financial dependency on the EU in the area of Roma becomes evident.

Apart from joint meetings and projects, the various units dealing with the Roma in the Commission and the FRA on the one side and the COE Secretariat on the other side are in contact and consult one another informally via e-mail and telephone. The relationship between the COE Secretariat and the FRA appears to be a particularly smooth and close one. What facilitates this relationship is the continuity of persons throughout the years of working within the COE Secretariat and the FRA, which has strengthened the trust between the involved counterparts. Additionally, due to the independent position that the FRA has within the EU system, it is easier for the COE to adopt joint statements with the FRA (I-1; I-24; I-27). In contrast, the staff within the Commission tends to change after some time due to the rotation principle, which in turn complicates the establishment of trustful working relationships. Moreover, as of January 2011, the antidiscrimination policy (and with it Roma issues) falls under the portfolio of the new DG JUSTICE, and this brings about, again, new counterparts. Additionally, joint statements between the COE and the Commission are out of question, since the involved Commission staff does not represent the entire Commission and accordingly cannot speak on behalf of it. Putting additional limits on this cooperation is the fact that the EU does not have a genuine competence for this topic (for example the EU cannot instruct member states' policy in education or housing), but can tackle Roma issues only indirectly through the nondiscrimination policy (I-6; I-22; I-27).

As previously mentioned, there are common projects in place with regard to the FRA. However, the *internal coordination mechanism* within the COE entails some challenges. The COE has placed an internal contact person for the FRA (see Chapter 8): the COE contact person's primary task is coordination, although especially in the beginning the contact person also had to raise awareness about the FRA. The coordination task entails, for example, collecting comments of the various COE units on the FRA's work program, collecting and selecting project proposals, and organizing COE visits to the FRA. Unfortunately, the internal coordination mechanism carries the potential for conflict. Due to the fact that the contact person is attached to an operational DG, more specifically to the DGHL, the staffs of the other DGs partly feel left out. One criticism is that the DGHL now has a privileged relationship with the FRA, which biases the FRA's selection of proposed projects (I-26; I-27; I-32).

An example of the potential for improved cooperation is the Roma and Travelers *activity calendar* set up by the Roma and Travelers Unit of the COE Secretariat within the past few years. The electronic calendar in theory lists activities of various IOs (for example COE, EU, OSCE, and UNHCR) and various NGOs. More specifically, the calendar announces the date, the venue, the event, and the contact persons, for example, listing that the European Roma Platform meets under the Hungarian EU Presidency (Report of the EC Task Force on Roma) in Budapest on 8–9 April 2011 (COE 2012c). Besides exchanging information on current activities, the ideal conception would be to coordinate these activities in advance (I-6; I-27). The advantage would be obvious: by learning about the activities of other IOs in advance, one would be able to choose to either focus on different aspects during a certain time frame or combine all the existing activities and highlight a specific issue in a certain time frame (for example housing). However, this currently seems a long way off. Additionally, the 2011 calendar primarily focused on COE activities, which might be explained by the fact that it is set up by the COE, but questions whether the calendar was indeed a calendar with information from all the partners. A 2012 calendar is not available online (June 2012).

What is noticeable from this section is the fact that cooperation between the EU and the COE in this policy field is much less distinct (as compared to the JHA field), especially when looking at cooperation within the internal human rights policy (targeted at EU member states). This might be explained by the fact that, for the EU, the COE is only one among the four or five most important actors in the field of social policy. It seems that much of the work is uncoordinated, and cooperation is, to some degree, random. In this regard, the COE fears that the EU is trying to reinvent the wheel, without considering the already existing COE documents on Roma on the one hand, and the meeting mechanisms and subsequent know-how already in place in Strasbourg (Roma expert meetings) on the other hand. Therefore, in order to improve the practical interorganizational cooperation between the EU and the COE in this field, it is necessary to either bring the parallel meeting mechanisms existing in the EU and the COE framework to an end, or to coordinate the current set up and decide on the tasks of each body. In a next step, the EU and the COE could inform each other of their future initiatives and priorities so that they either join forces or – at least – not direct the general public's attention away from Roma discrimination.

Finally, this section recalls the COE's fear of duplication through the EU and sets out a possible explanation. The EU's engagement in Roma issues attracts much more attention than that of the COE, even though the COE has been working on Roma issues for much longer. Besides these questions of visibility and media attention, the COE feels a kind of phantom (and real financial) pain in the sense that many of the countries that joined the COE in the beginning of the 1990s have become EU member states in the meantime and are therefore no longer applicable areas for joint programs. The problems of Roma discrimination in the new (and old) EU member states are anything but settled; however, the COE's engagement is repressed through its budget limitations now that the EU money is lacking. Lastly, the Commission might not always be very keen on relying on the work of the COE, as suggested by the following quotation:

> The Commission has its own power which comes with an attitude. [...] Sometimes it's good to keep in mind the other interests as well. There are other actors in this area. So we build on something that exists already, it's not terra incognita, it's not brand new. (I-16)

Therefore, the COE sees the need to remind the EU of what already exists in Strasbourg. However, instead of dismissing the EU's activities, the COE tries to push – as the staff says – 'in a way against their self-interest' (no organization wants another to interfere in its programs) the EU and FRA to do more on Roma (I-6). Concluding this empirical part, the subsequent section reviews and analyzes the fight against Roma discrimination case against the background of the theoretical framework.

6.6   IOR in the fight against Roma discrimination – analysis and explanatory factors

This section attempts to link the empirical results to the factors facilitating (hindering) interorganizational cooperation established in the theoretical framework in order to examine what the IOR between the EU and the COE means in terms of IOR theory.

6.6.1   Interest (policy and organizational)

This section looks at the differing histories of both IOs in terms of their respective commitments to protecting human rights, and examines whether this has had any impact on the two IOs' contemporary approach to human rights.

In the fight against Roma discrimination case, the policy interest of both IOs is congruent in most instances. This is due to the fact that the EU is building on the work of the COE. Yet, difficulties arise, given that the COE's norms do not appear as 'COE norms' in these documents. Therefore, the COE's organizational self-interest is at stake: the COE fears that the EU is reinventing the wheel and accuses the Commission of wanting to 'own' the process without letting the COE to be part of it. Nevertheless, the COE tries to push the EU and FRA to do more on Roma, 'in a way against their self-interest' – as the staff says. Returning to the policy congruence, this research identified instances of substantive disagreement between the COE and the EU, for example, on the Italian Roma policy. However, in this case, the COE's counterpart was not the Roma unit in DG EMPL as was previously the case, but a DG JLS unit.

6.6.2 Organizational characteristics

In the fight against Roma discrimination case, we have been able to observe that internal coordination mechanisms carry conflict potential. Due to the fact that the FRA contact person within the COE is attached to an operational DG, the staff of the other DGs feels partly left out. One point of criticism is that this DG now has a privileged relationship with the FRA, which biases the selection of projects proposed to the FRA. Additionally, heavy bureaucracies in the COE as well as in the FRA impede the joint funding of projects.

As opposed to what one might expect, one could therefore conclude that internal coordination mechanisms, like DG RELEX for general IOR between the EU and the COE or more specifically the coordination mechanism within the COE for relations with the FRA, do not always facilitate cooperation. In such settings, circumventing the coordination units through informal bilateral contacts might be a more promising way to go.

6.6.3 Socialization

This section considers one of the two aspects of the socialization factor: trust (at the individual level between persons involved in the IOR). In the fight against Roma discrimination case, a meeting mechanism, the Informal Contact Group, was set up and has been in place since 1999. The Informal Contact Group ideally brings together representatives of the COE, EU, OSCE, UNHCR, and the World Bank in order to exchange information and coordinate activities. In recent years, participation from the other IOs has declined and the meeting has transformed into some kind of exclusive COE–EU meeting. Yet, a trustful relationship did not develop between the (previously) involved counterparts (DG EMPL and COE Secretariat). This may be due to the fact that, over the years, different EU units participated in the meeting (if they participated at all), which reflects that the former 'accession country issue' became an internal issue in 2004 and/or that the meetings themselves remained at a superficial level.

6.6.4   Physical opportunity

To recall, the physical opportunity factor looks at the existing infrastructure in the external environment (transport system) as well as the intraorganizational resources available for IOR.

We have seen in Section 6.4 that there are many institutionalized meetings on the Roma in different contexts, within and beyond the COE and the EU framework. Accordingly, the staff is already accustomed to attending these meetings, despite the costly and time-consuming journey to and from Strasbourg (if non-COE staff is in attendance in Strasbourg or if COE staff is attending meetings elsewhere). Moreover, one can say that Liaison Offices on site in Brussels and Strasbourg are negligible for the IOR in fighting Roma discrimination. Since the Liaison Office of the COE in Brussels and the Delegation of the Commission to the COE are understaffed, the staff is unable to follow all the IOR (in the different subject areas), but instead can only concentrate on a few. Hence, officials tend to oversee the IOR according to their previous backgrounds. The focus is often put on JLS (as opposed to, for example, social policy). Additionally, similarly to the data protection case, officials have had to concentrate on conflictive relations while ignoring others due to staff shortages. Hence, the fight against Roma discrimination did not attract as much attention as, for example, the fight against terrorism.

Moving on to the second aspect, the intraorganizational resources, the EU and the COE have highly differing financial resources at their disposal. The fight against Roma discrimination case shows the COE's dependency on EU funding in order to conduct (joint) programs and the shrinking area of application of joint programs and therefore the diminishing available EU money as a result of the 2004 enlargement.

6.7   IOR in the fight against Roma discrimination – conclusions

The preceding sections set out to shed light on the IOR between the EU and the COE with regard to combating Roma discrimination, the third policy issue to be analyzed in addition to data protection and the fight against terrorism. It has been pointed out that, before the fall of Communism, there was hardly any interest in the Roma's social, political, and economic marginalization in their countries of residence. Scholars argue that the sudden interest of IOs – particularly of the OSCE and the EU – in Roma around the early-to-mid 1990s can be explained by the open security concerns in European countries about Roma immigration triggered by the fall of Communism.

The sections have shown that the COE has been the first European organization – alongside with the OSCE – addressing minority issues. Although the COE had adopted resolutions and recommendations on Roma as far back as the 1960s, the COE intensified its activities only from the beginning of the 1990s when many former Communist countries applied for COE membership. The EU also increased its attention to the Roma in the beginning of the 1990s, though only in the context of accession negotiations with candidate countries, while neglecting the topic of minority protection in the EU's internal affairs. With antidiscrimination becoming EU policy and accession expanding to ten Central and Eastern European countries, EU attention has further increased since 2000. The perspective of the EU Roma policy only changed from a security-oriented approach to a more rights-based approach when the accession in 2004 caused the situation of the Roma to become an internal issue. In 2007, the European Council gave the political signal for the EU to begin work in the field of Roma, which resulted in the set up of European Roma Summits and a European Roma Platform. In both cases, the COE has expressed concerns that the EU is trying to reinvent the wheel without taking into account the work done by the COE in this field and the existing meeting mechanism in Strasbourg. For example, there was not enough thought given to the question of what the added value of these new bodies would be or how the new bodies would fit into the already existing framework. This leaves the participants with a time-consuming situation of an exponentially increased number of meetings, conferences, and events on Roma. Fear of marginalization plays a role in the EU–COE relationship as well; even though the COE has been working on Roma issues much longer, the EU's work within Roma issues attracts much more attention. On the cooperative side, one can see that there are joint projects between the EU and the COE dealing with Roma issues. Yet, the COE is symbolically (and financially) dragged down by the fact that many of the countries that joined the COE in early 1990s have since joined the EU and therefore are no longer in the area of application for joint projects. Given the fact that problems with Roma discrimination in the new (and old) EU member states are anything but settled, the COE tries to engage in joint projects with the FRA as an alternative. In practice, however, the number of joint projects with the FRA has so far fallen short of the COE's expectations. Besides joint projects, the FRA and the COE counterparts are in contact and they consult each other informally or release joint statements. In conclusion, it is worth highlighting that the cooperation between the EU and the COE in this field is much less distinct (as compared to the JHA field), especially with regard to the internal human rights policy. This might be explained by the fact that, for the EU, the COE is only one among the four or five most important actors in the field of social policy.

In terms of IOR theory, the fight against Roma discrimination case has shown that the interest factor (in particular the organizational self-interest) plays a major role in the EU–COE relations, and that if the organizational self-interest is high in one of the IOs, the IOR are most probably conflictive. However, instead of dismissing the EU's activities in the fight against Roma discrimination case, the COE tries to push the EU and the FRA to do more for the Roma at their own expense. Two factors, complexity and socialization, reinforce the direction pre-determined by the interest factor: at the same time, they are unable to override it and reverse the trend. The fight against Roma discrimi-nation case has shown that internal coordination mechanisms (within each organization) do not always facilitate cooperation. Due to the different EU units (in the Commission) that have dealt with Roma issues over the years, a trustful relationship has not evolved at the individual counterpart level. In contrast, one can see a smooth rela-tionship between the COE and the FRA, facilitated by the independent position of the FRA within the EU system and the continuity of the involved counterparts, which strengthened the trust at the individ-ual level. The physical opportunity factor, the environmental features, and the intraorganizational resources do not have a direct impact on whether the relations are cooperative or conflictive, but instead indi-rectly exert influence on the extent of the IOR by creating additional challenges for the staff, who cannot control these conditions but must continue to cope with them (for example the COE's dependency on EU money due to lack of resources).

Part III
Institutional Cases

The case studies examined in this part of the book – the Memorandum of Understanding (Chapter 7) and the Fundamental Rights Agency (Chapter 8) – deal with institutional issues in the EU–COE relationship. In contrast to the preceding case studies focusing on policy issues, relations dealing with institutional issues can be regarded as politically sensitive and high level. The issues under analysis are structured as follows: The chapters start by providing the reader with a brief introduction to the use of MOUs in public international law on the one hand, and the antecedent situation of the establishment of the FRA on the other hand. They highlight the origins of the respective institutional innovations and examine the interorganizational contacts between the EU and the COE concerning the negotiation of the MOU and the FRA. Subsequently, the chapters present the final text of the MOU and the final setup of the FRA. At the core of these chapters is the subsequent analysis of the interorganizational relations between the EU and the COE surrounding the MOU and the FRA. The empirical cases are concluded with an analysis of the results against the background of the theoretical framework.

7
The Memorandum of Understanding

This chapter scrutinizes the IOR between the EU and the COE concerning the negotiation of the MOU, the Cooperation Agreement between the two organizations. The MOU is an interesting case to look at, as it has at its core the empirical focus of this research, namely EU–COE relations. Once committed to the idea of successfully adopting an agreement that would foster cooperation between them, the EU and the COE were confronted with a relatively long and difficult negotiation process (with many different actors involved). The controversy over the FRA heavily complicated the MOU negotiation process. In general, one can say that the COE was looking for a binding document with systematic cooperation mechanisms, while the EU, in contrast, wanted to maintain as much room for maneuver while simultaneously placating the COE. Prior to analyzing the contentious matters in detail, the subsequent section tackles the use of MOUs in public international law.

7.1 The use of MOUs in public international law

In public international law and practice, one often comes across the MOU. In fact, within public international law, the MOU is a well-accepted legal instrument. As early as the 1960s, it was recognized as 'an informal but nevertheless legal instrument' (McNair 1961: 15). In other words, the MOU does not appropriately qualify as a formal instrument, but, in contrast, can be seen as an *informal* instrument as it represents an 'instrument which is not a treaty because the parties to it do not intend it to be legally binding' (Aust 1986: 787).

The scholarly literature broadly describes the MOU as a excellent example of a 'non-treaty' or more specifically as a 'gentleman's agreement', 'non-binding agreement', '*de facto* agreement', and 'non-legal agreement' (Aust 1986: 787; Redgwell 2000: 104). In diplomatic terminology, it is generally called an MOU, since this is the most commonly used phrase. However, calling an instrument an MOU does not reveal its legal status nor reveal whether the instrument in question is binding or nonbinding: confusingly, one will also find (binding) treaties that are likewise called 'Memoranda of Understanding'. From this one can conclude that merely studying the title or other designation does not allow one to determine whether an instrument is of a legally binding nature. Even though there are different perspectives on whether a document should be called an 'agreement' when it is not legally binding (McNeill 1994: 823), this research follows Aust (2007: 21) in loosely referring to an MOU as an 'agreement', even though the parties to it have no intention that it should be legally binding. In conclusion, for the purpose of this research, which is not legal in nature, it is sufficient to define the MOU as an agreement intended to have political (or moral) weight.

When looking at possible consequences of informal instruments, one immediately thinks in terms of political or moral effects. Besides these obvious effects, one might contemplate whether an instrument, which is not in itself legally binding, can give rise to legal consequences. There are different views on this question: some scholars argue that the incentives for complying with informal instruments – so to say 'soft-law' – are essentially non legal. Following this view, compliance with them is a question of 'bureaucratic habit' (Baxter 1980: 556) and the MOU therefore lacks the binding power of a contract. In contrast, other scholars take the view that even an informal instrument might become legally binding, depending on the circumstances, for example, their association with a treaty.

So what are the advantages of informal instruments such as the MOU? First and foremost is the lack of formality: since the clauses are not entered into in the context of a treaty, parties worry less about elaborating final clauses or the formalities in relation to treaty making. Second, there is no requirement to publish it or register it with the UN, which accommodates the quest for confidentiality (for example for reasons of national security). Third, an informal instrument is easier to amend or even terminate.

By examining the form and the wording of an instrument, it is easy to establish whether the parties had a binding or a nonbinding status in mind with regard to a specific document. The wording of an informal instrument typically avoids terms that denote an intention to conclude a treaty, such as 'shall', 'agree', and 'enter into force'. Most probably, 'shall' gives way to less mandatory terms such as 'will', and the instrument is supposed to 'come into operation' or 'come into effect' instead of requiring the parties to 'agree' or 'undertake'. Most often designated as 'MOU' or 'arrangement', even the name points out the intention to create something less than a treaty. Finally, what is often missing in MOUs are terminological elements such as 'the parties' and final clauses noting the terms and the date of entry into force (Aust 1986: 789–812; McNeill 1994: 824). Table 7.1 summarizes the treaty and the MOU terminology.

To conclude, this section discusses the subject matter or content of MOUs. An MOU may be used as a 'confirmation of agreed-upon terms when an oral agreement has not been captured into a formal contract' (CAP 2010: 158). They often set out operational arrangements under an international framework agreement (for example a treaty) or regulate technical or detailed matters. Parties also deploy MOUs as contracts entailing all the basic principles and guidelines under which they will work together to accomplish their goals. Typically, the MOU takes the

Table 7.1 Treaty and MOU terminology – comparison

Treaty	MOU
article	paragraph
agree(d)	decide(d), accept(ed), approve(d)
agreement	arrangement(s), understanding(s)
authentic, authoritative	equally valid
clause	paragraph
conditions	provisions
continue in force	continue to have effect
done	signed
enter into force	come into effect, come into operation
mutually agreed	jointly decided
obligations	commitments
parties	participants, governments
preamble	introduction
rights	benefits
shall	will
terms	provisions
undertake	carry out
undertakings	understandings

Source: Aust (2007: 496).

form of a single instrument that does not require ratification and is concluded by either states or IOs. For instance, on the one hand, the UN negotiates MOUs with member states in order to organize peacekeeping operations or to arrange conferences. On the other hand, the UN adopts MOUs specifically regarding cooperation with other IOs (CAP 2010: 158; Paclii 2012).

It is exactly in this latter sense – the framework for the cooperation between different IOs – that this research will look at the MOU. The subsequent sections set out the origins of the MOU (7.2), explain the negotiation process (7.3), scrutinize the final text (7.4), and single out issues of interest in the IOR between the EU and the COE when negotiating the MOU (7.5).

7.2   Warsaw Summit: impulse for the MOU between the EU and the COE

When looking at the history of the MOU, one has to start with the Third Summit of Heads of State and Government of the COE, which took place in Warsaw on 16–17 May 2005 and gave the impetus for the reconstruction of the relations between the COE and the EU. On the agenda was the realignment of the principal tasks of the COE for the future. Therefore, the so-called Warsaw Summit dealt with major issues and challenges for the future of the COE. Within the Summit, the long-term positioning of the COE within the European integration process was an issue, particularly its assertiveness toward the EU. The participants of the Summit decided to establish a new framework for the COE's interorganizational relationship with the EU by stating:

> We are resolved to create a new framework for enhanced co-operation and interaction between the Council of Europe and the European Union in areas of common concern, in particular human rights, democracy and the rule of law.
>
> (COM 2005a: Paragraph 10.1)

To put the Warsaw Declaration into practice, the participants adopted an Action Plan. The Action Plan, inter alia, substantiated the intention to establish a new framework regarding relations with the EU, which had previously been formulated in a rather general way. To foster cooperation with the EU, the Action Plan put forward the plan to adopt a framework for cooperation in the format of an MOU:

Based on the appended guidelines, a memorandum of understanding will be drafted between the Council of Europe and the European Union to create a new framework of enhanced co-operation and political dialogue.

(COM 2005b: Chapter IV.1)

According to the Action Plan, the MOU has to seek out new ways for the EU and its member states to better benefit from COE instruments and institutions, and for all COE member states to gain more from closer links with the EU. The ten 'appended guidelines', forming the basis for the intended MOU, stress the common interest and aims of the COE and the EU and the fact that the partnership is based on complementarity. Also, they place emphasis on an early accession of the EU to the ECHR and argue the need for a reinforcing cooperation and extending joint activities. Finally, the guidelines call upon the EU to access COE expertise whenever tackling issues involving COE core competence:

The European Union shall in particular make full use of Council of Europe expertise in areas such as human rights, information, cybercrime, bioethics, trafficking and organised crime, where action is required within its competence.

(COM 2005b: Appendix 1.7)

According to Walter Schwimmer, a former COE SG, these guidelines are particularly noteworthy, since they were adopted by all COE member states, and therein the 25 EU member states. Likewise the Commission, represented by Benita Ferrero-Waldner, the then Commissioner for External Relations, had a presence. Consequently, Schwimmer (2008: 1327) argues that the guidelines – albeit not officially – constitute a self-imposed commitment of the EU toward the COE.

Finally, the discussion on the new framework for the IOR between COE and EU gained new impetus when the Heads of State and Government of the COE commissioned Jean-Claude Juncker to develop a report on the current state of relationship between the COE and the EU. Following this request, Juncker (2006) 'in his personal capacity' prepared the report 'Council of Europe – European Union: "A sole ambition for the European continent"', which he submitted less than a year later, in April 2006. According to Schwimmer (2008: 1327) the future of the COE depends to a great extent on the readiness to put exactly these Juncker proposals into practice. To see the ways in which the Juncker report left its mark on the Cooperation Agreement, refer to Section 7.5.

7.3 Interorganizational contacts in the MOU negotiation process

This section traces the general timetable of the MOU negotiations, or, in other words, the roadmap during the negotiation process. It sets out the actors involved in the negotiations and aims to give insight into the formal workings of these negotiations. What this section does not do is scrutinize the content of the negotiations (and explain why they were difficult), which will be the topic of Section 7.5 dealing with the IOR with regards to the MOU.

To give a brief overview, the drafting and negotiation process of the MOU began soon after the Warsaw Summit. On the EU side, the EU Presidency and the Commission (DG RELEX, Special Representative of the Commission to the COE) formed the negotiation team. On the COE negotiation team could be found the COE Presidency and the Secretariat of the COE (DER, Liasion Office in Brussels). The negotiation and drafting process took relatively long (over two years) and was very difficult, since the discussion on the EU FRA (see Chapter 8) coincided with the negotiations on the MOU and therefore made an agreement difficult to achieve (Agence Europe 2007; Taylor 2008: 1253) (I-5; I-17; I-20; I-31). While the British Presidency of the EU submitted a first draft of the MOU as early as late 2005, the MOU was not concluded until May 2007 (PACE 2006a: 4; COM 2007a). Accordingly, one finds various rotating Presidencies on the EU as well as the COE side, as pointed out in Table 7.2, which shows the eight Presidencies that were involved in the drafting and concluding of the MOU.

Table 7.2 Presidencies of the EU and the COE negotiating the MOU

Presidencies of the Council of the EU/Chairmanships of the COM			
Date	European Union	Date	Council of Europe
2005		2005/06	
Second half-year	United Kingdom	November–May	Romania
2006		2006/07	
First half-year	Austria	May–November	Russia
Second half-year	Finland	November–May	San Marino
2007		2007	
First half-year	Germany	May–November	Serbia

Source: COM (2012), Council (2012).

Having briefly reviewed the overall framework of the process, this section traces the chronological development of the MOU in depth. As a consequence of the Warsaw Summit, the British Presidency of the EU drew up a draft MOU together with the Commission. The draft mirrored not only the position of the Presidency and the Commission, but also the opinion of other EU member states found its way into the text. Additionally, it was clear to the Presidency and the Commission that the document did not represent the EU's final position, but was instead subject to further bargain. The first draft of the MOU was submitted to the Romanian Presidency of the COE in December 2005. In January 2006, the Romanian Presidency transmitted the draft to the COE member states, calling for their comments. From January on, the COE discussed the draft extensively in the meetings of the Follow-up Committee on the Third Summit (CM-SUIVI3 2006a). While the non-EU member states issued their statements on a partly-individual and partly-coordinated basis, the Austrian Presidency of the EU faced the need to coordinate – in drawn-out negotiations – a joint position of all EU member states.

To achieve an agreement on the text before the handover of the COE Presidency to Russia, the Romanian Presidency – with the help of the COE Secretariat – compiled a new draft of the MOU, which was presented to the public in March 2006. Although the new draft was based on the original draft of the British Presidency, it incorporated a number of proposals from non-EU member states: in the document of the CM-SUIVI3 meeting in March 2006, which represents the consolidated version of the then-state of work on the draft MOU, one can see the original text of the EU as well as the COE amendment proposals and their origin. Most often, the amendments came from the COE SG and Armenia, although Azerbaijan, Serbia and Montenegro, and Switzerland contributed as well (CM-SUIVI3 2006b). Following the presentation of the new draft, some EU member states complained that the draft was – according to their view – too 'COE-friendly' and voiced their fear that it would constrain the EU's room for maneuver.

After tough negotiations in the EU coordination meetings (see Section 3.2.3 of Chapter 3 for details), the Austrian Presidency of the EU eventually managed to put forward a joint EU position. However, despite the vigorous efforts – among others, a new draft developed by the Romanian Presidency in April 2006 – it was not possible to agree on one text until May 2006, when Russia took over the COE Presidency. During the Russian Presidency of the COE, it was equally impossible to agree on a draft. Observers trace this difficulty back to the Russian

Presidency, which – according to them – was too contingent on national interests. Only the subsequent COE Presidency, San Marino, was successful in bringing the negotiations to an end after over two years (Ettmayer 2008: 1194; Taylor 2008: 1253). From January 2007 on, San Marino undertook new endeavors to end the MOU stalemate by organizing informal consultations with the COE member states 'aimed at identifying the main difficulties linked to the drafting of the Memorandum of Understanding' (CM-SUIVI3 2007a) and drawing up a new draft. The informal consultations went on until April 2007, when San Marino presented a new version of the draft MOU. The schedule was to involve the COE PACE and to submit the document to the COM for adoption in May 2007 (CM-SUIVI3 2007b). Indeed, on 11 May 2007, Fiorenzo Stolfi, Foreign Minister of San Marino and, Terry Davis, COE SG, signed the MOU. The President of the Council of the EU, Gunter Gloser, and the Commissioner for External Relations, Benita Ferrero-Waldner, signed the document nearly two weeks later on 23 May 2007 (COM 2007a). The two-week delay was necessary due to a non-timely conclusion of an internal EU procedure (Ettmayer 2008: 1194).

Besides the above-mentioned milestones in the MOU negotiation roadmap, the EU and the COE discussed the MOU and tried to come to terms with each other in meetings specifically dedicated to this purpose. These meetings normally took place in Strasbourg during the above-mentioned negotiation time frame, 2006–2007, and were relatively small, consisting, at most, of ten participants. On the EU side, representatives from the Troika Presidency and the Commission attended the meetings, and on the COE side, the Presidency and the COE Secretariat delegated staff to the meetings. Given that the EU had access to and information on the internal COE negotiations through its own member states in the COE, the meetings between the EU and the COE served to communicate information on the state of affairs of the internal EU negotiations and sort out difficulties (I-14).

7.4   The final text – the MOU

Before continuing on to the issues of interest in the IOR between the EU and the COE in their negotiations of the MOU and the compromises that needed to be found in order to resolve these issues, this section takes a closer look at the document itself and scrutinizes its form, terminology, and content.

The MOU covers a broad spectrum ranging from topical priorities to institutional specifications. The final Cooperation Agreement, the MOU agreed on by the EU and the COE in May 2007, is split into the following chapters: Preamble, Purposes and Principles of Cooperation, Shared Priorities and Focal Areas for Cooperation, Arrangements for Cooperation, Visibility of the Partnership, and Follow-Up (COM 2007a). The *Preamble* highlights the ultimate goal of the document, namely greater unity between European states through the respect for human rights, and recognizes the contribution of specific bodies, instruments, and standards of the COE (for example ECtHR and ECHR) and the EU (for example the Charter of Fundamental Rights). Moreover, it recalls the development process, inter alia the Warsaw Summit and the Juncker Report, and the decision to create a new framework for cooperation (Paragraphs 1–8). The second chapter – *Purposes and Principles of Cooperation*– gives a preview on the issue areas, which will be subject to (enhanced) cooperation while stressing the principle of complementarity and resource efficiency (Paragraphs 9–13). Furthermore, Paragraph 10 acknowledges that '[t]he Council of Europe will remain the benchmark for human rights, the rule of law and democracy in Europe' (COM 2007a).

The chapter *Shared Priorities and Focal Areas for Cooperation* sets out the following five issue areas (grouped by this research): first, human rights and legal affairs (rule of law, and legal cooperation) (Paragraphs 16–26); second, democracy and good governance, and democratic stability (Paragraphs 27–32); third, intercultural dialogue and cultural diversity (Paragraphs 33–35); fourth, education, youth, and promotion of human contacts (Paragraphs 36–38); fifth, social cohesion (Paragraphs 39–40). According to the interests of this research, the parts of this chapter that outline cooperation in human rights as well as in social cohesion are particularly worth highlighting as in the following section.

In the part outlining cooperation in human rights and legal affairs (Paragraph 17), '[t]he European Union regards the Council of Europe as the Europe-wide reference source for human rights' (COM 2007a). Additionally, the two IOs affirm that they will draw on each other's expertise when drafting new initiatives and consult each other (Paragraph 18, 25). While it aims at coherence between the EU and the COE law (Paragraph 19, 24), the MOU 'does not prevent the [...] European Union law from providing more extensive protection' (COM 2007a). Thereafter, the section names some of the issue areas for cooperation: the protection of national minorities, the fight against discrimination and racism, the fight against torture, the fight against trafficking in human beings, the protection of children's rights, the promotion of human rights education and the freedom of expression, the fight against terrorism, organized crime, corruption, and money laundering, and other modern challenges, including those arising from the development of new technologies (such as cybercrime) (Paragraphs 21, 26). Finally, the EU and the COE briefly address the issue of EU accession to the ECHR on the one hand, and the cooperation between the COE and FRA on the other hand. The first issue will be 'examined further', while the second issue is subject to a bilateral Cooperation Agreement (Paragraph 20, 21).

In contrast to the detailed paragraphs on cooperation in the field of human rights and legal affairs, the part on cooperation in social cohesion is rather short. Paragraph 39 highlights the COE Social Charter and 'relevant EU texts' as the basis for their cooperation. According to Paragraph 40, the two IOs will support the efforts by their member states to exchange good practices on social cohesion with the aim of developing 'more efficient policies' in this field. Also, the section names some of the issue areas: the fight against violence, poverty, and exclusion and, more generally, the protection of vulnerable groups (Paragraph 40).

The chapter explaining the *Arrangements for Cooperation* touches upon the meeting mechanisms, the interinstitutional presence, and the joint programs. According to Paragraph 40, the practical realization of the cooperation takes place through regular and close consultation between the two IOs at the political and operational levels. The EU and the COE agree on further developing joint activities as well as enhancing cooperation between specialized COE structures and the respective EU counterparts. This cooperation should include dialogue on policy goals and the development of mid- or long-term strategies, as well as the (enhanced) coordination of operational activities in the priority areas. Besides the quadripartite meetings, the MOU offers the possibility of more frequent meetings between the Troika of the EU on the one hand, and the Presidency and the SG of the COE on the other hand in order to reinforce the political dialogue (Paragraph 41–50). Finally, and with reference to the future, Paragraph 51 states that the COE and the EU 'will consider how best to enhance and strengthen their presence in Brussels and Strasbourg respectively' (COM 2007a).

To increase the *Visibility of the Partnership*, which means the visibility of the two IOs and in particular that of the COE, both IOs assure that they will consult each other on the calendar (comparing appointments) of their respective awareness-raising campaigns and consider the possibility of organizing joint events. Additionally, both IOs aim at focusing on a better marketing strategy for the joint programs (Paragraphs 53–54).

The last part of the MOU is the *Follow-Up*: the implementation of the MOU will be subject to regular evaluations. On the basis of these evaluations, the MOU will – if necessary – be revised no later than 2013 with a view toward incorporating new priorities for cooperation (Paragraph 55).

When looking at the terminology used in this document, one finds many elements of the typical 'MOU terminology' described above. Generally speaking, the provisions of the MOU are scarcely binding and remain, for the most part, rather vague. The indecisiveness not only limits itself to the cooperation in the human rights field, but also applies to the institutional questions (Brummer 2008b: 76–7). Even though there is a preamble (and not an introduction), the other elements fit perfectly to the 'MOU terminology'. The Preamble lays out that the EU and the COE have reached the following 'understanding' (instead of 'agreement'). There is no 'shall' in the entire text, while 'will' is used no less than 55 times. One also finds some linguistic weakening of commitments such as 'where possible', 'to the extent necessary', and 'if necessary', or vague obligations per se, such as 'cooperation should be further developed', 'will continue to strive for appropriate forms of cooperation', and 'will examine this further'. An excellent example of this vagueness is the above-mentioned statement that both organizations '*will consider* how best to enhance and strengthen their presence in Brussels and Strasbourg respectively'. Finally, the document is 'signed' (and not 'done') in Strasbourg. From a linguistic point of view, one can conclude that the wording used is typical for an informal document and that one barely sees terms that denote an intention to conclude a treaty (the only exception being the Preamble).

7.5 IOR with regard to the MOU

Having introduced the form and content of the MOU and discussed the terminology used, the next step is to scrutinize the relations between the EU and the COE during the negotiation process. This section reviews the issues of interest in the relations between the EU and the COE in the field of the MOU. Accordingly, this section touches upon the legal nature of the document, the question of who sets human rights standards in Europe, cooperation in the standard-setting field, and the 'single legal space'. It also examines which of Juncker's recommendations finally entered into the MOU. Last but not least, it brings up the plan of a separate MOU in the JHA area, which failed to realize due to EU internal disagreement.

Before even considering the content, one contentious issue is related to the *legal nature of the document*. Originally, the COE wanted to have a legally binding document that would replace all previous agreements (I-5; I-30). This can also be seen from statements on the MOU like the following from COE staff members (emphases added): '*Though not being a legally binding agreement*, but expressing a political commitment, the MoU constitutes a framework for "enhanced co-operation and political dialogue"' (Polakiewicz 2009). The 'draft memorandum of understanding between the Council of Europe and the European Union stays *only as a political document*' (PACE 2007a: 1). Jan Kleijssen, at that time Secretariat of the PACE, 'pointed out that *one could not rely on a MoU alone, as it was not binding*. Mere declarations of intent were not enough' (Konrad Adenauer Stiftung 2006: 5). Therefore, he demanded a text that was legally binding. The EU, however, was not willing to go beyond the document that was eventually concluded (I-12; I-17; I-20). The tenor within the EU was to 'use the COE as long as it brings added value' (Konrad Adenauer Stiftung 2006: 4) but not to bind itself and/or create obligations. Also, the EU argued that having a legally binding text would complicate the adoption of the document because it would then have to be a kind of treaty in need of ratification. Being confronted with a tedious ratification process, the COE dropped this idea (I-17). The end result was a document on which all parties could seemingly agree, despite its not being legally binding. Moreover, the document does not replace previous cooperation agreements, but only adds another document to the preexisting number of cooperation agreements (see Section 3.1 of Chapter 3).

By the time the MOU was negotiated, the EU had increased its activities in the field of human rights, which included the adoption of the EU Charter of Fundamental Rights and the creation of the EU FRA (see Chapter 8). These activities fueled the anxiety in Strasbourg that the COE was losing its role as the European benchmark for human rights. Hence, the COE circles especially awaited the results – in the form of the MOU – with great anticipation. Accordingly, these concerns and the question – *who would be the ultimate human rights standard setter in Europe* – were subject to the negotiations on the MOU. While the MOU partly repeats what previous documents already stated, the recognition of the COE as the 'benchmark for human rights, the rule of law and democracy in Europe' is new, as is the EU's recognition of the COE 'as the Europe-wide reference source for human rights'. To meet this obligation, relevant COE norms should be cited as references in EU documents, and relevant activities of the COE monitoring structures should be taken into account by the EU. With this acknowledgment, the EU intended to reassure the COE that the EU would not try to replace or challenge the COE (for example through FRA), as is acknowledged by an EU staff member:

> I think the COE simply before the MOU was in this thinking that probably the EU after continuing [...] its enlargement and the enlargement of its capacities, also of its mandate [...] would progressively kill the COE. I think the MOU is, at least for some time, giving them the assurance that it is not going to be the case, and that we agree that there is a complementarity between the two organizations. (I-17)

Understandably, the COE was pleased with the EU's recognition of the COE as the benchmark in the human rights field. However, some of the COE staffs added that this was difficult to agree upon, and that the benchmark – for the EU – would apply first and foremost to non-EU member states (I-14; I-31). At the same time, and this is to some extent reminiscent of the 'Disconnection Clause' (Chapter 5), the MOU (Paragraph 19, 24) explicitly and repeatedly expresses the possibility that the EU will provide more extensive human rights protection, while, of course, ensuring coherence between EU law and COE *acquis*. To ensure this coherence, the two IOs need to *cooperate in the standard-setting (normative) field*. The question of how to ensure coherence between EU law and COE *acquis* was one of the most controversial topics in the MOU. Therefore, the EU and the COE should contact and inform each other before drafting new legal initiatives. By doing so, the other IO would have the possibility of intervening beforehand in case the new initiative contradicts preexisting law in Strasbourg or Brussels. Paragraph 25 states: 'To this end and to the extent necessary the Council of Europe and the European Union will consult each other at an early stage in the process of elaborating standards' (COM 2007a). Paragraph 25 was the most difficult to achieve and caused the negotiators to engage in a great deal of words. Every single word in this Paragraph is crucial, especially the wording 'to the extent necessary' and 'at an early stage in the process'. Only these restraints made the Paragraph acceptable to the EU. The background to this disputed issue is the following: while the COE strove for systematic consultation of COE officials in the EU decision-making process (at least within Commission), the EU wanted to maintain as much room for maneuver as possible (I-20; I-31), as stated by an EU official:

Yeah that's true they [the COE] are never happy because they think they should be consulted systematically. We wanted always to avoid systematization, we don't want to be blocked like that, I mean it's normal, we are partners – we are not married together! So [...] most of the time there are good reasons for consulting them but there might be also good reasons for not consulting them on certain issues. (I-20)

The COE took a different view and rejected the EU's idea of 'a relationship à la carte', which for the COE equals cherry-picking. Instead, the COE argues that consultations need to be systematic, given that the EU has to have a broader range of considerations in mind, in particular the Common Market. This point of view may lead the EU to different solutions than one would arrive at in Strasbourg. Accordingly, discrepancies would arise between the norms of the EU and the COE (I-31). Therefore, parts of the COE called for a setup of 'a co-ordination committee in the field of standard setting with a view to increasing co-operation in the drafting of new international legal instruments' (PACE 2006b: 9.5.7). The COE SG also proposed so-called 'genuine consultation procedures' (COM 2006b: 2). As one can tell by looking at the final MOU, these proposals did not meet with approval.

Related to this question, and equally disputed, was the issue of *'single legal space'* for human rights. Non-EU member states (inter alia Russia) especially felt discomfort with the situation of a 'two-tier regime' that they feared was developing. But before going into this issue with regard to content, one needs to bring up the rotating Presidencies of the EU and the COE: generally speaking, the negotiation process of the MOU was complicated due to the rotating Presidencies. As in other cases, the relationship between the COE's member state Russia and the EU is especially difficult, and likewise, the Russian's COE Presidency (May–November 2006) did not facilitate the negotiation process (I-5; I-17). The 23rd Quadripartite Meeting (see Section 3.3.1 of Chapter 3), which took place during the Russian Presidency, reflects this complicated relationship. The EU noted that the Russian Presidency further delayed the conclusion of the MOU due to 'remaining difficulties and legal implications of some of the elements of the dossier [...]. The latest proposals of the Russian Chairmanship would now have to be examined carefully, as some affected the European Union's institutional constraints' (COM 2006b: 1). Seemingly the latest proposals at that time included the request to combine the two legal orders and create one legal space by submitting the legal order of the EU to that of the COE in certain fields. For the EU, the idea of merging the two legal orders was unacceptable and, according to them, showed that not everyone in the COE actually understood the concept of European integration (I-17; I-20; I-28; I-31). On the contrary, the Russian Presidency of the COE, which strove for a strengthened role and authority of the COE in all its fields of activity, 'regretted that the European Union had shown so little flexibility so far' (COM 2006b: 2). According to the Russian Presidency, whose positions were supported by then-President of the PACE René van der Linden, there should be no dividing lines in Europe, but instead a common legal area. Furthermore, the principles of reciprocity, complementarity, and partnership on an equal footing had to be at the core of this cooperation. Therefore, agreeing on a text would require compromises from both parties, which, following this view, was missing from the EU. Furthermore, the 'discussions in Strasbourg had confirmed this inflexibility, as the Finnish Presidency had reiterated the European Union's initial proposals, with only scarce advances on the questions of education, culture and social cohesion' (COM 2006b: 2).

Besides the COE Presidency and PACE President, the COE SG Terry Davis also expressed criticism on how the negotiations proceeded. He underlined that he was surprised to hear that the EU Presidency planned to withdraw his proposals, which appeared (amended) in the text prepared by the COE Presidency. To satisfy all the signatories of the MOU, he called for putting his proposals back on the table (COM 2006b: 2). Since both sides accused each other of not being willing to compromise, only the subsequent COE Presidency of San Marino brought the negotiations to the breakthrough.

In the chapter 'Arrangements of Cooperation', one discovers an innovation related to the MOU's coverage: due to the fact that the MOU was signed, for the first time, by the Commission as well as by the EU Presidency, the MOU formally expands cooperation and responsibility from the Commission to the Council of the EU. Concerning the implementation of the MOU, the document envisages a mere commitment of both organizations to evaluate the implementation regularly. According to Paragraph 55, on the basis of these evaluations, the parties may decide to revise, if necessary, the MOU by 2013. As the negotiation process was rather complicated, the COE feels the need to additionally scrutinize the implementation of the MOU through a yearly stocktaking (see for example (COM 2008a), (COM 2009a), (COM 2009b), (COM 2010a) (COE 2011c)), as a COE official highlights in the following citation.

So it explains also why we follow so closely the implementation because we witnessed the hesitations, the reluctance of the Commission to accept some amendments that we included in the memorandum so it's clear that for them they did not do it with a great pleasure so then you could assume that maybe there would not do their best to implement those elements of the MOU that do not please them so much. So that's why we insisted so much about the implementation. (I-31)

So which of the *15 final recommendations of Juncker* (2006: 30–3) finally entered into the MOU? The recommendations that hold the most interest for this research are the following: EU accession to the ECHR (1), recognition of the COE as the Europe-wide reference source for human rights (EU should draw on COE expertise and consult COE whenever drafting new legal initiatives) (2), the FRA's need to deal with human rights only with respect to EU law and COE representation in the FRA's Management Board (4), creation of a joint platform for coordinating legislative initiatives in the legal and judicial area (6), making institutional relations between the EU and the COE more substantial (regular meetings between senior officials) (10), introduction of medium-term budget planning to ensure that the COE has adequate resources (14), and EU membership of the COE (15).

According to the supporters of the Juncker report, it did not receive the implementation its quality merited. Paragraph 20 incorporates Junckers' first recommendation, the claim for the EU's accession to the ECHR. However, even though Paragraph 20 aspires for an early accession, it does not set up any binding requirements. Negotiations on the EU's accession to ECHR started only three years after the adoption of the MOU in 2010 (COE 2010e). The second recommendation calls for EU bodies to recognize the COE as the Europe-wide reference for human rights. The above-mentioned Paragraphs 10 and 17 pick up this recommendation. The fourth recommendation deals with the mandate of the then future FRA: following Juncker, the mandate should be limited to human rights solely in relation to the implementation of EU law. Paragraph 22 secures that the FRA activities stay within the framework of the EU law and that a concrete Cooperation Agreement would be negotiated between the COE and the EU. Recommendation 6 calls for a joint platform for the assessment of standards and the complementarity of documents. However, there is no such facility introduced into the MOU. Recommendation 10 discusses the quadripartite meetings' format and sets out ideas for improvement; however, the MOU does not modify the setting of the quadripartite meetings, but only stipulates that further meetings may be organized informally on an adhoc basis. Also, efforts on budget planning are missing in the MOU, as proposed by Recommendation 14. Finally, COE membership to the EU (whatever form it may take) is not planned in the MOU either. The illustration shows that overall the MOU fell short of Juncker's expectations. Juncker (2006: 6) anticipated this development by stating that his recommendations had been ambitious and, 'deliberately optimistic'.

Besides the horizontal MOU described, there was the idea to set up a separate MOU in the JHA area, more specifically in the area of the fight against crime. In 2007, a framework for cooperation between the COE and DG JLS was developed. The separate, specific MOU would deviate from the general MOU in establishing more binding mechanisms for cooperation and early warning for forthcoming legal initiatives. For example, the specific MOU would have obliged the Commission to systematically invite COE officials to the relevant expert meetings and would have established senior coordinators for the fight against crime similar to the senior officials for the external relations area. While being a priority for the COE, the specific MOU met with disapproval in the Commission: the DG JLS management was not very keen on it and DG RELEX opposed it. Hence, eventually the JLS MOU was not processed (I-16; I-17).

> That [specific MOU] didn't happen and I partly regret it because we have a very formalistic exchange of views twice a year with the COE [...]. The Article 36 Committee [...], which meets [...] with the COE twice and it's not enough. It would be better to have a more, sort of proactive dossier-based coordination, that is the desk officers talk to each other and say, hey we have a text coming here, what do you think, it's compatible, would you have any problems with this? This is not happening for the moment. I do my best [...] to help this process happen but it is not always easy. There are some institutional barriers in the Commission. (I-16)

According to supporters, the specific MOU would have helped to ensure good partnership between the two IOs because, in practice, relations are not always free of conflict. Due to its strong institutional self-interests, in some areas, the EU tends to overlook the interests of the COE, an organization with less political weight. In these cases, the COE needs to approach the EU in complaint; then perhaps the EU will take into account the COE's interests as well.

At the present time, some of the DG JLS units informally implement the specific MOU to some extent. Yet, to fully comply with the defunct MOU would raise some eyebrows in the Commission. In the view of the DG RELEX (now EEAS), one has to be careful not to affect what took a great deal of difficult work to negotiate in the umbrella MOU. The terms in the MOU were heavily deliberated and the parts that are rather vague are not that way simply by chance. Hence, due to the difficulty of the MOU negotiation, one should stick to the existing framework rather than attempt something new. The fact that DG RELEX (now EEAS) prefers to maintain the overview of the relations between the various DGs and Services and the COE may also be significant. Accordingly, decentralized cooperation agreements are eyed suspiciously (I-16; I-17).

The last part of this section addresses *the question of how the MOU was perceived* by the media and scholarly literature one the one hand and the two IOs (and their staffs) themselves on the other hand. On the adoption of the MOU, the Agence Europe (2007) headline read 'Cooperation between EU and Council of Europe is timidly reactivated'. The MOU not being an 'over-zealous' agreement is the basic tenor to be found in the scholarly literature. The criticism is that the provisions are hardly ambitious and remain, overall, rather vague (Brummer 2008b: 76, 2008a: 232), and that the MOU 'somewhat confirms the existing relationship, instead of introducing genuine novelties' (Joris and Vandenberghe 2008/2009: 35). Also, Juncker (2006: 6) had hoped that the MOU would be more ambitious. Some observers described the Cooperation Agreement as a 'truce concluded between two international organizations, bound to agree to cooperate because of their overlapping membership', while others saw the MOU as 'a first step towards full normalization of the situation of the EU vis-à-vis the Council of Europe – a normalization which shall be complete only when the EU shall have become one member among others of the Council of Europe' (De Schutter 2008: 512).

Finally, the literature adds that there were some important issues that the MOU did not tackle. Among these unsettled issues is the question of a future institutional form of the partnership. In 2003, the then COE SG insisted that a wholly new approach regarding relations between EU and COE was needed and proposed a form of 'institutional partnership' (Schwimmer 2003), but the MOU remains silent on the possibility of an 'institutional partnership' let alone EU accession to the COE (as proposed inter alia by Juncker). The idea of a financial and administrative framework agreement complementing the MOU (Joris and Vandenberghe 2008/2009: 40) as well as the Juncker recommendations on budget planning and the efforts in increasing the COE budget failed to bear fruit.

Similarly, the MOU's shortcomings prevail in the view of the PACE (2007b), as can be seen from the following critical statement, which challenges the MOU's benefit for the interorganizational relationship between the EU and the COE as a whole.

> [T]he Assembly is disappointed by the overall content of the draft memorandum. It does not contain precise and concrete commitments requiring the parties to make substantial additional efforts to enhance co-operation. It does not provide an innovative or ambitious approach to challenges faced by European construction. Neither does it reflect a genuine political determination to advance the process of co-operation. Consequently, it will not pave the way for more extensive and intensive co-operation between the two institutions. [...] Furthermore, the draft text does not sufficiently reflect either the proposals and recommendations contained in the Juncker report or the proposals made by the Assembly and reiterated by its President and representatives on several occasions in the drafting process.

The PACE counterpart, the EP (2008a), welcomed the conclusion of the MOU, but has urged both parties to put the Agreement into practice. Moreover, the EP insisted that the EU and the COE (further) improve cooperation and coordination.

The opinion of the EU and the COE staff toward the MOU, obviously, is not homogeneous. One can distinguish between four (not mutually exclusive) types of staff assessment on each side: first, staff satisfaction with the MOU and the new possibilities it creates for cooperation; second, staff belief that the MOU brings nothing new and that the relationship would be the same without the MOU; third, staff disappointment with the MOU given its overall vagueness; fourth, staff disregard for the importance of the MOU in their daily work. Moreover, the COE staff especially sees the need for the MOU to be put into practice. The general tenor can be summarized as follows: enough with the political agreements (they are full of nice words), what is needed now is their implementation. Without going into an evaluation of the implementation, the MOU seemingly has now become the document referred to by the COE whenever the COE aims at expanding cooperation with the EU or strives for involvement in drafting processes of EU instruments (I-2; I-3; I-4; I-5; I-12; I-14; I-15; I-16; I-17; I-20; I-22; I-26; I-28; I-29; I-30; I-31; I-32; I-36; I-37).

Concluding this empirical part, the subsequent section goes on to review and analyze the IOR with regard to the MOU against the background of the theoretical framework.

7.6   IOR with regard to the MOU – analysis and explanatory factors

As can be seen from the above Section 7.5, the IOR between the EU and the COE during the negotiation of the MOU have been rather conflictive, but the Cooperation Agreement was successfully concluded in the end. So what does this mean in terms of IOR theory? To answer this question, this section aims at linking the empirical results to the factors facilitating (hindering) interorganizational cooperation established in the theoretical framework. For the sake of completeness, it should be added that not all factors are equally important to all cases. The MOU case omits two factors, that is the socialization factor and the physical opportunity factor, since they are not decisive in this case.

7.6.1   Interest (policy and organizational)

In the MOU case, both IOs share the policy interest of protecting and promoting human rights in Europe; there are only some minor differences of opinion regarding policy aspects. Similarly, both IOs are interested in formulating a Cooperation Agreement. However, the contemporary FRA conflict influenced and complicated cooperation in the MOU case. Additionally, the EU's organizational self-interest had some effect on the binding character of the Cooperation Agreement: the EU wanted to maintain for itself as much room for maneuver as possible: 'we are partners – we are not married'.

7.6.2   Organizational characteristics

The above-described interests represent a very simplified unitary view of the actors, which needs to be complemented. Since this project treats IOs as multiple actors, we also have to consider the possibility of different actors pursuing diverging or even conflicting goals (complexity). Additionally, and leaving aside the interest aspect, the IOR become more difficult as the sheer number of actors increases.

In the MOU case, the negotiation process was complicated by the wide variety of actors and the rotating presidencies on the EU as well on the COE side. The IOR are particularly difficult when Russia holds the COE presidency or when COE officials with Russian origin participate. Furthermore, an initiative in the JLS area to establish a specific MOU – with more binding mechanisms for cooperation and early warning for forthcoming legal initiatives – was not realized due to institutional barriers to deepening the IOR. DG RELEX, which previously had the function of overseeing IOR with the COE, wanted to maintain as much room for maneuver as possible for itself, namely adhoc cooperation instead of institutionalization, and opposed the plan.

Interestingly enough, the unit dealing with the COE within the Commission was – as previously mentioned – part of DG RELEX, which means that relations with the COE were seen as external, whereas the internal dimension (the majority of the COE member states are EU member states as well) was neglected. This allocation results in a somewhat peculiar situation in which the unit responsible for IOR with the COE in the Commission was in practice only able to oversee the external dimension, leaving the internal dimension hanging in the air. The focus on the external relations has not changed with the establishment of the EEAS, which now looks after the relations with the COE.

7.7   IOR with regard to the MOU – conclusions

The preceding sections set out to scrutinize the relations between the EU and the COE by tackling in depth an institutional issue of utmost importance for their relationship, namely the Cooperation Agreement called the MOU. They have shed light on the origins of the MOU during the Third Summit of Heads of State and Government of the COE, which took place in Warsaw in May 2005. The realignment of the principal tasks of the COE for the future (including the long-term positioning of the COE within the European integration process and its assertiveness toward the EU) had been on the agenda of the Warsaw Summit. The participants of the Warsaw Summit gave the impetus for the MOU by deciding to establish a new framework for the relations between the EU and the COE. To proceed with this idea, they adopted an Action Plan setting out guidelines to form the basis for the intended MOU and commissioned Jean-Claude Juncker to write a report on this issue, bringing forth 15 recommendations for the EU–COE relationship.

Even though the two IOs were committed to the idea of setting up a new framework for their relations, the negotiation process took relatively long and led to numerous difficulties. For one, the discussion on the EU's FRA coincided with the negotiations on the MOU, and therefore made an agreement difficult to achieve. As a result, the negotiations, which began in 2005 and ended in 2007, involved various rotating presidencies on the EU side as well as on the COE side. While not over-ambitious, the text that was finally adopted does entail some innovations, such as its treatment of the COE as the Europe-wide reference source for human rights and the benchmark for human rights, and the institutional enlargement of relations (from the Commission only) to the Council of the EU as well. The main contentious issues of the MOU were the legal nature of the document, the question of who sets human rights standards in Europe, cooperation in the standard-setting field, and the single legal space. Generally, one can say that the COE was looking for a binding document that included systematic cooperation, for example, in the standard-setting field, while the EU preferred a document that did not involve too many serious obligations for the EU. The sections also examine which of Juncker's recommendations finally entered into the MOU and how the MOU was perceived by the media and scholarly literature on the one hand, and the staff of the two IOs themselves on the other hand. The scholarly assessment can be summarized with the statement that the MOU was not 'over-zealous', and omitted some important issues like future institutional form of the partnership. Given the vagueness of the Cooperation Agreement, opinions within the staff ranged from satisfaction to disappointment, with indifference in between. Moreover, the sections bring up the plan of a separate MOU with more binding mechanisms for cooperation and early warning for forthcoming legal initiatives in the JHA area, which failed to be realized due to EU internal disagreement.

In terms of IOR theory, the sections reveal factors facilitating and aggravating the IOR in the case of the MOU. The fact that both IOs shared an interest in adopting such a Cooperation Agreement – although the COE probably had a greater interest in it than the EU – facilitated negotiations. However, the organizational self-interest of the EU posed limits on the liabilities in the document. In addition, the high number of actors involved in the negotiations – from the rotating presidencies to single leaders in the COE (PACE President and COE SG, at that time René van der Linden and Terry Davis) and specific parts of the Commission – especially complicated the negotiation process. The relationship between the Russian Presidency of the COE and the EU was particularly conflict laden. Only the subsequent Presidency of the COE (San Marino) was successful in bringing the negotiations on the Cooperation Agreement to an end. The other two factors, namely the socialization factor and the physical opportunity factor, were not decisive in this case.

8

The Fundamental Rights Agency

This chapter scrutinizes the IOR between the EU and the COE with regard to the EU FRA, whose establishment, so far, has caused the biggest conflict between the EU and the COE. The case of the FRA is particularly interesting as the EU's decision to set up an agency tackling human rights in Europe directly affects the core business of the COE. In the wake of a potential competitor, the COE – fearing marginalization and duplication of tasks already in existence in Strasbourg – took a critical stance toward these EU developments. This reaction, however, was not understandable to EU staff that saw the Agency as a way to fill a gap in human rights protection with regard to EU institutions. This chapter inter alia sheds light on how the COE tried to intervene in order to block the set up of the FRA and in what ways the EU tried to placate the COE, via the mandate of the Agency and the FRA–COE Cooperation Agreement. Before tackling these issues in depth, the following section starts out by highlighting the antecedent situation, by introducing the FRA's predecessor.

8.1 The antecedent situation

Institutionally speaking, the FRA was not set up from scratch. On the contrary, since the mid-1990s at the latest, one finds a number of bodies (of the EU and the COE) dealing with human rights, more precisely with the fight against racism and xenophobia. Specifically, one has to mention the EU predecessor upon which the FRA was built, which was the European Monitoring Centre on Racism and Xenophobia (EUMC) established in 1997. As early as 1993, the COE set up the European Commission against Racism and Intolerance (ECRI). Given the resemblance of ECRI and the EUMC, they can be seen as natural counterparts and their relationship can be seen as a predecessor of the COE–FRA relationship. Accordingly, this section analyses the antecedent situation (preceding the establishment of FRA) by focusing on the two bodies, the COE's ECRI and the EU's EUMC, and the interorganizational relationship between the two. It proceeds as follows: first, it goes into the details on the two bodies, the COE's ECRI and the EU's EUMC by highlighting their structures and fields of activity. Subsequently, it focuses on the interorganizational relationship between ECRI and EUMC.

8.1.1   The Council of Europe's European Commission against Racism and Intolerance

The ECRI was set up in Vienna in 1993 by the First Summit of Heads of State and Government of the COE member states in order to combat racism, racial discrimination, xenophobia, anti-Semitism, and intolerance. To perform this duty, ECRI reviews the member states' respective legislation and policies, proposes future action on various political levels, formulates policy recommendations to member states, and studies international legal instruments. The Second and Third Summit of Heads of State and Government of the COE further strengthened the position of ECRI and the importance of its activities, and since 2002 ECRI has had its own statute (COM 2002b: 1–5).

According to this statute, ECRI's main tasks consist in combating racism, racial discrimination, xenophobia, anti-Semitism, and intolerance. Therein, it is explicitly mentioned that ECRI should apply the perspective of the protection of human rights. In principle, in accordance with Article 1, ECRI has the following tasks:

- to review member states' legislation, policies and other measures to combat racism, xenophobia, anti-Semitism and intolerance, and their effectiveness;
- to propose further action at local, national and European level;
- to formulate general policy recommendations to member states;
- to study international legal instruments applicable in the matter with a view to their reinforcement where appropriate.

(COM 2002b)

To implement its work program, ECRI, first, adopts a country-by-country monitoring approach, and, second, works on general themes. In the framework of its country-by-country approach, ECRI monitors phenomena of racism, racial discrimination, xenophobia, anti-Semitism, and intolerance in all COE member states. The examinations and contact visits that are therefore necessary in the countries concerned are expanded into country reports. According to Article 11, these reports entail 'factual analyses as well as suggestions and proposals as to how each country might deal with any problems identified' (COM 2002b). The ECRI's four- to five-year monitoring cycles consider all COE member states on an equal footing. In 2008, ECRI began its fourth-round cycle (2008–2012), in which ECRI visited approximately ten countries per year. In 2010, ECRI carried out nine contact visits to Armenia, Azerbaijan, Bosnia and Herzegovina, Cyprus, Italy, Lithuania, Monaco, Serbia, and Spain, and published eight reports on the fourth monitoring cycle. Within the context of the work on general themes, ECRI adopts general policy recommendations, which are submitted to all COE member states. These recommendations are intended to serve as guidelines for national policy makers when drawing up national policies. The latest General Policy Recommendation Nr. 13, adopted in June 2011, concerns anti-Gypsyism, and currently ECRI is working on a new recommendation dealing with racial discrimination in employment (CRI 2011: 17–9).

8.1.2 The European Union's European Monitoring Centre on Racism and Xenophobia

With the Council Regulation (EC) Nr. 1035/97 of 2 June 1997, the EU decided to establish a EUMC. It was only at a later point in time the European Council agreed that the EUMC should have its seat in Vienna (Commission 2003: 2). According to Article 2, the primary goal of the EUMC is to provide the EU and its member states with 'objective, reliable and comparable' data on the phenomena of racism, xenophobia, and anti-Semitism in order to help them when they take measures or adopt policies within their respective spheres of competence. The EUMC also studies the extent and the development of these phenomena, and analyzes their causes, consequences, and effects. Last but not least, the EUMC examines examples of good practice in dealing with these issues.

To these ends, the EUMC inter alia collects, records, analyzes, and distributes information and data on racism, xenophobia, and anti-Semitism. At the request of the EP, the Council of the EU or the Commission, the EUMC carries out scientific research and surveys, as well as preparatory and feasibility studies. On the basis of this research, the EUMC draws up conclusions and opinions for the EU and its member states. On an annual basis, the EUMC drafts reports on the situation regarding racism, xenophobia, and anti-Semitism in the EU, highlighting also examples of good practice.

In addition to the annual reports, the EUMC conducted and published a number of comparative baseline studies in order to implement
its work program. These EU-wide studies inter alia covered topics such
as employment, education, and racist violence (FRA 2012). In 2005,
the EUMC also published an opinion on the application of the EU
Anti-Discrimination Directive 2000/43/EC (EUMC 2005).

Besides these tasks, the EUMC is obliged to promote and facilitate
information exchange, organize events, and help with raising awareness. Finally, the EUMC establishes and coordinates a network, the
European Racism and Xenophobia Information Network (Raxen), for
cooperating with various bodies dealing with racism, xenophobia, and
anti-Semitism.

Regarding the previously existing bodies in this field and in particular
the COE, Paragraph 20 of the Regulation Nr. 1035/97 establishing the
EUMC states the following:

> [I]n order to enhance cooperation and avoid overlap or duplication
> of work, the tasks assigned to the Centre *pre-suppose close links with
> the Council of Europe*, which has considerable experience in this field.
>
> (Emphasis added)

To this end, the EU and the COE concluded an Agreement in 1999,
which had the purpose of establishing close cooperation between the
EUMC and the COE. The subsequent section goes into detail on this
Cooperation Agreement.

8.1.3   The Cooperation Agreement between ECRI and the EUMC

The legal basis for the contact between ECRI and the EUMC dates back
to the Council Decision 1999/132/EC, in which the EU and the COE
concluded an agreement for the purpose of establishing close cooperation between the EUMC and the COE (and in particular ECRI).
Apart from the Agreement of 1987 (see Section 3.1.1.2 of Chapter 3),
this Cooperation Agreement constitutes – at the time of adoption –
the first international treaty concluded directly between those two IOs
(Polakiewicz 1999: 67). The Cooperation Agreement splits into three
parts: exchange of information and data, cooperation, and appointment of an independent person by the COE to the EUMC's Management
Board. The following paragraph goes into detail on these parts.

The first part of the Cooperation Agreement foresees regular contact
between the EUMC and the COE Secretariat, in particular ECRI. EUMC
and ECRI would provide each other with information and data and use
them in their own respective activities. They would also hold regular

meetings during which they would exchange information on activities that are to be proposed or that are already under way. The second part, defining the interorganizational cooperation, stipulates regular consultations in order to coordinate the activities of the EUMC and ECRI and, in particular, draw up the EUMC's work program. It goes without saying that this should ensure complementarity of the two bodies' programs and avoid unnecessary duplication. On the basis of these consultations, EUMC and ECRI could carry out joint and/or complementary projects on subjects of common interest. The third part provides for an independent person from among the members of ECRI to be appointed by the COE SG to serve on the EUMC's Management Board.

When the EUMC was transformed into the FRA in 2007, the relations between ECRI and EUMC served as a model for the forthcoming contacts (I-8). Hence, parts of the 1999 Agreement can be found in the Council Regulation (EC) Nr. 168/2007 of 15 February 2007, which establishes a European Union Agency for Fundamental Rights, and the subsequent Agreement on Cooperation between the FRA and the COE.

Having started this empirical case by highlighting the antecedent situation of the FRA's establishment, the subsequent sections continue on the origins of the EU's 'Human Rights Agency' (8.2) and the interorganizational contacts in the negotiations of the FRA establishment as well as of the Cooperation Agreement between the FRA and the COE (8.3), before scrutinizing the final set up of the FRA and the Cooperation Agreement (8.4), and the IOR between the EU and the COE surrounding the FRA (8.5).

8.2 The idea to set up an EU 'Human Rights Agency'

The idea of an EU 'Human Rights Agency' dates back to the second half of the 1990s, when different sides brought forward the idea almost contemporaneously. Among these innovative thinkers were Philip Alston and Joseph Weiler (1999: 3–66), who elaborated comprehensively on the idea of a full-fledged EU 'Human Rights Agency' within the framework of a report for the Comité de Sages for an EU human rights agenda for the year 2000. The following quotation is an excerpt from their report.

> It is proposed either that a separate monitoring agency [should] be created or that the jurisdiction of the Vienna Monitoring Centre on Racism and Xenophobia [EUMC] should be enhanced so as to make into *a fully-fledged agency with monitoring responsibility over all human rights in the field of Community law*.
>
> (Alston and Weiler 1999: 55, emphasis added)

Alston and Weiler also add that '[t]he latter proposal is put forward because it seems likely to be more politically palatable and less administrative challenging than the creation of an entirely new agency' (Alston and Weiler 1999: 55). Even though the advance was given a boost within the political arena, the idea did not get a strong impetus until, unexpectedly, the Austrian (Haider) crisis triggered a new dynamic (Toggenburg 2007b: 86). In Paragraph 119 of these visionaries' report, which ended the EU sanctions against Austria, Ahtisaari et al. (2000) called for 'the extension of the activities, budget and status of the existing EU Observatory on racism and xenophobia [EUCM], which is based in Vienna, in order to make possible the *establishment of a full EU Agency on Human Rights*' (emphasis added).

However, neither the Council of the EU nor the Commission acted on this suggestion. Accordingly, in December 2003, the decision of the European Council to establish a 'Human Rights Agency' on the basis of the EUMC and to invite the Commission to submit a proposal raised many eyebrows. On the basis of this decision, the Commission promoted the idea of an agency, especially through a communication of the Commission (2004) in October 2004, and the proposal for a Council regulation in June 2005 (Commission 2005a).

Even to insiders, the decision of December 2003 came as a complete surprise, and was criticized as political horse-trading (Bell 2007: 196). Following Toggenburg (2007b: 87), the abrupt starting signal may be one of the reasons for the later political difficulties at the stage of the practical realization of the EU 'Human Rights Agency'.

This U-turn might be linked to the question of what should be done with the EUMC. The EUMC experienced considerable difficulties that can be summarized into two categories: finding an institutional identity and fulfilling its mandate. Since the EUMC's growing pains challenged its viability (De Schutter and Alston 2005: 1–3; Bell 2007: 193–5), the Commission proposed a number of amendments in order to improve the EUMC's effectiveness and strengthen its coherence. However, despite the Commission's (2003: 9) finding that the 'Centre [EUMC] should continue to concentrate on racism and that an extension to other fields would be an unwelcome distraction within the limits of the resources likely to be available to the Centre [EUMC] and that it would lead to a weakening of the emphasis on racism', the European Council decided to transform this body into a broader and full-fledged 'Human Rights Agency'.

De Schutter and Alston (2005: 3) point out that, although this decision resolved the question of what to do with the EUMC, it posed yet another question, namely what would be the contribution of the new 'Human Rights Agency'. The short and cryptic formula of the European Council (2004a) lacks an idea of how the Agency would improve the monitoring of human rights in the EU and how the new body would relate to preexisting bodies in the field of promotion and protection of the human rights in Europe.

From December 2003 on, more than three years had passed before there was a final agreement on the Agency. The Commission exercised its right of initiative within the first part of this genesis, within which one can further distinguish three phases. In the first phase, the preparation phase, the Commission elaborated documents and background information for the subsequent phase of consultation. Within the framework of this public consultation, the Commission received and analyzed over 100 written comments, in particular from civil society and NGOs. The consultation phase ended with a public hearing on 25 January 2005, after which the Commission assessed the impacts and implications of the establishment of such an agency (Commission 2005b). Six months later, the Commission presented the finalized proposal for a regulation establishing an EU Agency for Fundamental Rights (Commission 2005a). However, hopes for speedy negotiations within the Council went unfulfilled.

8.3 Interorganizational contacts in the FRA negotiations and the negotiations on the FRA Cooperation Agreement

The negotiations on the founding regulation of the Fundamental Rights Agency, as the EU was to call the Agency (pursuant to the EU Charter of Fundamental Rights, of which the Agency was intended to undertake the promotion and monitoring), took place in the Council of the EU from the second half of 2005 until the end of 2006. In December 2006, the EU Justice and Home Affairs Council reached a political agreement on the establishment and functioning of the new Agency (Council 2006: 10).

Officially, the COE itself did not take part in the negotiations, as these were limited to EU member states. Accordingly, after the consultation process mentioned above, in which the COE contributed with a written comment on the proposal for an EU Agency (COE 2004b), the COE needed to find other ways to influence the negotiations. As a result, the COE first and foremost relied on specific member states that were EU member states as well and were therefore taking part in the negotiations. The subsequent section demonstrates that the COE particularly worked the communication channels with Germany and the Netherlands. Along with these indirect contacts, there were also bilateral contacts between the EU and the COE, since the establishment of the FRA was also on the agenda in the negotiations on the MOU (see Chapter 7) and came up in the quadripartite meetings (see Section 3.3.1 of Chapter 3). Additionally, there had been informal contacts at the staff levels of the EU and the COE (be it Commission or FRA with COE Secretariat) throughout the process (I-10; I-12; I-17; I-20; I-24; I-34; I-37). There were also contacts at the political level, for example, the meeting in July 2005 between the then COE SG Terry Davis and then Commissioner for Justice, Freedom, and Security Franco Frattini. In the framework of this meeting, the COE SG agreed to provide the Commission with an analysis, undertaken by the COE Secretariat, of the proposals for the establishment of the FRA. This analysis was finalized in September 2005 (De Schutter 2008: 521–2).

The negotiations on the Cooperation Agreement began as soon as the negotiations on the Regulation came to an end. The EU promoted the idea of a Cooperation Agreement between the FRA and the COE in order to placate the COE and to clarify that the FRA would not duplicate the COE's tasks. As foreseen in the Regulation establishing the FRA (Article 9), the EU should enter into an Agreement with the COE for the purpose of establishing close cooperation between the later FRA, and therefore the Council of the EU provided the Commission with a mandate to negotiate. The negotiations on the Cooperation Agreement took place in the first half of 2007. The negotiations were essentially completed in June 2007, but on the EU side it took some time to go through the internal law-passing procedure in order to finalize this decision. Formally, the Cooperation Agreement was not signed and did not enter into force until June 2008. Coming back to the negotiations in the first half of 2007, it should be mentioned that, on the EU side, the negotiation team came from DG JLS (Commission), and on the COE side, the negotiation team came from the DG JLS equivalent in the COE, namely DGHL (COE Secretariat). The three rounds of negotiation (with meetings lasting a couple of hours) took place in both locations, in Brussels as well as in Strasbourg (I-26; I-37).

8.4   The final set up

Before moving on to the questions of how the COE responded to the overall idea of an EU 'Human Rights Agency', what topics in the proposal were particularly controversial, and how the EU and the COE tried to come to terms (see Section 8.5 on the IOR in the FRA case), this section gives a brief overview on how the FRA was designed in the Council Regulation that established it and how the Cooperation Agreement between the FRA and the COE was arranged.

8.4.1   The Fundamental Rights Agency

The Council Regulation (EC) Nr. 168/2007 of 15 February 2007 establishing a European Union Agency for Fundamental Rights sets out the mandate, functioning, and structure of the FRA. In broad terms, one could say that the first part of the Regulation tackles the mandate and tasks of the FRA, while the second part elaborates on how it fits into the preexisting framework of actors dealing with human rights and engages in relations with them. The last part of the Regulation deals with the structure (organization) of the FRA, the way it operates, and how it functions.

According to Article 3, the new Agency deals with fundamental rights issues in the EU and in the EU member states when implementing EU law. To meet this objective, the FRA – similarly to the EUMC's tasks – primarily collects, analyzes, and disseminates information and data on human rights issues. The FRA can also issue opinions on specific thematic topics (regarding EU law, for example, on a proposal by the Commission), either on its own initiative or on request. Last but not least, an important task of the FRA is publishing: the FRA publishes annual reports on fundamental rights issues as well as on its own activities on the one hand, and thematic reports on the other (Article 4). Multiannual frameworks determine the FRA's areas of activities for a five-year period (Article 5). To ensure 'objective, reliable, and comparable' data, the FRA sets up and coordinates information networks and uses existing networks, organizes meetings of external experts, and sets up ad hoc working parties when necessary. Whenever available, the FRA has to take into account preexisting information from bodies working in the human rights field, for example, provided by the COE (Article 6). Articles 7–10 deal with the relations and cooperation with various bodies, inter alia, the COE. On the cooperation with the COE, the Regulation Nr. 168/2007 already states in the introduction (Paragraph 18):

> The Agency should collaborate closely with the Council of Europe. *Such cooperation should guarantee that any overlap between the activities of the Agency and those of the Council of Europe is avoided, in particular by elaborating mechanisms to ensure complementarity and added*

value, such as the conclusion of a bilateral cooperation agreement and the participation of an independent person appointed by the Council of Europe in the management structures of the Agency with appropriately defined voting rights.

(Emphasis added)

This is one of a couple of explicit references to the COE within the Regulation. With the interorganizational cooperation, overlap should be avoided while ensuring complementarity and added value. For more information on how the cooperation should be organized (for example the independent person of the COE in the management structures of the FRA) and carried out, refer to Section 8.4.2 scrutinizing the Cooperation Agreement between the FRA and the COE.

The last part of the Regulation lays out the bodies of the Agency, consisting of a Management Board, an Executive Board, a Scientific Committee, and a Director (Articles 11–15). The structure of the FRA goes back not only to the previous form of the EUMC but also to an external evaluation of the EUMC and the subsequent Commission (2003) proposal to reform the EUMC (Toggenburg 2007b: 91–2). Finally, the Regulation deals with the operation of the FRA (Articles 16–19), financial provisions and budget implementation (Articles 20–22), general provisions (Articles 23–28), and final provisions (29–34), such as the evaluations of the Agency.

8.4.2   The Cooperation Agreement between the FRA and the COE

After the successful adoption of the Council Regulation (EC) Nr. 168/2007 in February 2007, the EU and the COE tried to come to terms with each other and to come to an agreement on cooperation between the FRA and the COE, as foreseen in the Regulation. In broad terms, one could say that the agreement between the European Community and the Council of Europe on cooperation between the European Union Agency for Fundamental Rights and the Council of Europe (June 2008) splits into four parts: the general cooperation framework, exchange of information and data, methods of cooperation, and the appointment by the COE of an independent person to sit on the FRA's management and executive boards. The subsequent paragraphs will go into detail on these parts.

On a general level, the cooperation framework aims at avoiding duplication while ensuring complementarity and added value, covering the whole range of the FRA's present and future activities. More specifically, the first part of the Cooperation Agreement foresees the establishment of regular contact at appropriate levels between the FRA and the COE, as well as the appointment of a contact person within the FRA and the COE, who deals specifically with matters relating to interorganizational cooperation. The Agreement also foresees the invitation of representatives of the COE to the meetings of the FRA's Management Board and that, vice versa, representatives of the FRA are – if interested – invited to meetings of the COE committees of experts.

The second part, dedicated to the exchange of data and information, dictates that the COE and the FRA provide each other with information and data and use them in their own respective activities. More specifically, it lists the ECtHR, the COE's human rights monitoring systems and expert committees, and the COE Commissioner for Human Rights as important data sources for the FRA. Fastidiously, the Agreement states that whenever the FRA uses COE data, it must indicate its origin and reference accordingly (and vice versa). Finally, the second part schedules regular meetings between the FRA and the COE, which aims at exchanging information on activities that are to be proposed or are already under way.

The third part, highlighting the methods of cooperation, envisages regular consultations between the FRA and the COE with the aim of coordinating their activities. This coordination notably concerns the preparation of the FRA's annual work program and the annual report on fundamental rights issues. On the basis of these consultations, the FRA and the COE can carry out joint and/or complementary projects on subjects of common interest. Most innovative, the Agreement, in theory, allows for temporary staff exchanges to be arranged by agreement between the COE SG and the Director of the FRA.

Concluding the Cooperation Agreement, the fourth part explicitly deals with the appointment by the COE of an independent person to sit on the FRA's management and executive boards. Regarding this issue, Paragraph 19 states:

> The person appointed by the Council of Europe to the Management Board shall be invited to participate in the meetings of the Executive Board. *His or her views shall be duly taken into account*, especially to ensure complementarity and added value between the activities of the Agency and those of the Council of Europe.
>
> (Emphasis added)

As discussed in Section 8.5 the question of whether the independent person, appointed by the COE to sit on the FRA's management and executive boards, has voting rights was a difficult one in the negotiations between the EU and the COE.

8.5 IOR surrounding the FRA

This section reviews the issues of interest in the relations between the EU and the COE concerning the establishment of the FRA. Accordingly, this section touches upon the initial hostile reaction of the COE to the decision of the EU to set up an agency dealing with human rights and the EU point of view. Furthermore, this section demonstrates the ways in which the COE tried to influence the negotiation process and in which ways the final Regulation on the FRA establishment meets COE demands. Subsequently, it discusses in detail the Cooperation Agreement and scrutinizes disputed questions. This section also analyzes how the cooperation between the FRA and the COE has worked in practice and what difficulties lay therein. Last but not least, it picks up the question of the potential renegotiation of the FRA's mandate.

The EU decision to set up the FRA gave rise to the biggest conflict that has arisen between the EU and the COE to date. From the beginning, the *COE took a critical, and in part even dismissive, stance toward these EU developments*. The COE feared that the Agency would intrude into the organization's core business, in terms of content as well as geography. Then COE SG Terry Davis expressed this concern with the following statement: 'With all the best will in the world, I can't understand what it [the Agency] is going to do' (Parker and Laitner 2005). In other words, the COE feared that the EU aimed at reinventing the wheel in human rights protection, thereby duplicating tasks already undertaken by the COE (PACE 2005; Toggenburg 2007b: 88–91; De Schutter 2007: 5–8, 2008: 517; Brummer 2008b: 69). The PACE (2006c: Paragraph 4), one of the most critical and outspoken actors within the COE, underlined the possible negative consequences of an agency for human right protection in Europe: 'Duplication could lead to inconsistencies and create the possibility of "forum shopping", with the countries that were subject to the different mechanisms giving preference to whichever took the more favourable position'. Besides the possibility of inconsistencies in human rights protection, the PACE also highlights possible negative effects for the European integration process and waste of resources by stating the following:

> The fact of having two parallel institutions engaged in similar activities within the same geographical region [...] would create new dividing lines in Europe by reference to states' institutional situation in bodies devoted to human rights, one of the very principles intended to unite Europe. The apparent incoherence of creating a

new European Union body to duplicate work already satisfactorily undertaken elsewhere would cause *confusion amongst a European public already uncertain about the process of European integration. Duplication would also waste public money at a time of general budgetary stringency,* thus further alienating citizens from European institutions, including the mechanisms of human rights protection.

(PACE 2006c: Paragraph 5, emphasis added)

Besides the fact that the COE was keen not to see the FRA become a competing monitoring mechanism, the enormous financial budget of the Agency caused a great disappointment (and jealousy of the EU) for the COE, which confronts hard budget constraints (I-1; I-5; I-12; I-26; I-29). In 2013, when the Agency's budget is scheduled to reach its peak, the FRA budget would represent – one-fifth of the COE budget (excluding the budget of the ECtHR supervising the ECHR). This situation is particularly disturbing because the COE's budget 'is widely perceived as insufficient to meet its mandate' (De Schutter 2008: 514) and the budget has not been growing at all for many years (Strasser 2000: 135; Taylor 2008: 1249). Aside from the budget figures, staff from the COE emphasized the collateral damages of this decision, meaning the movement of labor, experts, and NGOs from the COE to the EU. Moreover, causing some frustration on the COE side was the fact that the EU decided to invest large amounts of money into the former EUMC, an agency that performed poorly on an overall level. Confronted with these major disappointments, the COE staff tended to joke that the COE was in fact the 'true' EU 'Human Rights Agency', given that it had the special monitoring mechanisms, the expert committees, and the knowledge to draft legal initiatives. Following this point of view, instead of creating a new agency, it would have been more reasonable to give the money directly to the COE. With this, the COE alleged that, to some extent, the decision to create the FRA was driven by EU ignorance of the COE. In the minority, there were also peaceful voices within the COE highlighting their understanding of the EU decision. For example, some of the COE staff took the view that the more bodies there were dealing with human rights, the merrier it would be for human rights protection (versus the view that more bodies would create confusion and compete for visibility) (I-1; I-5; I-14; I-26; I-32).

For the EU, the outspoken negative reaction of the COE toward the decision to set up the FRA was not understandable. However, it did not come as a surprise to the EU staff, since the feeling that 'the COE is always very much hesitating to see the EU developing a new file having a fundamental rights dimension' (I-10) prevails in the EU. The EU staff wondered whether their counterparts in Strasbourg had really understood the EU's purpose for creating the Agency. According to the EU's line of reasoning, the objective was never to reinvent the wheel or to engage in competition with the COE, but to fill a gap in human rights protection by undertaking research for, and to give advice and opinions to, the EU institutions. Following this point of view, the Agency was seen as a national agency (like, for example, the German national agency), a strong agency with many competences but exclusively within the EU's field of competences. In the pre-drafting phase, EU staff went to Strasbourg in order to explain to their counterparts what the Agency's mandate would and would not be (I-10; I-12; I-24; I-37). Also, the EU tried to calm the COE down by formally recalling, on several occasions, that '[t]he Agency is expected *to bring real added value* to the EU institutions and will contribute to more coherence and consistency in the EU human rights policy' (COM 2006a: 4, emphasis added).

Nevertheless, the controversial opinions did not dissolve so easily: during the negotiation process in the EU, the COE *did everything in its power to block the process* and thus intervened in order to modify the agencies' mandate according to its concerns (I-5; I-10; I-12; I-23; I-24; I-37). In June 2005, the former PACE President René van der Linden, for instance, telephoned the German Chancellor Angela Merkel and obtained a German blockage of the question of the FRA in the Council meeting in Luxembourg. The former PACE President argued that this project would be a great strain on the EU budget, while simultaneously would not bring added value compared to what was already in existence in Strasbourg. In the end, the German authorities were convinced of the project's usefulness but the COE had been successful in delaying the decision-making process. The general decision to set up an agency, however, was already made in December 2003. Aside from the communication channels with Germany, the former PACE President also worked the links with the national parliament of the Netherlands (I-10; I-30; I-34; I-37).

As previously mentioned, the COE feared that the FRA would intrude into the organization's core business, in content as well as geography. The former referred to whether the Agency would monitor human rights ('advisory monitoring') or eventually set human rights standards ('normative monitoring'). Another question related to this was whether the Agency's mandate would be limited to the application of EU law or include member states acting autonomously. The latter referred to whether the Agency's tasks would be limited to EU member states or would include non-EU member states (yet COE member states) as well. Whether it was actually caused by the COE interventions or conversely could be explained by member states' similar requests to those of the COE (I-5; I-22; I-26), the *final provisions concerning the Agency's tasks and mandate largely comply with the COE requests* (De Schutter 2007: 8–14; Toggenburg 2007b: 91; Brummer 2008b: 70), and the most important point to note is that – the scope of the FRA is limited to EU law and mainly to EU member states and the main task is collecting data and providing expertise for EU institutions, which means that the COE standard-setting task remains untouched. Due to its narrow mandate, the new agency is rather distinct from the 'monitoring centre for human rights' first envisaged by Philip Alston and Joseph Weiler (1999: 55–9). Accordingly, the COE's dismissive attitude toward the Agency dissolved, as can be seen from the following statement of the COE SG Terry Davis in February 2007 (COE 2007c):

I welcome the decision by the EU Council of Ministers to create a new Fundamental Rights Agency with a mandate to scrutinise EU institutions and the application of EU laws. This is an important and challenging task, and the new Agency can make a useful contribution in helping the EU to comply with the Council of Europe standards based on the European Convention on Human Rights.

The involvement of non-EU member states in the FRA is one of the few things that did not change according to the COE's point of view: within the quadripartite meetings, the COE argued heavily for limiting the Agency's scope solely to human rights in the framework of EU law within the EU member states, by stating that '[a]ny other attitude would be extremely dangerous for the principle of a single human rights system in Europe and could lead to the fragmentation of human rights protection' (COM 2006b: 2). In contrast, the EU explained 'that the negotiations were generally heading in the direction desired by the Council of Europe, but recalled that the agency could also have to deal with partner countries' (COM 2006b: 3). Eventually, Article 28 of the Regulation decided that the FRA would be open to EU candidate countries as observers.

In the end, the Regulation – more specifically Article 9 – attached great importance to the cooperation between the FRA and the COE. The aim was to avoid duplication and ensure complementarity and added value. To achieve these aims, an independent person appointed by the COE is involved in the management structures of the Agency. Subsequently, in

2008 the COE announced its first independent person to participate in the FRA's decision-making bodies.

The *Agreement between the EU and the COE on cooperation between the FRA and the COE*, as foreseen in the MOU (see Chapter 7), was concluded in June 2008. One highly disputed issue in the negotiation process revolved around the question as to whether the independent person appointed by the COE should be able to vote in the Management as well as in the Executive Board (I-26; I-37). Although the Regulation anticipated most of the guidelines of the Cooperation Agreement, it was imprecise on the question of the independent person's voting rights. Paragraph 18 of the Regulation talked vaguely of 'the participation of an independent person appointed by the Council of Europe in the management structures of the Agency with *appropriately defined voting rights*' (emphasis added). Seemingly, during the negotiation process of the Cooperation Agreement, it was no longer clear what opinion the Council of the EU and the member states originally took when drafting the Regulation, as a compromise had eventually been concluded. Regarding the independent person's voting rights in the Executive Board, Paragraph 19 of the Cooperation Agreement states: '*His or her views shall be duly taken into account*, especially to ensure complementarity and added value between the activities of the Agency and those of the Council of Europe' (emphasis added). In practice, it turned out that the whole discussion was rather useless, since the Executive Board hardly ever voted, given that it consists only of six members. Aside from this aspect, the negotiations transpired rather quickly and took place mainly during the first half of 2007. Hence, the Cooperation Agreement could have been concluded earlier, but translation problems and a wrongly adopted version of the Agreement triggered a delay in the EU decision-making process (within the Council of the EU).

Generally speaking, at present, the COE is satisfied with the Regulation as well as with the Cooperation Agreement. Accordingly, the FRA case is often mentioned and referred to when talking about the 'good' interorganizational relationship between the EU and the COE. However, it is said within Strasbourg that one should distinguish between what is written on paper, how it is put into practice, and how it will develop in the future, since an institution – once established – develops a life of its own and increases its mandate. Regarding the latter, the COE worries specifically about forces within the EU (for example EP) that strive for widening the Agency's scope (I-3; I-5; I-26; I-30; I-32; I-37).

Having discussed the different perspectives and expectations on the establishment of the FRA, the subsequent part of the section analyzes *how the interorganizational cooperation between the FRA and the COE worked in practice.* The interorganizational contact of the Agency (EUMC) with the COE broadened by a great deal, progressing from a very small part of the COE, which was the ECRI, to covering the entire COE, including the Commissioner for Human Rights. So it expanded massively. In addition, the interorganizational contact, which can be ad hoc or organized in advanced, takes place at various levels, from the operational to the political, and involves mutual visits, e-mails, and phone calls, as well as informal joint lunches or 'good-natured drinks' after official meetings. Additionally, while the decision to establish the FRA resulted in a big dispute at the political level, everything remained the same for the staff working in the FRA and ECRI, at least during the starting phase: the same staff working in the former EUMC became the staff of the later FRA (before the recruitment process started), and, of course, due to the long-lasting working relationship, trust has developed over the years at the staff level. Consequently, the involved EU and the COE staffs did not understand the commotion about the Agency. Moreover, and most interestingly, the agitation concerning the Agency was not new to the staff, given that the establishment of EUMC (vis-à-vis ECRI) had already caused similar reactions in the second half of the 1990s (I-1; I-8; I-24; I-26; I-29).

That being said, there are some points in the working relationship that in practice *cause displeasure on both sides.* Since the FRA itself was not involved at all in the negotiations for the Cooperation Agreement, the Agreement is something external to which the personnel of the Agency must adapt. Nonetheless, parts of the FRA staff have the feeling that the reciprocity of the two parties, the FRA and the COE, is unbalanced, for example, the COE's one-sided involvement in the Management Board of the FRA as well as the COE's possibility to propose joint projects to the FRA. Also, since the Cooperation Agreement is, in part, not very specific, it raises some practical questions, for example, what joint projects entail and how do they work. In response to these kinds of questions, there may be different opinions (from the FRA and the COE) on how to interpret the contract. Generally speaking, the COE is unsatisfied with the small number of joint projects with the FRA. Also, a recurring point of discussion is the delayed delivery of FRA documents. Some of the documents that the COE needs to work on are delivered only 24 or 48 hours before deadline, which makes it difficult for the COE, on the one hand, to actually have a look at it, and, on the other hand, devaluates cooperation. In one case, the COE was even asked for its opinion after the document had already been sent out to the board members (I-24; I-26; I-37).

Concerning the *respective knowledge that exists in both IOs* generally, it is further seen that there still is room for improvement. Already at the beginning of the interorganizational relationship between the FRA and the COE, the FRA needed to clarify its role, since some of the COE staff heard of the big FRA budget and had the – misleading – expectation that the Agency, like some kind of donor, would close the COE budget gaps. As foreseen in the Cooperation Agreement, the Directors of the FRA and the COE each appointed a contact person to deal specifically with matters relating to their cooperation. The COE contact person's task is coordination, although the contact person also had to raise awareness about the FRA, especially in the beginning. The coordination task entails, for instance, collecting comments of the various COE units on the Agency's work program, collecting and selecting project proposals, and organizing COE visits to the FRA. Unfortunately, the internal coordination mechanism carries conflict potential. Due to the fact that the contact person is attached to an operational DG, more specifically to DGHL, the staffs of the other DGs partly feel left out. One criticism is that DGHL now has a privileged relationship with the FRA, which biases the selection of projects proposed to the FRA. Similarly to the COE contact person's task, the FRA contact person's task is coordinating contacts, visits, meetings, and written contributions to the COE expert committees or projects. However, in contrast to the COE, internal awareness-raising is not as important to the FRA, since the long-term staff of the FRA (and the former EUMC) is already well informed on the COE. Outside the FRA, for example, within the Commission, the FRA contact person stresses – as a kind of advocate – the importance of other actors in the field of human rights protection, such as the UN, the COE, and the OSCE (I-1; I-24; I-26; I-27; I-32).

Regarding how cooperation works in practice, there are a few things that do not run smoothly, but overall both the COE and the FRA are pleased with their cooperation. The involvement of the COE in the management structures of the Agency is working out fairly well and there is very little in the way the cooperation is working about which the COE can complain. A minor difference in the way that the interorganizational cooperation works can be found between different COE units: seemingly, the relationship between the FRA and DGHL (COE Secretariat) runs more smoothly than the relationship between the FRA and DG III (COE Secretariat). Aside from that, the former leaders within the COE (COE SG and PACE President, at that time Terry Davis and René van der Linden), who were skeptical toward the establishment of the FRA, left their posts, and the interorganizational relationship appears to be much easier with their successors. Moreover, the FRA Director Morten Kjaerum takes a conciliatory point of view and is eager to have good relations with the COE (I-29; I-32; I-34; I-37).

In conclusion, this section points to the possible *renegotiation of the FRA mandate*. In December 2006 under the Finnish Presidency of the EU, the 'agreement to disagree' did foresee that EU member states would renegotiate the mandate of the FRA (with the idea to expand it into the former third-pillar area) prior to December 2009 (Toggenburg 2007a: 7). The issue in question was, inter alia, whether the FRA should have the right to formulate opinions on legislative proposals in the third-pillar area on its own initiative. One can refer to this situation as a typical EU (Commission) strategy: first, set up an agency with a limited scope; second, see how it works; and third, if member states are satisfied with it, broaden the mandate. Interestingly, this is – as previously mentioned – exactly what the COE staff feared would happen with the Agency's mandate, once established. The FRA staff expected the Swedish Presidency to raise this issue in autumn 2009 (I-16; I-24). However, the Swedish Presidency's proposal concerning this matter was turned down, and accordingly was not included into the Stockholm Program (Marcher 2009: 14–5). Consequently, a possible renewed discussion between the EU and the COE on the FRA mandate did not occur. Interestingly, according to the Commission, there is no need to extend the Agency's mandate, while in the EP voices have been raised to do so. They argue that the environment has changed since the creation of the FRA: due to the Lisbon Treaty and with it the abolition of the pillar structure, the EU has gained considerable competences in the JHA area, in which consistent focus on fundamental rights is clearly needed. Therefore, they maintain, the Agency's mandate should be expanded for the FRA to be able to address exactly these issues (Bychawska-Siniarska and Warso 2011). It remains to be seen how the question of the renegotiation of the FRA's mandate further develops.

Concluding this empirical part, the subsequent section goes on to review and analyze the IOR with regard to the FRA against the background of the theoretical framework.

8.6   IOR surrounding the FRA – analysis and explanatory factors

As discussed the IOR between the EU and the COE during the process of establishing the FRA have been rather conflictive, but an Agreement on cooperation between the FRA and the COE was successfully concluded in the end. To examine what this means in terms of IOR theory, this section aims at linking the empirical results to the factors facilitating (hindering) interorganizational cooperation established in the theoretical framework.

8.6.1   Interest (policy and organizational)

In the FRA case, the policy interest, the protection of human rights, is beyond question, at least from a superficial point of view. This may also be due to the fact that human rights and their protection have a very positive connotation. Nobody would publicly declare 'we are against human rights' or 'we prefer less protection'. However, the question in dispute is how to best achieve this aim. The views range from the idea that the more bodies tackling human rights, the better it would be for human rights protection, to the support for simply giving all funds to the COE in order to avoid duplication and parallel standards. The organizational self-interest of both IOs is evident: for the EU, human rights have a legitimating function, whereas the COE is driven by the fear of marginalization and jealousy of the FRA's extensive budget. One can see that organizational self-interest plays a major role in the IOR between the EU and the COE: most of the conflicts between the EU and the COE arise when self-interest is at stake in one of the organizations.

8.6.2   Organizational characteristics

As mentioned previously, as the sheer number of actors increases, the IOR become more difficult. In the FRA case, many actors are involved on both sides (and occasionally at different points in time). These actors may not even be involved in the bilateral relations between the counterparts, but may still exert an external influence. On the COE side, the former PACE President opposed the FRA and actively lobbied against its establishment, which not only confused the issue of IOR but even delayed and complicated EU internal negotiations. Moreover, the COE SG issued hostile press releases hindering the establishment of a trustful cooperation. One can infer from this observation that, in addition to the counterparts involved at the operational level, one must consider the behavior of leaders and notabilities in order to fully grasp the IOR.

Similarly to the fight against the Roma discrimination case, where one can see internal coordination mechanisms (within the COE for relations with the FRA) that carry conflict potential, it becomes apparent that heavy bureaucracies in the COE as well as in the FRA impede the joint funding of projects. Consequently, it can be assumed that the organizational characteristics factor is particularly decisive for the institutional relations (politically sensitive and high level). In these cases, the FRA and the MOU, cooperative relations are most often hindered by complex settings, in which many actors – often with conflicting goals – are involved.

8.6.3 Socialization

This section considers the two aspects of the socialization factor: culture (views of seeing the world) and trust (at the individual level between persons involved in the IOR).

At the political level, there was not enough time for socialization processes in the FRA case. The views differed and the two IOs reproached one another for not knowing enough about the respective unit in the other organization (the creation of the FRA driven by EU ignorance on the one hand, and the COE not knowing what political integration means on the other hand). The practical working relationships between the COE, the EUMC, and later the FRA (operational level) are not affected by the developments at the political level. Since the staff has remained the same, trust has developed over the years. Regarding the common procedures, there is an independent person appointed to the FRA Management as well as the Executive Board who can bring the COE's view closer to that of the FRA. Additionally, specific contact persons (one in the COE and one in the FRA) raise awareness of the respective unit of the other organization and provide information. The fact that this task is needed shows that knowledge about one another is still lacking.

The first aspect of the factor at hand, the *organizational culture*, is difficult to analyze on a one-to-one basis. Conversely, it seems reasonable to scrutinize this aspect from a cross-case perspective. In general, the fact stands out that a lack of clarity prevails in both IOs regarding the working methods and tasks of the other organization. For example, while the EU complains that the COE does not understand what political integration means, at the same time the COE accuses the EU of being ignorant and not acknowledging that it is not 'terra incognita'. Different terminologies (different labels for identical terms) do exist, the most prominent example being 'human rights' and 'fundamental rights', but this does not pose any challenges to the IOR, since the IOs treat these terms synonymously. Within the EU framework, the origin of the 'fundamental rights' label is explained as follows: the name change from EU 'Human Rights Agency' to EU Fundamental Rights Agency should be seen pursuant to the EU Charter of Fundamental Rights, the promotion and monitoring of which is intended to be done by the Agency.

Accordingly, one has to ask from where does the term 'Charter of Fundamental Rights' come. Seemingly, it was promoted by the Convention drafting the Charter in order to ensure gender-neutral language: in the French language, originally, it would have been 'droits de l'homme', which can be understood as 'men's rights'. In order to avoid this association, the Convention put forward the term 'droits fondamentaux', which, equally, covers men and women. Different ways of seeing the world can be found more broadly in the differentiation of civil servant and diplomatic agent, interior and justice ministry orientation, and international law perspective and community perspective.

8.6.4 Physical opportunity

To recall, the physical opportunity factor looks at the existing infrastructure in the external environment (transport system) as well as the intraorganizational resources available for IOR.

Also in the case of the FRA, the deficient transport system in Strasbourg handicaps the possibility of short-notice meetings: staffs really need to be convinced of the need for attending considering the costly and time-consuming journey. Without having any Liaison Office to compensate for these difficulties in the FRA case, the COE and the FRA decided to take another path and establish the aforementioned contact persons. Finally, the reciprocal representation of the EU in Strasbourg is limited to the Commission, given that the General Secretariat of the Council of the EU decided to abstain from this activity.

8.7 IOR surrounding the FRA – conclusions

The preceding sections set out to shed light on the IOR between the EU and the COE with regard to the FRA, the EU 'Human Rights Agency', which is the second institutional issue to be analyzed along with the MOU. When looking at the antecedent situation of the FRA establishment, one needs to mention ECRI, established by the COE as early as 1993, in order to combat racism and xenophobia. A couple of years later, in 1997, the EU followed the COE by introducing the EUMC, which dealt with racism and xenophobia as well. Given the resemblance of the two bodies, ECRI and the EUMC can be seen as natural counterparts and their relationship as a predecessor to the COE–FRA relationship.

The sections have shown that the idea of setting up an EU 'Human Rights Agency' dates back to the second half of the 1990s, during which Alston and Weiler (1999) comprehensively elaborated on the idea of a full-fledged EU 'Human Rights Agency' within the framework of the EU human rights agenda for the year 2000. Even though the idea received strong impetus from the Austria (Haider) crisis, the EU did not act on this suggestion. So when the European Council publicized the decision to install a 'Human Rights Agency' on the basis of the EUMC in December 2003, even political insiders were taken by surprise. This U-turn has to be seen in relation to the question of what should be done with the EUMC, which had considerable difficulties challenging its viability. Yet, the decision to transform the EUMC into a new agency did not give sufficient thought to what the contribution of the new 'Human Rights Agency' would be. Due to the abrupt signal and the existing ambiguity over the new agency's mandate, it is no great wonder that the practical realization of the EU 'Human Rights Agency' was not free of political difficulties.

While examining the interorganizational contacts in the negotiations on the FRA establishment, it becomes clear that, although the COE itself did not participate in negotiations, the COE found other ways to influence negotiations according to its needs. In particular, the COE worked the communication channels with Germany and the Netherlands. Besides this indirect attempt to activate and engage its lobby, there were also bilateral contacts between the EU and the COE, for example, in the framework of the MOU negotiations and the quadripartite meetings, where the FRA was on the agenda as well.

The sections have shown that the initial hostile reaction of the COE toward the decision of the EU to set up an agency dealing with human rights can be explained by the COE's fear of marginalization and duplication. In contrast, for the EU, the COE's outspoken negative reaction was not understandable. Furthermore, the preceding sections have shown the ways in which the COE tried to influence the negotiation process and how the final Regulation on the establishment of the Agency met with COE demands. Whether actually caused by COE interventions or explained by member states' requests that were similar to those of the COE, for the most part the final provisions concerning the Agency's tasks and mandate did ultimately comply with COE requests. On the operational level, one could see that the staff did not share in the big dispute that occurred on the political level, since the personnel remained essentially the same (at the beginning) and trust had developed over the years at the staff level. The sections highlighted a few aspects in the working relationship that cause displeasure on both sides, and pointed out the way in which the FRA and the COE work to increase the respective knowledge of one another and manage the IOR. Overall, COE and the FRA are pleased with their cooperation and, accordingly, the FRA case is often mentioned and referred to when talking about the 'good' interorganizational relationship between the EU and the COE in terms of 'from a rough start to a successful interorganizational cooperation'. However, this is of course an oversimplified picture.

In terms of IOR theory, the FRA case has shown that the interest factor (in particular, the organizational self-interest) plays a major role in the EU–COE relations, since whenever organizational self-interests are at stake they tend to override the shared policy interest. Once again, a high degree of organizational self-interest in one of the IOs tends to create a high degree of conflict in the IOR, as simultaneously the complexity and socialization factors reinforce the direction predetermined by the interest factor without the ability to override it and reverse the trend. In the FRA case, the level of complexity was high and increased the trend (of the interest factor) toward conflict. On the political level, there was not enough time for socialization processes in the FRA case. The physical opportunity factor, the environmental features, and the intraorganizational resources do not have a direct impact on whether the relations are cooperative or conflictive, but have an indirect influence on the extent of the IOR through the staff's inability to control these conditions and simultaneous obligation to cope with these challenges (for example lacking resources).

Part IV
Conclusion

9
Conclusion

> Human rights are too important in the construction of Europe
> to justify one body (the EU) trying to reinvent the wheel. Like-
> wise, they are too important for the other body (the Council
> of Europe) to stand on the past and not to recognize that the
> future is constantly being made.
>
> (Quinn 2001: 874)

This observation describes quite accurately the main problem in the IOR
between the EU and the COE, namely, the EU's power and attempts to
reinvent the wheel and the COE's skepticism about the EU's engagement
in human rights. Speaking to this assessment, this chapter, by bringing
together the empirical results and the theoretical framework, identifies the interest-based factor as the primary factor determining the IOR
between the EU and the COE. Before going into the discussion, the following paragraphs describe the full variance of the dependent variable.

The empirical case studies have shown both instances of conflict as
well as cooperation in the EU–COE relations. *Conflictive relations* involve
differences in opinion that result in missing political support, such
as hostile press releases and documents (for example FRA, terrorism),
motivation of one's own 'lobby' (for example national parliaments and
member states' politicians), and interventions in order to block the initiative of the other organization (for example FRA). Also, one can see
complaints about the behavior of the counterparts on a personal or
an organizational level (for example terrorism, data protection, general access of COE to EU meetings and documents). The fight against
terrorism case reveals a kind of 'race' for who can come up with a
legal initiative first. Linked to this are discussions on duplication and
reinvention of the wheel (for example Roma). Also in dispute is the

question of the 'Disconnection Clause' with which the EU defies control of the COE convention system (for example terrorism).

As regards *cooperative relations*, the case studies have highlighted information sharing through liaison offices and reciprocal representation. Nevertheless, the information-sharing process is criticized as being one sided (for example COE cannot access the restricted EU documents). The two IOs organize joint press conferences or initiatives, conduct joint projects (for example Roma), and conclude cooperation agreements (for example FRA, MOU). They also support each other politically, for example, by referring to each other's work or bearing out a convention (for example terrorism). The study emphasizes the importance of informal features of cooperative relations, as cooperation often depends on how well the counterparts get along with each other (which implies that relations are not institutionalized). Moreover, informal relations might be more successful precisely because the institutional frameworks of the two IOs do not always support formal cooperation (for example Roma).

The findings show *differences between policy areas*: cooperation between the EU and the COE is much more advanced in the JHA field than in the social policy field, in which the COE is merely named as one of the four or five most important actors. Also, specific coordination meetings between the EU and the COE are in place in the JHA field, highlighting the importance of the relations within this field.

9.1   IOR and explanatory factors

Bringing the empirical data in line with the theoretical framework, Table 9.1 attempts to summarize the main theoretical results of this research study. The attempt is to show what factors predominantly impact on which cases and account for which results (level of conflict). It goes without saying that to achieve this objective, one needs to simplify matters and, therefore, Table 9.1 cannot reflect the data exactly as they are. Thus, this table highlights the determining factors for the cases analyzed and their effect, without implying that factors not listed for a specific case are nonexistent. In fact, this research did find instances of, for example, shared policy interest for the FRA and the terrorism cases, but the shared policy interest did not prevail for these cases and did not hold back the conflict. For the sake of completeness, it should be added that the socialization factor works in both directions: socialization facilitates interorganizational cooperation, whereas the lack of socialization hinders interorganizational cooperation.

Table 9.1   Patterns of dominant factors influencing interorganizational relations

Pattern 1: Highly conflictive relations

Cases	Explanatory Factors			
	Org. self-interest	Policy interest	Complexity	Lack of socialization
FRA	X		X	
Terrorism	X			X
MOU	X		X	

Pattern 2: Less conflictive relations

Cases	Explanatory factors			
	Org. self-interest	Policy interest	Complexity	Socialization
Roma		X		X
Data protection		X		X

The empirical data identify the *interest-based factor* (grayshaded) as the most relevant for explaining the EU–COE relations. The interest factor splits into the shared policy interest and the organizational self-interest. On the face of it, the shared policy interest (for example protection of human rights in general or more specifically an issue area such as data protection) was given in all cases analyzed. Of course, the extent of shared policy interest varied slightly from one case to another (for example one could find some differences of policy interest in the terrorism case). However, it proves crucial whether the actors pursue organizational self-interest: despite similar policy interests in the protection of human rights; serious conflicts between both sides have arisen whenever organizational self-interest is at stake. In particular, this was the case when the COE perceived the EU as intruding into some of its core areas of competence, thus threatening its organizational survival. Hence, if the organizational self-interest is high in one of the IOs, the IOR are most probably conflictive. If the organizational self-interest is low or not present at all, the IOR are cooperative or at least conflict free. In a nutshell, the theoretical results of this research show that Downs (1967: 16, 215) – who, as early as the 1960s, underlined the organizations' inherent tendency to expand and the organizations' sensitivity to 'invasions' of their core areas of competence – can indeed still be consulted for an explanation of a great deal of contemporary IOs' behavior. Though not particularly highlighted by Table 9.1 cooperation between the two IOs took place as well. However, it seems that first IOs must continuously overcome their organizational self-interest.

Linking these theoretical results to the hypotheses drawn up in Chapter 2, one can state the following: the data strongly confirm the hypothesis stressing the role of interests in the IOR (H 1.). However, one can further distinguish between the hypothesis that puts the focus on shared policy interest (H 1.1.) and the hypothesis highlighting the organizational self-interest (H 1.2.). The data show that organizational self-interest is the most significant independent variable, overriding the shared policy interest variable (as well as all the other independent variables). Accordingly, the shared policy interest hypothesis (H 1.1.) proves to be far less important than the organizational self-interest hypothesis (H 1.2.). Future research will show whether, and, if so to what extent, the weakness of the former hypothesis can be attributed to the fact that 'human rights' have a strong positive connotation and both IOs – at least on the surface – support the protection of human rights.

The factors *organizational characteristics* (complexity) and *socialization* (trust) only play a secondary role; they only reinforce the main trend toward cooperation or conflict arising from the constellation of interests. The organizational characteristics factor (complexity) has a strong influence on institutional relations that are often characterized as politically sensitive and high level. A higher value of complexity indicates a high number of actors/decision points and complex settings in which units involved in the IOR – to a greater or lesser extent – depend on other units. If the level of complexity is high, this factor increases the trend (of the interest factor) toward conflictive relations, as is the case with the FRA and MOU. Compared with the institutional cases, the present factor has a minor impact on the operational relations dealing with policy issues.

In contrast, the socialization factor has a strong influence on the (low-level) operational relations dealing with policy issues that are institutionalized, but not so strong an influence on the (high-level) institutional relations. Socialization indicates trust at the individual level between the counterparts involved in the IOR. Conversely, missing socialization indicates a lack of trust. If trust has been established, this factor strengthens the trend (of the interest factor) toward cooperative relations, as is, in part, true for the Roma and the data protection case. If trust is lacking, this factor increases the trend (of the interest factor) toward conflictive relations, which applies to the terrorism case.

The data yield mixed results for the hypothesis drawing attention the organizational characteristics (complexity) (H 2.). One the one hand, the data confirm this hypothesis for the institutional cases; on the other hand, the data refute this hypothesis for the policy cases. Likewise, the data give way to mixed results on the hypothesis emphasizing the extent of socialization between the two IOs (H 3.): the data confirm the socialization hypothesis for the policy cases, while the data refute this hypothesis for the institutional cases. Whenever the organizational self-interest hypothesis (H 1.2.) and either the organizational characteristics hypothesis (H 2.) or the socialization hypothesis (H 3.) contradict each other and predict a different outcome, the organizational self-interest hypothesis (H 1.2.) wins, is far more significant for explaining the IOR.

Table 9.1 also displays the outcome (Pattern 1 and Pattern 2) – the dependent variable, which is conceived of as a continuum ranging from conflict to cooperation – as a dichotomy of highly conflictive and less conflictive relations. This strong simplification omits the question of whether the lack of conflict automatically implies cooperation. It should be added that conflict and cooperation vary not only across cases but also within cases during the observed time frame, a fact that cannot be accurately captured by the table. A high level of conflict can be observed in the FRA case, the fight against terrorism case, and the MOU case; however, to some extent, all three 'conflictive cases' transformed into more cooperative situations over the analyzed time frame.

When recalling Chart 1, one notices that the fourth factor, physical opportunity, is not listed in Table 9.1. The results show that the environmental features and the intraorganizational resources do not have a direct impact on whether the relations are cooperative or conflictive (H 4. emerges as an intervening variable that influences the extent of IOR). The staff involved in IOR cannot control these conditions, but must still cope with these challenges (for example lacking resources), and thus this factor has an indirect influence on the extent of the IOR. Equally missing from the table is the first aspect of the socialization factor, the organizational culture, given the difficulty to analyze it on a one-to-one basis. This implies that several organizational cultures would exist within one organization (for a discussion on this topic see Section 8.6.3 of Chapter 8).

The subsequent section illustrates the patterns of dominant factors influencing IOR by examining the case studies and briefly reproducing the highly conflictive cases (FRA, terrorism, and MOU) and the less conflictive cases (Roma and data protection).

9.2 Pattern 1: organizational self-interest and complexity/lack of trust

In the FRA case, the terrorism case, and the MOU case, one can see highly conflictive relations resulting from the IOs' organizational self-interest and high complexity, or in the case of terrorism, the lack of socialization. This section gives details on the cases belonging to Pattern 1.

When the EU decided the set-up of its own *Fundamental Rights Agency*, the COE took a critical, in part even dismissive, stance toward these EU developments. Although the policy interest – the protection of human rights – is beyond all questions, the issue in dispute is how to best achieve this aim. The views range from the idea that the more bodies tackling human rights the merrier it would be for human rights protection, to the viewpoint of diverting all funds simply to the COE in order to avoid duplication and parallel standards. The organizational self-interest of both IOs is evident: for the EU, human rights have a legitimating function, whereas the COE is driven by the fear of marginalization and jealousy of the FRA's substantial budget. As regards the complexity, many actors are involved on both sides (and occasionally at different points in time) in the FRA case. These actors may not even be involved in the bilateral relations between the counterparts at the operational level, but may exert influence from the outside. On the COE side, the then PACE President opposed the FRA and actively lobbied against its establishment, which not only confused the issue of IOR but also delayed and complicated EU internal negotiations. Also, the then COE SG issued hostile press releases hindering the establishment of a trustful cooperation. One can infer from this observation that, besides the counterparts involved at the operational level, researchers have to consider the behavior of leaders and notabilities in order to fully grasp the IOR.

The *terrorism* case reveals a kind of 'race' for who can be the first to come up with a legal initiative. Therein, one might ask whether one can observe different approaches to human rights issues (for example law enforcement versus human rights approach). The data show that this is not the case. The COE Convention on the Prevention of Terrorism, in fact, goes very far in terms of criminalization compared with other (previous) anti-terrorism treaties. What one can find, however, are differences of opinion on how to achieve the best human rights protection in Europe, for example, whether the inclusion of a 'Disconnection Clause' or the EU Framework Decision, which basically transforms the COE consensus into an EU instrument, is needed. While emphasizing policy interest, the line of argument of both IOs actually reflects underlying organizational self-interest. Moreover, as in the FRA case, the COE SG issued hostile press releases hindering the establishment of a trustful cooperation. In the terrorism case, the so-called CATS meetings bring together the General Secretariat of the Council with the COE Secretariat, and they were to some extent attended by the Commission. Although the issue of the Terrorism Framework Decision was often on the agenda in the meetings, conflict was not avoided. However, the conflict mainly arose between the Commission and the COE Secretariat. While the official dealing with terrorism in the COE Secretariat was the same for several years, the high staff turnover in the responsible Commission unit impeded the establishment of trust. Also, due to the principle of rotation, staff may deal with very different topics during their career in the Commission, while staff in the COE Secretariat often grows to be an expert in a specific issue area. This may lead to diverging assessments, especially during drafting processes.

In the *MOU case*, both IOs share the policy interest of the protection and promotion of human rights in Europe; there are only some minor differences of opinion regarding policy aspects. Similarly, both IOs are interested in formulating a Cooperation Agreement, namely the MOU. However, the contemporary FRA conflict influenced and complicated the cooperation in the MOU case. Additionally, the EU's organizational self-interest had some effect on the binding character of the Cooperation Agreement: the EU wanted to maintain for itself as much room for maneuver as possible: 'we are partners – we are not married'. The many different actors, the rotating presidencies on the EU as well as on the COE side, complicated the negotiation process. The IOR are particularly difficult when Russia holds the COE presidency or when COE officials with Russian origin participate. Furthermore, an initiative in the JLS area to establish a specific sub-MOU – with more binding mechanisms for cooperation and early warning for forthcoming legal initiatives – was not realized due to institutional barriers regarding a deepening of the IOR. DG RELEX, which had the function of overseeing IOR with the COE, again wanted to maintain as much room for maneuver as possible, namely ad hoc cooperation instead of institutionalization, and opposed the plan.

9.3 Pattern 2: policy interest and socialization

In the fight against Roma discrimination case and the data protection case one can see less conflictive relations. This research argues that, first and foremost, the high extent of shared policy interest (and the lack of organizational self-interest) account for this result. The socialization factor shows the importance of trust at the individual level for the IOR in these cases. This section gives details on the cases belonging to Pattern 2.

In the *fight against Roma discrimination case,* the policy interest of both IOs is congruent in most instances, due to the fact that the EU is building on the work of the COE. Yet, difficulties arise, given that the COE's norms do not appear as 'COE norms' in these documents. Therefore, the COE's organizational self-interest is at stake: the COE fears that the EU is reinventing the wheel and accuses the Commission of wanting to 'own' the process without letting the COE to be part of it. Nevertheless, the COE tries to push the EU and the FRA to do more on the Roma, 'in a way against their self-interest' as the staff says. Returning to the policy congruence, this research identified instances of substantive disagreement, for example, on the Italian Roma policy, between the COE and the EU. However, in this case, the COE's counterpart was not, as is usual, the Roma unit in DG EMPL, but a DG JLS unit. A meeting mechanism was set up in 1999 on the issue of Roma, the Informal Contact Group, which ideally brings together representatives of the COE, EU, OSCE, UNHCR, and the World Bank in order to exchange information and coordinate activities. In recent years, participation of the other IOs has declined and the meetings have transformed into some kind of exclusive COE–EU meetings. However, a trustful relationship did not develop between the involved counterparts (DG EMPL and COE Secretariat). This may be due to the fact that, over the years, different EU units participated in the meetings (if they participated at all), which reflects that the former 'accession country issue' became an internal issue in 2004 and/or that the meetings themselves remained at a superficial level. In contrast, trust characterizes the relationship between the COE Secretariat and the FRA, with counterparts working together for years. Thus, one can see joint statements and projects resulting from the FRA–COE relationship.

As in the other cases, one can see policy congruence in the *data protection case*. In addition, both IOs have the same angle, since EU legislation is inspired by the COE Data Protection Convention. There are some conflicts that resulted from the organizational self-interest, yet they lay dormant and without eruption: first, the EU accused the COE of acting in a defensive way when the EU developed the first directive dealing with data protection in the mid-1990s. Second, the plan for the EU to become a member of the COE convention did not materialize due to the fact that non-EU member states (and implicitly also the COE Secretariat) feared that the EU would then 'dictate' data protection policy in Strasbourg. This case is a clear example of the importance of the individual level, namely the officials involved in the IOR. On the one hand, when there is 'good chemistry' between the counterparts, relations run smoothly (for example regular reciprocal representation, exchange of restricted documents); on the other hand, when 'good chemistry' between the counterparts is lacking, the IOR tend to lapse (for example EU, feeling superior, does not see the need to participate in COE meetings or follow COE developments, while at the same time the COE can access neither EU meetings nor documents). From this one can infer that relations are not institutionalized and depend – to a great extent – on the personal will of the counterparts.

9.4 The question of standard setting and outlook

This section aims at embedding the results of Chapters 4–8 into the big picture, and focusing on the research's broad implications and ideas for further research. This research began by asking what would happen if one organization enters into the competence sphere of another organization, and two IOs consequently occupy the same policy space (organizational overlap). Keeping in mind a world of scarce resources, one would expect IOs to be skeptical about intruders. Accordingly, one part of the literature suggests that the COE is driven by the fear of marginalization and sees the EU's increasing interest in the human rights field as a threat (De Schutter 2008: 510–7). Hence, the expected outcome is rather conflictive. This view is bolstered by the asymmetry between the two IOs, namely the EU's substantially greater power, in terms of financial (and human) resources as well as autonomy over its member states and political weight (for example through media attention). Another strand of literature identifies a different asymmetry within the IOR between the EU and the COE: while human rights form the core policy of the latter, the former only sees human rights as a peripheral policy. In this line of reasoning, one can expect the opposite outcome, that is, cooperation between two IOs, since the EU does not threaten the position of the COE (Brosig 2010: 15–6).

So what does the data tell us? Not surprisingly, the imbalance (in resources) is reflected in the IOR between the EU and the COE and constitutes a distinct feature of their relationship. While the EU can access COE documents and meetings in Strasbourg without difficulty, the COE struggles for the same systematic access to information, for example, the EU working groups are not open to COE officials and consultation of the COE is merely ad hoc and on the same footing as NGOs.

But what about the other asymmetry, that of core policy versus peripheral policy? Does the EU – as put forward by the argument – not interfere with the COE's role as guardian of human rights, or does the COE fear marginalization, and, if so, is it justified?

When asked about the added value of the COE, EU officials (as well as some COE officials) immediately refer to the antechamber function of the COE. Thus, the EU would benefit from the COE's larger membership (for example in terms of providing a forum for talks with (future) candidate countries) and the COE's possibility to transfer EU norms to the 'larger Europe' (for example through joint projects). Moreover, the EU would benefit from the COE in terms of the COE's expertise on specific member states at which the EU's progress reports are targeted. Once in a while EU officials mention the importance of the ECHR and the ECtHR in Strasbourg.

In contrast, the COE's work on EU member states (for example through the monitoring function) is mentioned rarely; even less so is the standard-setting function in terms of legal initiatives, for example, in the JHA field. Why is it that the EU does not see the norm-setting role of the COE as added value? Is it because they lack knowledge or is it because the EU increasingly wants to set human rights norms itself? To answer these questions, the subsequent five paragraphs scrutinize the empirical cases at hand, beginning with the institutional cases.

In the *FRA case*, one observes conflictive relations for the very reason that the COE feared the Agency's intrusion into the COE's core business in terms of content as well as geography, and thus feared that the Agency would outstrip its norm-setting function. Whether caused by the COE's big outcry or not, the final provisions concerning the Agency's tasks and mandate largely comply with the COE requests, the most important being the limitation of the FRA's scope to EU law and EU member states; the main task becomes data collection and the provision of expertise for EU institutions, which means that the COE standard-setting task remains untouched.

The question of standard setting was also at stake in the *MOU*. Even though the COE did not achieve the binding agreement it had hoped for, the final document seems rather COE-friendly (despite its vagueness). Several points of the document underline that the COE remains the benchmark and reference source for human rights in Europe. Given the COE's hostile reaction toward the establishment of the FRA, the EU intended to use the aforementioned confirmation in the MOU to reassure the COE that it did not want to challenge it. The policy cases will show whether this acknowledgment remains an empty claim or is put into practice.

The example of the *data protection case* dates back to the mid-1990s, when the EU adopted its Data Protection Directive. Where did the standards incorporated in the Directive come from? The EU Directive was clearly inspired by the COE Convention of 1981. Once implemented by the EU member states, the EU Directive replaced the COE Convention in terms of data protection standards. However, since then, the data protection has not been further strengthened in either the COE or the EU. 9/11 and the fight against terrorism particularly pushed the protection of personal data into the background; however, the EU 2009 Stockholm Program brings about this issue's rebound and puts data protection back on the EU agenda (Council 2009e: 18–9). Following the Stockholm Program, the EU aimed at modernizing the Data Protection Directive and integrating it with other existing EU data protection instruments (Commission 2010d: 5; 2010a), and the COE ushered in the process of modernizing Convention 108 soon thereafter. The reform of data protection instruments is still ongoing in both IOs (June 2012); therefore, the question of who is now setting the standards is difficult to answer at the moment. However, given the cumbersome nature of the COE convention system and the binding nature of EU instruments, the EU will go on setting and interpreting data protection standards in Europe and will eventually outrun the COE leadership in this policy issue, if it has not already done so. The COE's budget limitations, of course, are not very helpful to counterbalance this development. Therefore, the COE's role, as some kind of EU assistant, will be limited to non-EU member states.

In contrast, the *terrorism case* shows a recent successful legal initiative (standard setting) of the COE in the JHA field. The COE Convention on the Prevention of Terrorism has been innovative in the sense that it is the first international treaty addressing terrorism from a preventive side. Not long after the treaty opened for signature, the EU announced its interest in adopting its own legal initiative. The EU took advantage of the COE consensus and stated that member states agreed to this project 'insofar as the criminalisation does not go further than the balance achieved in the Council of Europe Convention on the Prevention of Terrorism' (Commission 2007: 5). As a matter of fact, the EU Framework Decision strongly resembles the COE Convention. The terrorism case demonstrates how easily IOs can utilize initiatives of the other organization and transform them into an initiative of their own, as copyright seemingly does not apply to international law (or IOs). The EU takes up the position that the COE should appreciate the EU's initiative from the point of follow-up and monitoring because it allows bypassing of the often operose COE ratification process. The possibility of adopting directives that are directly binding on its member states (since the adoption of the Lisbon Treaty, even in JHA matters) is of course an advantage that the EU has as compared to the COE. However, COE officials who share the EU's point of view are in the minority. What the COE regretted was the lack of clear reference to the COE *acquis* on the one hand, and the potential slowing down of the ratification process on the other. Although actively involved in the negotiations, the EU agreed to reaffirm the importance of the COE ratification process publicly only after its own initiative had successfully been concluded. To sum up, the terrorism case highlights the COE's satisfaction of its function as the standard setter. However, the EU clearly and powerfully interfered in this case when suddenly putting forward its own initiative based on the COE consensus. On the one hand, this kind of conflict arguably derogates the effectiveness of human rights protection, given that EU member states tend to 'forget' about the COE ratification process the moment the EU puts forward an initiative. On the other hand, one can stress that – in the long run – human rights are protected more effectively within EU member states due to the EU Framework Decision, which, of course, applies to EU member states only.

In the *fight against Roma discrimination case* the EU, again, builds on COE policy recommendations that have been developed in order to improve the Roma's daily-life situation in the 1990s: access to housing, education, employment, and health care. The EU's Roma strategy and documents deal with these principles; however, as in other cases, a clear reference to the COE *acquis* is missing. The EU's possibility for standard setting is constricted due to the fact that the competence at the EU level is missing (the present-day basis is antidiscrimination legislation), which is why the EU has to find other ways to act: organizing European Roma Summits, setting up the European Roma Platform, and examining existing EU instruments that could be used in order to promote Roma inclusion. All these EU activities attract a great deal of attention, and push the COE in the background. In addition, the COE sees itself confronted with an area of application for joint projects that continues to shrink, and therefore so does available EU money on which the COE depends. From the Roma case, one can assess that in some areas the COE still has an edge over the EU, whose limited competences prevent it from setting new legal initiatives. Yet, even in these issues, the EU, having money at hand, manages to affect the inclusion of Roma by setting up new activities. In this regard, the COE complains that the EU, wanting to be the owner of the process, reinvents the wheel without taking into account the existing work done by the COE.

In terms of standard setting, the empirical cases showed that the EU took its inspiration from COE conventions and recommendations.

In those cases, the ideas came from the COE, while the EU picked them up and transferred them into its own legal initiatives that often have the upper hand over COE initiatives in terms of binding character, follow-up, and monitoring. From this observation one might conclude that the EU is threatening the COE's standard-setting role and therefore the COE might rightly fear marginalization. However, beyond the cases analyzed by this research, the picture is not as black and white as it seems at first glance. Tracing the development of selected legal initiatives of the COE and the EU in the JHA field (see Table 11 in the Appendix), one can detect a distinct parallel evolution of legal initiatives with both IOs borrowing from each other reciprocally. In some policy issues, one faces the well-known pattern of the EU borrowing from the COE: in the empirically analyzed issues of data protection and fight against terrorism, the COE inspired the EU in fighting environmental crime, corruption, cybercrime, and money laundering. However, one can also observe a new pattern, namely the COE borrowing from the EU in terms of mutual legal assistance in criminal matters, the fight against trafficking in human beings, and sexual exploitation of children. On a general level it can be assumed that the EU – at least for the time being – relies on the COE *acquis* to a larger extent than vice versa. Juncker highlighted (2006: 13) that, from the COE's 200 conventions (2006), EU policy makers had incorporated about thirty COE clauses in directives and framework decisions. Accordingly, one can conclude that borrowing from each other is – in the case of the EU and the COE – a two-way street. However, the extent to which the EU and the COE draw inspiration from one another varies. In contrast to this observation, it can be argued that, since 2000, the EU has been increasingly setting standards to which the COE has had to align itself.

This research has shown that the COE rightly fears marginalization given the steadily increasing activity of the EU in the human rights field. Accordingly, one might, perhaps provocatively, conclude that the EU – from the COE's point of view – has turned from friend to foe. The empirical cases show that the EU has remarkably changed its attitude toward human rights over time, a development that can most clearly be observed in the data protection case, the Roma case, and the FRA case. In the data protection case, the EU has changed from its 1980s' perception of personal data as a simple good to be circulated to its dedication of an entire article of the EU Charter of Fundamental Rights to the protection of personal data (Article 8) in 2000. The Roma started out as being considered – to put it bluntly – a security concern for the EU after the collapse of Communism. With the enlargement in 2004, the Roma – previously seen as an external issue concerning EU candidate countries – became an internal issue for the EU. The EU now strongly dedicates itself to improving the situation of the Roma. In the FRA case, the following statement of the Commission best demonstrates the EU's U-turn on the question of its own EU 'Human Rights Agency':

> [T]he Commission considers that the European Union *does not lack for sources of advice and information.* It can draw on reports from the United Nations, the *Council of Europe* and a variety of international NGOs. [...] The real challenge for any institution is to use the information in a productive manner, and to have the political will to take difficult decisions. *An additional advisory body would not overcome this challenge.* The Commission does not therefore intend to pursue this suggestion.
>
> (Commission 2001a: 20, emphasis added)

Two years later, the defensive attitude of the Commission toward an additional body tackling human rights gave way to the European Council's decision to establish a 'Human Rights Agency', which the Commission said it supported fully. The transformation must be seen in the context of the *EU's attempt to establish a human rights policy on its own.* This development is accompanied by the retrospective setting up of a foundational EU fundamental rights myth and free-riding on the reputation of the COE (Smismans 2010). Already at the turn of the millennium, Simitis (2001) classified these 'human rights steps' as the EU's slow, but clear, shift from an economic to a political union. Von Bogdandy (2000: 1337) attempts to explain this development by pointing out that, with the Common Market exhausted as a vision for further integration, the EU is searching for a new raison d'être, and human rights provide an intriguing prospect.

Summing up, this section has shown that the strand of literature suggesting conflictive relations between two IOs occupying the same policy space is more accurate for the relations between the EU and the COE. Despite the fact that the human rights field is 'only' a peripheral policy for the EU, the COE fears marginalization and acts in a defensive and hostile way when the EU interferes in its field of activity. Additionally, the asymmetry in the two IOs' resources also plays a role: the EU has plenty of resources at its disposal and constantly expands in competences and member states, whereas the COE is forced to cut back and again focus on core policies.

Regarding future research, one can see the human rights protection system develop further as the EU becomes increasingly active in the human rights field. Research has shown that the EU challenges the COE's standard-setting role and that both IOs will similarly set standards on the one hand, and will have to align themselves with the standards set by the other organization on the other hand. However, further research is needed regarding the specific design and refinement of the future human rights system, for example, to explain how and in what ways the IOR between the EU and the COE impact on the efficiency of human rights protection in general. In the terrorism case, the ratification process of the COE Convention came to a halt, as the EU negotiated its own Framework Decision. As in other cases (beyond the ones in this analysis), there has been the tendency of EU member states to 'forget' about the ratification of COE instruments the moment the EU puts forward a similar initiative. Only after the successful adoption of its own initiative does the EU publicly call upon member states to sign, ratify, and implement the respective COE conventions. One could argue that this kind of conflict derogates the effectiveness of human rights protection.

This research aims at producing findings that have implications on our understanding of IOs in general and the relationship between the EU and the COE in particular. Therefore, the subsequent two paragraphs discuss and ask why the results produced by this research can be applied to other contexts. To this end, it seems reasonable to distinguish between theoretical and empirical results that could potentially travel across contexts.

Regarding the *empirical results*, it seems reasonable to claim that the results in this study are applicable to relations between the EU and the COE in other issue areas as well. The intensity of IOR might vary across other issue areas (whether the EU/the COE is more or less interested in an issue), but the two distinct features of the relationship – the fear of marginalization (boosted by the power asymmetry) and the EU's tendency to reinvent the wheel – are also expected to apply. The EU will threaten – to a greater or lesser extent – the COE's role in other issue areas, if not through standard setting, then through the set up of other activities (in cases in which the EU lacks competence). Whether it results from a lack of knowledge or from a feeling of superiority on side of the EU, the EU tends to overlook the interests of other actors presuming that a specific issue area is 'terra incognita'.

Turning to the *theoretical results*, this research presumes that they might be applied to other IOs under specific conditions. The question of whether the results are applicable has to take into account the organizations under analysis. First, it is conceivable that the organizations to be analyzed include the EU (or another powerful organization) on the one hand, and another smaller regional organization (for example OSCE) or an organization dealing with a specific subtask (for example International Maritime Organization) on the other hand. Hence, one potentially faces a kind of 'crowding-out situation'. In this specific setting, this research expects the interest factor – more specifically the organizational self-interest – to be equally important. Second, it is conceivable that the organizations to be analyzed are equally powerful, for example, the EU on the one hand, and the UN or the World Trade Organization, or another regional organization of another part of the world (for example Mercado Comúndel Sur), on the other hand. Since in these kinds of settings the fear of marginalization might not be present at all, the organizational self-interest may be of less importance. It goes without saying that these IOs also have organizational self-interest; however, one can hypothesize that they are not as often or to a lesser extent at stake since the other organization is not as threatening as in 'crowding-out situations'. Besides the interest factor, it is assumed that the socialization factor (particularly the importance of trust between individual actors), and the organizational characteristics factor also play a role in the relations of other IOs in other parts of the world.

9.5 The future development of the EU–COE relations

As the EU continues with its standard-setting activities, one might wonder what will be the long-term future task of the COE? Will the COE remain the main guardian for the protection of human rights and keep setting human rights standards for Europe, or will its role be limited to non-EU member states at some point in the future? This text argues that the answers to these questions, to some extent, depend on the COE itself, whether it will be able to realign and position itself for this new development. In order to better keep up with the EU, the COE would need much more resources (financial and human) and media attention. This is what the COE is clearly lacking. To make the COE 'more politically relevant, effective, and influential', the new COE SG Thorbjørn Jagland introduced a major reform in January 2010 with the aim of revitalizing the COE as a political body and innovative organization, concentrating on only a few core areas of competence, and developing a more flexible organization that is both visible and relevant within Europe (COE 2011b: 3–5).

Apart from this ambitious undertaking, which is currently underway, the COE already has a few strengths that give it an edge over the EU: first, due to the fact that the staff within the COE remains on a specific post for a longer period of time, the COE personnel often has more expertise than the EU staff. The COE staff grows to be an expert, so to speak. In joint meetings, this leaves the EU personnel astonished by the knowledge of their counterparts. Second, the EU officials are also astonished by the big 'lobby' of the COE. On the one hand, it is the member states that inform, support, and reclaim the COE's involvement in EU activities. On the other hand, it is personal advocacy of some of the EU officials themselves, who worked for the COE before switching to the EU and/or have a close relationship with the COE. They refer to the COE's *acquis* in EU documents, organize joint meetings, and involve the COE staff in the drafting process of legal initiatives. Accordingly, in order to gain standing vis-à-vis the EU, the COE would need to focus and rebuild on these strengths.

However, what complicates a balanced IOR between the two IOs is that they differ in their self-competence and appearance. One can describe the COE as an honorable and highly qualified, yet not very powerful, organization (Zikmund 2008: 919; Petaux 2009). The EU, on the other hand, is very powerful and this power comes with an attitude, namely Brussels feeling strong enough to ultimately handle all agendas on its own. It is probably for this reason that past attempts to enforce a stronger interorganizational cooperation ran off into sand (Ettmayer 2008: 1196). This EU attitude is reflected in the data: when asked about the future vision of the EU and the COE, the EU staff's opinions range from the EU having its own human rights monitoring mechanisms, to some kind of potential merger between the two IOs, to the perception that the COE will soon become obsolete and merely be responsible for a couple of non-EU member states. Against this background, it does not come as a complete surprise when some COE staff say that the IOR with the EU have been 'extremely exhausting, due to the fact that one has to constantly insist on one's existence [the COE's existence], so to speak. Thus, it is very rare that this is already taken for granted'. It remains to be seen in the future whether the new attempts to bring the EU and the COE closer together will ultimately be successful. For the time being, it is already evident that the recent developments in the IOR between the two IOs – such as the MOU and the FRA – have helped, at least, to increase knowledge and raise awareness of each other.

Appendix

Table A.1 Overview of the conducted interviews

Interviewed experts (total: 40)	Location	Date	Type of interview
European Union (18 Interviews)			
Fundamental Rights Agency	Vienna	30.10.2008	On site
Fundamental Rights Agency	Vienna	08.04.2009	On site
European Commission (DG JLS)	Brussels	30.03.2009	On site
European Commission (DG JLS)	Brussels	01.04.2009	On site
European Commission (DG JLS)	Brussels	02.04.2009	On site
European Commission (DG JLS)		18.12.2009	Telephone
European Commission (DG RELEX)	Brussels	02.04.2009	On site
European Commission (DG RELEX)	Brussels	02.04.2009	On site
European Commission (DG RELEX)	Strasbourg	11.06.2009	On site
European Commission (DG SG)	Brussels	02.04.2009	On site
European Commission (DG EMPL)		08.12.2009	Telephone
European Commission (DG ELARG)	Brussels	03.04.2009	On site
General Secretariat of the Council of the EU	Brussels	03.04.2009	On site
General Secretariat of the Council of the EU (DG E)	Brussels	03.04.2009	On site
General Secretariat of the Council of the EU (DG E)	Brussels	23.04.2010	On site
General Secretariat of the Council of the EU (DG H)	Brussels	31.03.2009	On site
General Secretariat of the Council of the EU (DG H)	Brussels	31.03.2009	On site
General Secretariat of the Council of the EU (DG H)	Brussels	01.04.2009	On site
Council of Europe (17 Interviews)			
Secretariat General of the COE		11. 2008	E-mail
Secretariat General of the COE	Strasbourg	12.06.2009	On site
Secretariat General of the COE (DGHL)	Strasbourg	25.11.2008	On site
Secretariat General of the COE (DGHL)	Strasbourg	09.06.2009	On site
Secretariat General of the COE (DGHL)	Strasbourg	11.06.2009	On site
Secretariat General of the COE (DGHL)	Strasbourg	11.06.2009	On site
Secretariat General of the COE (DER)	Strasbourg	25.11.2008	On site
Secretariat General of the COE (DER)	Brussels	31.03.2009	On site
Secretariat General of the COE (DER)	Brussels	23.04.2010	On site

Secretariat General of the COE (DG III)	Strasbourg	26.11.2008	On site
Secretariat General of the COE (DG III)	Strasbourg	26.11.2008	On site
Secretariat General of the COE (DG III)	Strasbourg	10.06.2009	On site
Secretariat General of the COE (Internal Audit)	Strasbourg	25.11.2008	On site
Secretariat General of the COE (DLAPIL)	Strasbourg	09.06.2009	On site
Secretariat General of the COE (SecCM)	Strasbourg	12.06.2009	On site
Secretariat General of the COE (Office of the Commissioner for Human Rights)	Strasbourg	26.11.2008	On site
European Commission against Racism and Intolerance	Strasbourg	26.11.2008	On site
Other (5 Interviews)			
NGO	Strasbourg	26.11.2008	On site
NGO	Brussels	30.03.2009	On site
Austrian public administration	Vienna	16.07.2009	On site
Austrian public administration	Vienna	07.12.2009	On site
Researcher		08.12.2009	Telephone

Table A.2   Selected initiatives of the COE and the EU in the JHA field

Issue	COE	COE	EU	EU
		Date of initiative		
Data protection	Convention 108	1981	1995	Directive 95/46/EC
Environmental crime	Convention 172	1998	2003	Framework Decision 2003/80/JHA
Corruption	Convention 173	1998	2001	Directive 2001/97/EC
Mutual Legal Assistance	2nd Addit. Protocol 182	2001	2000	Conv. on Mutual Assistance
Cyber crime	Convention 185	2001	2005	Framework Decision 2005/222/JHA
Fight against Terrorism	Convention 196	2005	2008	Framework Decision 2008/919/JHA
Trafficking	Convention 197	2005	2002	Framework Decision 2002/629/JHA
Money Laundering	Convention 198	2005	2005	Directive 2005/60/EC
Protection of children	Convention 201	2007	2003	Framework Decision 2004/68/JHA

Source: COE (2012e), Commission (2012c).

References

Agence Europe. 2007. 'EU/Council of Europe: Cooperation between EU and Council of Europe is timidly reactivated.' *Europe Daily Bulletin, No. 9426,* 14 May 2007.

Aggarwal, Vinod K. 1998. 'Reconciling Multiple Institutions: Bargaining, Linkages, and Nesting.' In *Institutional Designs for a Complex World: Bargaining, Linkages, and Nesting,* ed. V. K. Aggarwal. Ithaca: Cornell University Press.

Ahtisaari, Martti, Jochen Frowein, and Marcelino Oreja. 2000. 'Report.' Adopted in Paris on 8 September 2000. Paris.

AI, Amnesty International. 2008. 'Public provocation to commit terrorism offences. Roundtable of European and National Parliaments – exchange of views on the revision of the Framework Decision 2002/475/JHA on combating terrorism – Monday 7 April 2008. Amnesty International Statement. Add more human rights protection – not less.' Brussels.

Alexander, Ernest R. 1995. *How Organizations Act Together. Interorganizational Coordination in Theory and Practice.* Luxembourg: Gordon and Breach.

Allison, Graham T. 1971. *Essence of Decision. Explaining the Cuban Missile Crisis.* Boston: Little, Brown and Company.

Alston, Philip, and Joseph H. H. Weiler. 1999. 'An "Ever Closer Union" in Need of a Human Rights Policy: The European Union and Human Rights.' In *The EU and Human Rights,* ed. P. Alston, M. Bustelo and J. Heenan. Oxford: Oxford University Press.

Alter, Karen J., and Sophie Meunier. 2006. 'Nested and Overlapping Regimes in the Transatlantic Banana Trade Dispute.' *Journal of European Public Policy* 13 (3):362–82.

Alter, Karen J., and Sophie Meunier. 2009. 'The Politics of International Regime Complexity.' *Perspectives on Politics* 7 (1):13–24.

Article 29, Data Protection Working Party. 2007a. 'Opinion 2/2007 on information to Passengers about the Transfer of PNR Data to US Authorities.' Adopted on 15 February 2007 and Revised and Updated on 24 June 2008. Brussels.

Article 29, Data Protection Working Party. 2007b. 'Resolution by the Article 29 Working Party on the 1st European Data Protection Day.' Version of 24 January 2007. Brussels.

Ashton, Catherine. 2011. 'SPEECH/11/31. Remarks at the Official Opening of the EU Delegation to the Council of Europe European Parliament Strasbourg.' 19 January 2011. Strasbourg.

Aust, Anthony. 1986. 'The Theory and Practice of Informal International Instruments.' *The International and Comparative Law Quarterly* 35 (4):787–812.

Aust, Anthony. 2007. *Modern Treaty Law and Practice.* 2nd edn. Cambridge: Cambridge University Press.

Bachmann, Reinhard, and Akbar Zaheer. 2008. 'Trust in Inter-organizational Relations.' In *The Oxford Handbook of Inter-organizational Relations,* ed. S. Cropper, M. Ebers, C. Huxham and P. S. Ring. Oxford: Oxford University Press.

Banisar, David. 2008. *Speaking of Terror. A Survey of the Effects of Counter-terrorism Legislation on Freedom of the Media in Europe.* Strasbourg: Council of Europe.

Barnett, Michael N., and Martha Finnemore. 1999. 'The Politics, Power, and Pathologies of International Organizations.' *International Organization* 53 (4):699–732.

Barnett, Michael N., and Martha Finnemore. 2004. *Rules for the World. International Organizations in Global Politics.* Ithaca: Cornell University Press.

Baxter, Richard R. 1980. 'International Law in "Her Infinite Variety".' *The International and Comparative Law Quarterly* 29 (4):549–66.

Bell, Mark. 2007. 'EU-Anti-Racism Policy; the Leader of the Pack?' In *Equality Law for an Enlarged Union. Understanding the Article 13 Directives*, ed. H. Meenan. Cambridge: Cambridge University Press.

Benson, Kenneth J. 1975. 'The Interorganizational Network as a Political Economy.' *Administrative Science Quarterly* 20 (2):229–49.

Benvenuti, Lodovico, and Walter Hallstein. 1961 [1959]. *Arrangement between the Committee of Ministers of the Council of Europe and the Commission of the European Economic Community*, concluded on 18 August 1959.

Biermann, Rafael. 2008. 'Towards a Theory of Inter-Organizational Networking. The Euro-Atlantic Security Institutions Interacting.' *The Review of International Organizations* 3 (2):151–77.

Bish, Robert. 1978. 'Intergovernmental Relations in the United States: Some Concepts and Implications from a Public Choice Perspective.' In *Interorganizational Policy Making. Limits to Coordination and Central Control*, ed. K. Hanf and F. W. Scharpf. London: Sage.

Bond, Martin. 2012. *Council of Europe. Structure, History and Issues in European Politics.* Abingdon: Routledge.

Borchert, Heiko 2001. 'Strengthening Europe's Security Architecture: Where Do We Stand? Where Should We Go?' In *Europe's New Security Challenges*, ed. H. Gärtner, A. Hyde-Price and E. Reiter. Boulder, CO: Lynne Rienner.

Brosig, Malte. 2006a. 'Human Rights in Europe: An Introduction.' In *Human Rights in Europe. A Fragmented Regime?* ed. M. Brosig. Frankfurt/M.: Peter Lang.

Brosig, Malte, ed. 2006b. *Human Rights in Europe: A Fragmented Regime?* Frankfurt/M.: Peter Lang.

Brosig, Malte. 2010. 'Governance between International Institutions: Analysing Interaction Modes between the EU, the Council of Europe and the OSCE.' In *Cooperation or Conflict? Problematizing Overlap in Europe*, ed. C. Gebhard and D. Galbreath. Farnham: Ashgate.

Brummer, Klaus. 2008a. *Der Europarat. Eine Einführung.* Wiesbaden: VS Verlag für Sozialwissenschaften.

Brummer, Klaus. 2008b. 'Konkurrenz um Menschenrechte in Europa: Die EU und der Europarat.' *Integration* 31 (1):65–79.

Brummer, Klaus. 2010. 'Enhancing Intergovernmentalism: The Council of Europe and Human Rights.' *The International Journal of Human Rights* 14 (2):280–99.

Bunyan, Tony. 2002. ' "The war on freedom and democracy". An analysis of the effects on civil liberties and democratic culture in the EU.' *Statewatch*, September 2002.

Bunyan, Tony. 2010. 'Commission: Action Plan on the Stockholm Programme. A bit more freedom and justice and a lot more security' *Statewatch*, Statewatch Analysis 95.

Burnham, Peter, Karin Gilland, Wyn Grant, and Zig Layton-Henry. 2004. 'Elite Interviewing.' In *Research Methods in Politics*, ed. G. B. Peters, J. Pierre and G. Stoker. Houndsmill: Palgrave Macmillan.

Bychawska-Siniarska, Dominika, and Zuzanna Warso. 2011. 'Doubts about the future scope of the EU Agency for Fundamental Rights.' http://humanrights.blogactiv.eu/2011/10/07/doubts-about-the-future-scope-of-the-eu-fundamental-rights-agency/, 7 October 2011.

Cannataci, Joseph A., and Jeanne Pia Mifsud-Bonnici. 2005. 'Data Protection Comes of Age: The Data Protection Clauses in the European Constitutional Treaty.' *Information & Communication Technology Law* 14 (1):5–15.

CAP, Capable Partners Program. 2010. *The Essential NGO Guide to Managing Your USAID Award*. Washington, DC.

Cardona, Meliton. 1992. 'The European Response to Terrorism.' *Terrorism & Political Violence* 4 (4):245–54.

Chalmers, Damian, Christos Hadjiemmanuil, Giorgio Monti, and Adam Tomkins. 2006. *European Union Law. Text and Materials*. Cambridge: Cambridge University Press.

CM-SUIVI3, Follow-up Committee on the Third Summit. 2006a. 'CM-SUIVI3(2006)4 18 January 2006. Draft memorandum of understanding on the strengthening of co-operation between the Council of Europe and the European Union.'

CM-SUIVI3, Follow-up Committee on the Third Summit. 2006b. 'CM-SUIVI3(2006)8 9 March 2006. Draft memorandum of understanding on the strengthening of co-operation between the Council of Europe and the European Union – consolidated version.'

CM-SUIVI3, Follow-up Committee on the Third Summit. 2007a. 'CM-SUIVI3(2007)CB1 22 January 2007. Synopsis. Meeting of 18 January 2007.'

CM-SUIVI3, Follow-up Committee on the Third Summit. 2007b. 'CM-SUIVI3(2007)CB4 12 April 2007. Synopsis Meeting of 10 April 2007.'

CODEXTER. 2004. 'CODEXTER (2004) 16. 2nd meeting 29 March – 1 April. Meeting Report.' Strasbourg.

CODEXTER. 2008. 'CODEXTER (2008) 01. Terms of Reference of the Committee of Experts on Terrorism (CODEXTER) for 2008–2010.' Strasbourg.

COE. 1949. 'ETS – No. 1. Statute of the Council of Europe. London, 5.V.1949.' London.

COE. 1950. 'ETS – No. 5. European Convention for the Protection of Human Rights and Fundamental Freedoms, Rome, 4.XI.1950.' Rome.

COE. 1977. 'ETS – No. 90. European Convention on the Suppression of Terrorism. Strasbourg, 27.I.1977.' Strasbourg.

COE. 1981. 'ETS – No. 108. Convention for the Protection of Individuals with regard to Automatic Processing of Personal Data. Strasbourg, 28.I.1981.' Strasbourg.

COE. 1992. 'ETS – No. 148. European Charter for Regional or Minority Languages. Strasbourg, 5.XI.1992.' Strasbourg.

COE. 1995. 'ETS – No. 157. Framework Convention for the Protection of National Minorities.' Strasbourg.

COE. 2003. 'ETS – No. 190. Protocol Amending the European Convention on the Suppression of Terrorism. Strasbourg, 15.V.2003.' Strasbourg.

COE. 2004a. 'DG-I (2004)5. Rapport de la réunion entre la Troïka du Comité de l'Article 36 de l'Union européenne et le Conseil de l'Europe. 27 mai 2004.' Bruxelles.

COE. 2004b. 'SG/Inf (2004)34. 16 December 2004. The Fundamental Rights Agency of the European Union – A Council of Europe Perspective. Contribution by the Secretary General of the Council of Europe.'

COE. 2005a. 'Council of Europe Treaty Series – No. 196. Council of Europe Convention on the Prevention of Terrorism. Warsaw, 16.V.2005.' Warsaw.

COE. 2005b. 'ETS – No. 196. Council of Europe Convention on the Prevention of Terrorism. 16.V.2005.' Warsaw.

COE. 2006a. 'DGI (2007) 01. Report of the Meeting between the Troika of the Article 36 Committee of the European Union and the Council of Europe.' Brussels.

COE. 2006b. 'Roma and Travellers Glossary.' Strasbourg.

COE. 2007a. 'Press release – 750(2007). Terry Davis: "Key parts of the EU Commission's anti-terrorist package duplicate the 2005 Council of Europe Convention on the Prevention of Terrorism".' Strasbourg.

COE. 2007b. 'Press Release – 847(2007). Signing of a cooperation agreement between PACE and EP.'

COE. 2007c. 'Press release – 102(2007). Council of Europe Secretary General: The new Agency should help the EU to better respect human rights.' Strasbourg.

COE. 2008. 'Press release – 558(2008). Italy: "Immigration policy must be based on human rights principles and not only on perceived security concerns", says Commissioner Hammarberg presenting a special report.' Strasbourg.

COE. 2009. 'Thorbjørn Jagland: European Union is Council of Europe's most important institutional partner.' http://www.coe.org.rs/eng/news_sr_eng/?conid=1433, 31 May 2012.

COE. 2010a. 'Council of Europe Activity report 2010.' Strasbourg.

COE. 2010b. 'Council of Europe response to privacy challenges Modernisation of Convention 108. Position paper, 27–29 October 2010.' In *32nd International Conference of Data Protection and Privacy Commissioners.* Jerusalem.

COE. 2010c. 'DP (2010) textes. Data Protection. Compilation of Council of Europe Texts.' Strasbourg.

COE. 2010d. 'PD-BUR (2010) RAP 21. Consultative Committee of the Convention for the Protection of Individuals with regard to Automatic Processing of Personal Data [ETS 108] (T-PD). 21st Bureau meeting. Lisbon, 13–15 April 2010.' Strasbourg.

COE. 2010e. 'Press Release – 545(2010). European Commission and Council of Europe kick off joint talks on EU's accession to the Convention on Human Rights.' Strasbourg.

COE. 2010f. 'T-PD (2010) RAP 26 Abr. Consultative Committee of the Convention for the Protection of Individuals with regard to Automatic Processing of Personal Data [ETS 108] (T-PD).' 26th Plenary Meeting, 1–4 June 2010.' Strasbourg.

COE. 2011a. 'Annual meeting of Senior Officials of the European Union and the Council of Europe under the Joint Declaration on Co-operation and Partnership Brussels.' 8th December 2010. Report.'

COE. 2011b. 'Council of Europe Reform: Heading into the Future.' Progress Review Report. 18 March 2011.

COE. 2011c. 'DPA/Inf (2011) 18. 5 May 2011. Implementation of the Memorandum of Understanding between the Council of Europe and the European Union: Overview of Activities' (1 January–31 December 2010).

COE. 2012a. 'Action Against Terrorism. Meetings of the CODEXTER.' http://www.coe.int/t/dlapil/codexter/meetings_en.asp, 1 June 2012.

COE. 2012b. 'Action Against Terrorism. The Multidisciplinary Group on International Action against Terrorism (GMT).' http://www.coe.int/t/dlapil/codexter/gmt_more_en.asp, 1 June 2012.

COE. 2012c. 'Calendar of Roma Related Upcoming Activities.' http://www.coe.int/t/dg3/romatravellers/source/documents/2011_calendar_of_Roma_related_upcoming_activities.doc, 1 June 2012.

COE. 2012d. 'COE Treaty Office. CETS No.: 196.' http://conventions.coe.int/Treaty/Commun/QueVoulezVous.asp?NT=196&CM=8&DF=01/06/2012&CL=ENG, 1 June 2012.

COE. 2012e. 'Complete List of the Council of Europe's Treaties.' http://conventions.coe.int/Treaty/Commun/ListeTraites.asp?CM=8&CL=ENG, 1 June 2012.

COE. 2012f. 'Data Protection. Calendar.' http://www.coe.int/t/dghl/standardsetting/dataprotection/Calendar_en.asp, 31 May 2012.

COE. 2012g. 'Data Protection. History.' http://www.coe.int/t/dghl/standardsetting/dataprotection/History_more_en.asp, 31 May 2012.

COE. 2012h. 'Data Protection. Reports and Studies.' http://www.coe.int/t/dghl/standardsetting/dataprotection/Reports_and_studies_en.asp, 31 May 2012.

COE. 2012i. 'Dosta Campaign. Dosta! Go beyond Prejudice, Discover the Roma!' http://www.coe.int/T/DG3/RomaTravellers/dosta_en.asp, 1 June 2012.

COE. 2012j. 'Making Human Rights for Roma a Reality.' http://www.coe.int/web/coe-portal/roma/, 1 June 2012.

COE. 2012k. 'T-PD-BUR(2012)01. Consultative Committee of the Convention for the Protection of Individuals with regard to Automatic Processing of Personal Data [ETS 108] (T-PD). Modernisation of Convention 108: new proposals.' Strasbourg.

COE. 2012l. 'T-PD (2012) Roadmap. Consultative Committee of the Convention for the Protection of Individuals with regard to Automatic Processing of Personal Data [ETS 108] (T-PD).' Strasbourg.

COE. 2012m. 'Treaty Office. CETS No.: 108.' http://conventions.coe.int/Treaty/Commun/QueVoulezVous.asp?NT=108&CM= 8&DF= 01/06/2012&CL= ENG, 1 June 2012.

COE. 2012n. 'Treaty Office. CETS No.: 157.' http://conventions.coe.int/Treaty/Commun/QueVoulezVous.asp?NT=157&CM=8&DF=01/06/2012&CL=ENG, 1 June 2012.

COM, Committee of Ministers. 1951. 'Resolution (51) 30 FE 3 May 1951 – Relations with International Organisations, both Intergovernmental and Non-governmental.'

COM, Committee of Ministers. 1973. 'Resolution (73) 22 on the Protection of the Privacy of Individuals vis-à-vis Electronic Data Banks in the Private Sector.'

COM, Committee of Ministers. 1974a. 'Resolution (74) 3 on International Terrorism'. (Adopted by the Committee of Ministers on 24 January 1974 at its 53rd Session).

COM, Committee of Ministers. 1974b. 'Resolution (74) 13 on the Establishment of a Liasion Office of the Council of Europe in Brussels'. (Adopted by the Committee of Ministers on 6 May 1974 at its 54th Session).

COM, Committee of Ministers. 1974c. 'Resolution (74) 29 on the Protection of the Privacy of Individuals vis-à-vis Electronic Data Banks in the Public Sector.'

COM, Committee of Ministers. 1978. 'Declaration on Terrorism.' (Adopted by the Committee of Ministers at its 63rd Session, on 23 November 1978).

COM, Committee of Ministers. 1982. 'Recommendation R (82) 1 Concerning International Cooperation in the Prosecution and Punishment of Acts of Terrorism.' (Adopted by the Committee of Ministers on 15 January 1982 at the 342nd meeting of the Ministers' Deputies).

COM, Committee of Ministers. 1989. ' Declaration on the Future role of the Council of Europe in European Construction' (Adopted and signed at the 84th Session of the Committee of Ministers, 5 May 1989, on the occasion of the 40th anniversary of the Organisation).' Strasbourg.

COM, Committee of Ministers. 1996. 'CM/Del/Dec(96)579/2.1/appendix5. 03 December 1996. Letter Inviting the Commission to Participate in Meetings of the Ministers' Deputies.'

COM, Committee of Ministers. 1999. 'Amendments to the Convention for the Protection of Individuals With Regard to Automatic Processing OF Personal Data (ETS No. 108) Allowing the European Communities to Accede.' Strasbourg, 15 June 1999. Strasbourg.

COM, Committee of Ministers. 2000. 'Resolution (2000) 2 on the Council of Europe's information strategy (11 April 2000).' (Adopted by the Committee of Ministers on 11 April 2000 at the 706th meeting of the Ministers' Deputies).

COM, Committee of Ministers. 2001. '109th Session of the Committee of Ministers, 7–8 November 2001.' Communiqué on International Action Against Terrorism. Strasbourg.

COM, Committee of Ministers. 2002a. 'CM(2002)164 final. 111th Session of the Committee of Ministers (6–7 November 2002). Communiqué.' Strasbourg.

COM, Committee of Ministers. 2002b. 'Resolution (2002) 8 on the Statute of the European Commission against Racism and Intolerance.' (Adopted by the Committee of Ministers on 13 June 2002 at the 799th meeting of the Ministers' Deputies).

COM, Committee of Ministers. 2005a. 'CM(2005)79 final. 17 May 2005. Third Summit of Heads of State and Government of the Council of Europe (Warsaw, 16–17 May 2005). Warsaw Declaration.' Warsaw.

COM, Committee of Ministers. 2005b. 'CM(2005)80 final. 17 May 2005. Action Plan.' Warsaw.

COM, Committee of Ministers. 2006a. 'CM/Inf(2006)16. 16 March 2006. 22nd Quadripartite meeting Council of Europe/European Union. (Strasbourg, 15 March 2006).'

COM, Committee of Ministers. 2006b. CM/Inf(2006)46 revised. 15 November 2006. 23rd Council of Europe/European Union Quadripartite meeting. (Brussels, 3 November 2006).

COM, Committee of Ministers. 2006c. 'GR-EXT(2006)15. 2 November 2006. 23rd Quadripartite meeting between the Council of Europe and the European Union (Brussels, 3 November 2006). Information document on quadripartite meetings.'

COM, Committee of Ministers. 2007a. 'CM(2007)74. 10 May 2007. 117th Session of the Committee of Ministers (Strasbourg, 10–11 May 2007). Memorandum of Understanding between the Council of Europe and the European Union.' Strasbourg.

COM, Committee of Ministers. 2007b. CM/Inf(2007)14. 16 February 2007. 24th Quadripartite meeting between the Council of Europe and the European Union (Brussels, 13 February 2007).

COM, Committee of Ministers. 2007c. 'CM/Inf(2007)44. 23 October 2007.25th Quadripartite Meeting between the Council of Europe and the European Union (Strasbourg, 23 October 2007).' Strasbourg.

COM, Committee of Ministers. 2008a. 'CM(2008)49 add. 30 April 2008.118th Session of the Committee of Ministers (Strasbourg, 7 May 2008) – Stocktaking of the implementation of the Memorandum of Understanding between the Council of Europe and the European Union.' Strasbourg.

COM, Committee of Ministers. 2008b. 'CM(2008)164. 1044 Meeting, 10 December 2008. CAHDI. Report on the Consequences of the So-Called "Disconnection Clause" in International Law in General and for Council of Europe Conventions, Containing such a Clause, in Particular.'

COM, Committee of Ministers. 2008c. CM/Inf(2008)14. 12 March 2008. 26th Quadripartite Meeting between the Council of Europe and the European Union (Brussels, 10 March 2008).

COM, Committee of Ministers. 2008d. CM/Inf(2008)39. 17 November 2008. 27th Quadripartite Meeting between the Council of Europe and the European Union (Brussels, 10 November 2008).

COM, Committee of Ministers. 2009a. 'CM(2009)52 addendum 1. 7 May 2009. 119th Session of the Committee of Ministers (Madrid, 12 May 2009). Co-operation between the Council of Europe and the European Union – Stocktaking of the Implementation of the Memorandum of Understanding between the Council of Europe and the European Union (1 January–31 December 2008).'

COM, Committee of Ministers. 2009b. 'CM(2009)52. 7 May 2009. 119th Session of the Committe of Ministers (Madrid, 12 May 2009) – Co-operation between the Council of Europe and the European Union – Report for the 119th Ministerial Session.' Madrid.

COM, Committee of Ministers. 2009c. CM/Inf(2009)26 revised. 22 May 2009. 28th Quadripartite Meeting between the Council of Europe and the European Union (Madrid, 11 May 2009).

COM, Committee of Ministers. 2009d. 'CM/Inf(2009)47 28 October 2009. 29th Quadripartite Meeting between the Council of Europe and the European Union (Luxembourg, 27 October 2009).'

COM, Committee of Ministers. 2009e. 'CM/Res(2009)21 Concerning the Ordinary Budget for 2010.' (Adopted by the Committee of Ministers on 25 November 2009 at the 1071st meeting of the Ministers' Deputies).

COM, Committee of Ministers. 2009f. 'GR-EXT(2009)2. 28 January 2009. Information Document on Quadripartite Meetings.'

COM, Committee of Ministers. 2010a. 'CM(2010)52 final. 6 May 2010. 120th Session of the Committee of Ministers (Strasbourg, 11 May 2010). Co-operation between the Council of Europe and the European Union – Report for the 120th Ministerial Session.' Strasbourg.

COM, Committee of Ministers. 2010b. 'CM(2010)133 final. Council of Europe High Level Meeting on Roma. Strasbourg, 20 October 2010. "The Strasbourg Declaration on Roma".' Strasbourg.

COM, Committee of Ministers. 2012. 'Chairmanship and Sessions of the Committee of Ministers.' http://www.coe.int/web/coe-portal/event-files/chairmanship-and-sessions-committee-of-ministers, 25 July 2012.

Commission, European. 1990. 'COM(90) 314 final. Communication on the Protection of Individuals in Relation to The Processing of Personal Data in the Community and Information Security.' Brussels.

Commission, European. 1996. 'Bulletin EU 9-1996. Joint Council and Commission Conclusions on Arrangements for Cooperation between the European Union and the Council of Europe (1/1).'

Commission, European. 2001a. 'COM(2001) 252 final. Communication on the European Union's Role in Promoting Human Rights and Democratisation in Third Countries.'

Commission, European. 2001b. 'COM(2001) 521 final. Proposal for a Council Framework Decision on Combating Terrorism.' Brussels.

Commission, European. 2003. 'COM(2003) 483 final. 2003/0185 (CNS). Communication on the Activities of the European Monitoring Centre on Racism and Xenophobia, together with Proposals to Recast Council Regulation (EC) 1035/97.' Brussels.

Commission, European. 2004. 'COM(2004) 693 final. Communication from the Commission. The Fundamental Rights Agency. Public Consultation Document {SEC(2004)1281}.' Brussels.

Commission, European. 2005a. 'COM(2005) 280 final. Proposal for a Council Regulation establishing a European Union Agency for Fundamental Rights. Proposal for a Council Regulation empowering the European Union Agency for Fundamental Rights to Pursue its Activities in Areas Referred to in Title VI of the Treaty on European Union {SEC(2005)849}.' Brussels.

Commission, European. 2005b. 'SEC(2005) 849. Annex to the Proposal for a Council Regulation establishing a European Union Agency for Fundamental Rights, and to the Proposal for a Council Decision empowering the European Union Agency for Fundamental Rights to Pursue its Activities in Areas Referred to in Title VI of the Treaty on European Union. Impact Assessment Report. {COM(2005)280 final}.' Brussels.

Commission, European. 2007. 'COM(2007) 650 final. Proposal for a Council Framework Decision amending Framework Decision 2002/475/JHA on combating terrorism (presented by the Commission).' Brussels.

Commission, European. 2008. 'SEC(2008) 2172. Commission Staff Working Document Accompanying the Communication from the Commission to the European Parliament, the Council, the European Economic and Social Committee and the Committee of the Regions. Non-discrimination and Equal Opportunities: A Renewed Commitment. Community Instruments and Policies for Roma Inclusion {COM(2008) 420 final}.' Brussels.

Commission, European. 2010a. 'COM(2010) 609 final. Communication from the Commission. A Comprehensive Approach on Personal Data Protection in the European Union.' Brussels.

Commission, European. 2010b. 'General Budget of the European Union for the Financial year 2010. The figures.' Brussels.

Commission, European. 2010c. 'Improving the Tools for the Social Inclusion and Non-Discrimination of Roma in the EU. Report.' Luxembourg.

Commission, European. 2010d. 'MEMO/10/139. European Commission Plan to Deliver Justice, Freedom and Security to Citizens (2010–2014).' Brussels.

Commission, European. 2012a. 'COM(2012) 9 final. Communication from the Commission. Safeguarding Privacy in a Connected World. A European Data Protection Framework for the 21st Century.' Brussels.

Commission, European. 2012b. 'Fundamental Rights at the Heart of Policy Making – 16/04/2012.' http://ec.europa.eu/news/justice/120416_en.htm, 22 May 2012.

Commission, European. 2012c. 'Policies. Justice and Citizens' Rights.' http://ec.europa.eu/policies/justice_citizens_rights_en.htm, 1 June 2012.

Commission, European. 2012d. 'Policy Areas. Human rights.' http://europa.eu/pol/rights/index_en.htm, 23 July 2012.

Commission, of the European Communities. 1989. 'COM (89) 124 final. 8 March 1989. Commission communication to the Council on Relations between the Community and the Council of Europe.' Brussels.

Commissioner, for Human Rights. 2008. 'CommDH(2008)18. Memorandum by Thomas Hammarberg Commissioner for Human Rights of the Council of Europe.' Strasbourg, 28 July 2008. Strasbourg.

Commissioner, for Human Rights. 2009. 'CommDH(2009)16. Report by Thomas Hammarberg, Commissioner for Human Rights of the Council of Europe, following his visit to Italy on 13–15 January 2009.' Strasbourg, 16 April 2009. Strasbourg.

Coolsaet, Rik. 2010. 'EU Counterterrorism Strategy: Value Added or Chimera?' *International Affairs* 86 (4):857–73.

Costa, Oriol, and Knud Erik Jørgensen, eds. 2012. *The Influence of International Institutions on the EU. When Multilateralism hits Brussels*. Basingstoke: Palgrave Macmillan.

Council, of the European Union. 1999. '13940/99. CATS 35. Brussels, 8 December 1999. Meeting between the Troika of the Article 36 Committee and the Council of Europe.' Brussels.

Council, of the European Union. 2000a. '8837/00. CATS 41. Consultation Meeting between the Troika of the Article 36 Committee and the Council of Europe.' 15 May 2000 in Strasbourg. Brussels.

Council, of the European Union. 2000b. '13909/00. CATS 70. Consultation Meeting between the Troika of the Article 36 Committee and the Council of Europe.' 13 November 2000 in Brussels. Brussels.

Council, of the European Union. 2001a. '5146/01. Presidency Programme Concerning External Relations in the JHA field (2001–2002).' Brussels.

Council, of the European Union. 2001b. '7980/01. CATS 10. 18 April 2001. Draft report of a Meeting between the Troika of the Article 36 Committee and the Council of Europe.' Brussels.

Council, of the European Union. 2002. '14261/02. CATS 67. COSCE 8. Troika Meeting with the Council of Europe on 22 October 2002.' Brussels.

Council, of the European Union. 2003. '8019/03. CATS 19 Réunion Troika/CATS avec le Conseil de l'Europe du 24 mars 2003.' Brussels.

Council, of the European Union. 2004. '7873/04. Meeting of the JHA Counsellors on 26 March 2004. Co-ordination of EU Member States and Acceding States to prepare the meeting of CODEXTER (29 March–1 April 2004).' Brussels.

Council, of the European Union. 2005. '8649/05. JAI 156. RELEX 202. Troika Comité Article 36 avec Conseil de l'Europe du 29 avril 2005 à Strasbourg.' Brussels.

Council, of the European Union. 2006. '15801/06 (Presse 341). Press Release. 2768th Council Meeting. Justice and Home Affairs.' Brussels, 4–5 December 2006. Brussels.

Council, of the European Union. 2007. '9938/07. JAI 263. RELEX 382. Meeting between the Troïka of the Article 36 Committee and the Council of Europe.' 21 May 2007. Brussels.

Council, of the European Union. 2008a. '10898/08. "CFSP Guide" – Compilation of Relevant Texts.' Brussels.

Council, of the European Union. 2008b. '11168/08. JAI 350. RELEX 478. Meeting between the Troïka of the Article 36 Committee and the Council of Europe, 24 June 2008.' Brussels.

Council, of the European Union. 2008c. '17016/08. JAIEX 7. JAI 700. RELEX 1009. Meeting between the Troika of the Article 36 Committee and the Council of Europe, 8 December 2008, Strasbourg.' Brussels.

Council, of the European Union. 2008d. 'Council Conclusions on Inclusion of the Roma. 2914th General Affairs Council Meeting.' Brussels, 8 December 2008. Brussels.

Council, of the European Union. 2009a. '5618/1/09 REV 1. Note. Proposal for a Council Framework Decision on the use of Passenger Name Record (PNR) for law enforcement purposes.' Brussels.

Council, of the European Union. 2009b. '10480/09. JAIEX 36. RELEX 520. CATS 60. Summary of conclusions of the meeting with the Council of Europe.' Brussels, 19 May 2009. Brussels.

Council, of the European Union. 2009c. '10480/09. Summary of conclusions of the meeting with the Council of Europe, Brussels.' 19 May 2009. In *Outcome of Proceedings*. Brussels.

Council, of the European Union. 2009d. '14390/09. JAIEX 72. RELEX 898. CATS 105. Summary of Conclusions of the Meeting between the Troika of the Article 36 Committee and the Council of Europe.' Brussels, 8 October 2009. Brussels.

Council, of the European Union. 2009e. '17024/09. The Stockholm Programme – An Open and Secure Europe Serving and Protecting the Citizens.' Brussels.

Council, of the European Union. 2009f. '17352/1/08 REV 1. Draft Council Conclusions Supporting the Council of Europe's Legislative Work in the Area of Criminal Justice.' In *Note*. Brussels.

Council, of the European Union. 2010a. '11473/10. JAIEX 64. RELEX 585. CATS 62. Summary of Conclusions of the Meeting between the Troika of the Article 36 Committee and the Council of Europe.' Strasbourg, 21 June 2010. Brussels.

Council, of the European Union. 2010b. '17498/10. JAIEX 97. RELEX 1071. CATS 103. Summary of the CATS – Council of Europe Meeting.' Brussels, 6 December 2010. Brussels.

Council, of the European Union. 2010c. 'Council conclusions on advancing Roma Inclusion. 3019th Employment, Social Policy Health and Consumer Affairs Council Meeting.' Luxembourg, 7 June 2010. Luxembourg.

Council, of the European Union. 2011a. '5091/12. JAIEX 1. CATS 1. RELEX 16. Summary of the CATS – Council of Europe Meeting.' Brussels, 16 December 2011.

Council, of the European Union. 2011b. '11780/11. JAIEX 62. RELEX 675. CATS 54. Summary of the CATS – Council of Europe Meeting.' Strasbourg, 15 June 2011.

Council, of the European Union. 2012. 'Council. Presidency Websites.' http://www.consilium.europa.eu/council/presidency-websites.aspx, 25 July 2012.

CRI, European Commission against Racism and Intolerance. 2011. 'CRI(2011)36. Annual Report on ECRI's Activities Covering the Period from 1 January to 31 December 2010.' Strasbourg.

Cropper, Steve, Mark Ebers, Chris Huxham, and Peter Smith Ring. 2008. 'Introducing Inter-organizational Relations.' In *The Oxford Handbook of Inter-organizational Relations*, ed. S. Cropper, M. Ebers, C. Huxham and P. S. Ring. Oxford: Oxford University Press.

Csonka, Peter. 1996. 'Council of Europe Activities Related to Information Technology, Data Protection and Computer Crime.' *Information & Communication Technology Law* 5 (3):197–214.

Dawar, Kamala. 2010. 'Disconnection Clauses: An Inevitable Symptom of Regionalism? Online Proceedings Working Paper No. 2010/11.' In *Second Biennial Global Conference*. 8–10 July 2010. The University of Barcelona and its IELPO Programme Barcelona.

De Schutter, Olivier. 2007. 'The division of tasks between the Council of Europe and the European Union in the promotion of Human Rights in Europe: Conflict, Competition and Complementarity.' In *Working paper series: REFGOV-FR-11*. Louvain: Catholic University of Louvain.

De Schutter, Olivier. 2008. 'The Two Europes of Human Rights. The Emerging Division of Tasks Between the Council of Europe and the European Union in Promoting Human Rights in Europe.' *The Columbia Journal of European Law* 14 (3):509–61.

De Schutter, Olivier, and Philip Alston. 2005. 'Introduction: Addressing the Challenges Confronted the EU Fundamental Rights Agency.' In *Monitoring Fundamental Rights in the EU: The Contribution of the Fundamental Rights Agency*, ed. P. Alston and O. De Schutter. Oxford: Hart Publishing.

Dinant, Jean-Marc 2010. 'PD-BUR(2010)09 (I) FINAL. Rapport sur les lacunes de la Convention n° 108 pou r la protection des personnes à l'égard du traitement automatisé des données à caractère personnel face aux développements technologiques.' ed. COE. Strasbourg.

Donnelly, Jack. 1986. 'International Human Rights: A Regime Analysis.' *International Organization* 40 (3):599–642.

Downs, Anthony. 1967. *Inside Bureaucracy*. 7th edn. Boston: Little, Brown and Company.

Egeberg, Morten. 2003. 'How Bureaucratic Structure Matters: An Organizational Perspective.' In *Handbook of Public Administration*, ed. B. G. Peters and J. Pierre. London: Sage.

EP, European Parliament. 2005. 'European Parliament resolution on the situation of the Roma in the European Union. P6_TA(2005)0151.' Brussels.

EP, European Parliament. 2006. 'European Parliament Resolution on the situation of Roma women in the European Union. P6-TA-PROV(2006)0244.' Brussels.

EP, European Parliament. 2008a. 'European Parliament resolution of 8 May 2008 on the Annual Report on Human Rights in the World 2007 and the European Union's policy on the matter. P6_TA(2008)0193.' Brussels.

EP, European Parliament. 2008b. 'European Parliament resolution of 31 January 2008 on a European strategy on the Roma. P6_TA(2008)0035.' Brussels.

EP, European Parliament. 2008c. 'Report on the proposal for a Council Framework Decision amending Framework Decision 2002/475/JHA on combating terrorism. 23.7.2008.'

EP, European Parliament. 2010. 'Budgets. European Parliament. Definitive adoption of the European Union's general budget for the financial year 2010 (2010/117/EU, Euratom).'

ERRC, European Roma Rights Centre, Open Society Institute, and Italian NGO OsservAzione. 2009. 'Memorandum to the European Commission. Violations of EC Law and the Fundamental Rights of Roma and Sinit by the Italian Government in the Implementation of the Census in "Nomad Camps" '. 4 May 2009.

Ettmayer, Wendelin. 2008. 'Das Europäische Modell und der Europarat.' In *Österreich im Europarat 1956–2006. Bilanz einer 50-jährigen Mitgliedschaft*, ed. W. Hummer. Wien: Böhlau.

EU COCEN. 1999. 'Recommendation on the Situation of Roma in the Candidate Countries: Background Document, 1999. Guiding Principles for Improving the Situation of the Roma based on the Recommendations of the Council of Europe's Specialist Group of Roma/Gypsy and on the Recommendations of the OSCE High Commissioner on National Minorities.' Adopted by the European Union (COCEN group) at the Tampere Summit, December 1999.

EUMC, European Monitoring Centre on Racism and Xenophobia. 2005. 'Application of Council Directive 2000/43/EC of 29 June 2000. Views of the European Monitoring Centre on Racism and Xenophobia.' Vienna.

European Council. 1993. 'SN 180/93. European Council in Copenhagen.' 21–22 June 1993. Conclusions of the Presidency.

European Council. 2004a. '5381/04. Presidency Conclusions of the Brussels European Council.' 12 and 13 December 2003. Brussels.

European Council. 2004b. 'Declaration on Combating Terrorism.' 25 March 2004. Brussels.

Evan, William M. 1966. 'The Organization-Set: Toward a Theory of Interorganizational Relations.' In *Approaches to Organizational Design*, ed. J. D. Thompson. Pittsburgh: University of Pittsburgh Press.

FRA, European Union Agency for Fundamental Rights. 2008. 'Opinion of the European Union Agency for Fundamental Rights on the Proposal for a Council Framework Decision on the use of Passenger Name Record (PNR) data for law enforcement purposes.'

FRA, European Union Agency for Fundamental Rights. 2009. 'Summary Report. The situation of Roma EU citizens moving to and settling in other EU Member States.' November 2009.

FRA, European Union Agency for Fundamental Rights. 2012. 'Research and analysis. 1999–2006 Publications.' http://fra.europa.eu/fraWebsite/research/publications/publications_per_year/previous_publications/previous_publications_en.htm, 1 June 2012.

Galbreath, David J., and Carmen Gebhard, eds. 2010. *Cooperation or Conflict? Problematizing Organizational Overlap in Europe*. Farnham: Ashgate.

Gehring, Thomas, and Sebastian Oberthür. 2004. 'Exploring Regime Interaction.' In *Regime Consequences. Methodological Challenges and Research Strategies*, ed. A. Underdal and O. R. Young. Dordrecht: Kluwer.

Gehring, Thomas, and Sebastian Oberthür. 2006. *Institutional Interaction in Global Environmental Governance. Synergy and Conflict among International and EU Policies*. Cambridge: MIT Press.

George, Alexander L., and Andrew Bennett. 2005. *Case Study and Theory Development in the Social Sciences*. Cambridge: MIT Press.

Gest, Nathaniel, and Alexandru Grigorescu. 2010. 'Interactions Among Intergovernmental Organizations in the Anti-corruption Realm.' *The Review of International Organizations* 5 (1):53–72.

Gläser, Jochen, and Grit Laudel. 2009. *Experteninterviews und qualitative Inhaltsanalyse*. Vol. 3. Auflage. Wiesbaden: VS Verlag für Sozialwissenschaften.

Grandori, Anna. 1987. *Perspectives on Organization Theory*. Cambridge: Ballinger.

Gray, Barbara. 2008. 'Intervening to Improve Interorganizational Partnerships.' In *The Oxford Handbook of Inter-organizational Relations*, ed. S. Cropper, M. Ebers, C. Huxham and P. S. Ring. Oxford: Oxford University Press.

Greer, Steven, and Andrew Williams. 2009. 'Human Rights in the Council of Europe and the EU: Towards "Individual", "Constitutional" or "Institutional" Justice?' *European Law Journal* 15 (4):462–81.

GS, General Secretariat of the Council of the European Communities. 1989. '5482/89 (Presse 44). 1308th Council Meeting – General Affairs – Brussels, 20 March 1989.'

Guglielmo, Rachel, and Timothy William Waters. 2005. 'Migrating Towards Minority Status: Shifting European Policy Towards Roma.' *Journal of Common Market Studies* 43 (4):763–86.

Hall, Richard H. 1972. *Organizations. Structure and Process*. Englewood Cliffs, New Jersey: Prentice Hall.

Hall, Richard H., John P. Clark, Peggy C. Giordano, Paul V. Johnson, and Martha Van Roekel. 1977. 'Patterns of Interorganizational Relationships.' *Administrative Science Quarterly* 22 (3):457–74.

Halpert, Burton P. 1982. 'Antecedents.' In *Interorganizational Coordination: Theory, Research, and Implementation*, ed. D. L. Rogers and D. A. Whetten. Ames, Iowa: Iowa State University Press.

Hanf, Kenneth. 1978. 'Introduction.' In *Interorganizational Policy Making. Limits to Coordination and Central Control*, ed. K. Hanf and F. W. Scharpf. London: Sage.

Hanf, Kenneth, and Laurence J. O'Toole. 1992. 'Revisiting Old Friends: Networks, Implementation Structures and the Management of Inter-organizational Relations.' *European Journal of Political Research* 21 (1–2):163–80.

Hibbert, Paul, Chris Huxham, and Peter Smith Ring. 2008. 'Managing Collaborative Inter-organizational Relations.' In *The Oxford Handbook of Inter-organizational Relations*, ed. S. Cropper, M. Ebers, C. Huxham and P. S. Ring. Oxford: Oxford University Press.

Hoffman, Bruce. 1999. 'Is Europe Soft on Terrorism?' *Foreign Policy* 115:62–76.

Hofmann, Rainer, and Erik Friberg. 2004. 'The Enlarged EU and the Council of Europe: Transfer of Standards and the Quest for Future Cooperation in Minority Protection.' In *Minority Protection and the Enlarged European Union: The Way Forward*, ed. G. N. Toggenburg. Budapest: Open Society Institute.

Hummer, Waldemar, and Andrea Schmid. 2008. 'Gesamtdarstellung der (Rechtsharmonisierungs-)Konventionen im Schoss des Europarates – unter besonderer Berücksichtigung der Teilnahme Österreichs.' In *Österreich im Europarat 1956–2006. Bilanz einer 50-jährigen Mitgliedschaft*, ed. W. Hummer. Wien: Böhlau.

Hunt, Adrian. 2006. 'The Council of Europe Convention on the Prevention of Terrorism.' *European Public Law* 12 (4):603–28.

Jönsson, Christer, and Maria Strömvik. 2005. 'Negotiations in Networks.' In *European Union Negotiations. Processes, Networks and Institutions*, ed. O. Elgström and C. Jönsson. London: Routledge.

Jørgensen, Knud Erik, ed. 2009. *The European Union and International Organizations*. Abingdon: Routledge.

Joris, Tony, and Jan Vandenberghe. 2008/2009. 'The Council of Europe and the European Union: Natural Partners or Uneasy Bedfellows?' *The Columbia Journal of European Law* 15 (1):1–41.

Juncker, Jean-Claude. 2006. 'Council of Europe – European Union: "A sole ambition for the European continent". Report by Jean-Claude Juncker, Prime minister of the Grand Duchy of Luxembourg, to the attention of the Heads of State or Government of the Member States of the Council of Europe.'

Kenis, Patrick, and Leon Oerlemans. 2008. 'The Social Network Perspective. Understanding the Structure of Cooperation.' In *The Oxford Handbook of Inter-Organizational Relations*, ed. S. Cropper, M. Ebers, C. Huxham and P. S. Ring. Oxford: Oxford University Press.

Klijn, Erik-Hans. 2008. 'Policy and Implementation Networks. Managing Complex Interactions.' In *The Oxford Handbook of Inter-organizational Relations*, ed. S. Cropper, M. Ebers, C. Huxham and P. S. Ring. Oxford: Oxford University Press.

Knodt, Michèle. 2005. *Regieren im erweiterten europäischen Mehrebenensystem. Internationale Einbettung der EU in die WTO*. Baden-Baden: Nomos.

Knoke, David and Xiangxiang Chen. 2008. 'Political Perspectives on Inter-organizational Networks.' In *The Oxford Handbook of Inter-organizational Relations*, ed. S. Cropper, M. Ebers, C. Huxham and P. S. Ring. Oxford: Oxford University Press.

Kohler-Koch, Beate. 1989. *Regime in den internationalen Beziehungen*. Baden-Baden: Nomos.

Konrad Adenauer Stiftung, Europabüro. 2006. 'Workshop Report. "The Relation between the European Union and the Council of Europe – Towards New Complementarity and Cooperation." ' February 7th, 2006. Brussels.

Koskenniemi, Martti. 2006. 'Report of the Study Group of the International Law Commission, UN Doc. A/CN.4/L.682 of 13 April 2006 and Add.1 of 2 May 2006.'

Kovats, Martin. 2001. 'The Emergence of European Roma policy.' In *Between Past and Future. The Roma of Central and Eastern Europe*, ed. W. Guy. Hatfield: University of Herfordshire Press.

Krasner, Stephen D. 1983. 'Structural Causes and Regime Consequences: Regimes as Intervening Variables.' In *International Regimes*, ed. S. D. Krasner. Ithaca: Cornell University Press.

Lagodny, Otto. 1989. 'The European Convention on the Suppression of Terrorism: a Substantial Step to Combat Terrorism.' *University of Colorado Law Review* 60 (3):583–600.

Lavenex, Sandra. 2006. 'The External Face of Europeanization: Third Countries and International Organizations.' In *The Europeanization of National Policies and Politics of Immigration*, ed. T. Faist and A. Ette. Houndmills: Palgrave Macmillan.

Lewin, Kurt. 1964. 'Behavior and Development as a Function of the Total Situation.' In *Field Theory in Social Science. Selected Theoretical Papers.* ed. D. Cartwright. New York: Harper Torchbooks.

Liégeois, Jean-Pierre. 2007. *Roma in Europe*. Strasbourg: Council of Europe Publishing.

Lugna, Lauri. 2006. 'Institutional Framework of the European Union Counter-Terrorism Policy Setting.' *Baltic Security & Defence Review* 8: 101–127.

MacMullen, Andrew. 2004. 'Intergovernmental Functionalism? The Council of Europe in European Integration.' *Journal of European Integration* 26 (4):405–29.

Marcher, Brigitte. 2009. 'Der gemeinsame Rechtsraum der EU: Wirklich ein europäischer Mehrwert für die BürgerInnen? Resümee der Tagung vom Freitag.' 4 December 2009, Renner-Institut, Wien.

Mattessich, Paul W., Marta Murray-Close and Barbara R. Monsey. 2004. *Collaboration: What Makes It Work.* 2nd ed. Saint Paul, MN: Fieldstone Alliance.

Mayring, Philipp. 2003. *Qualitative Inhaltsanalyse. Grundlagen und Techniken.* 8th ed. Weinheim: Deutscher Studien Verlag.

McNair, Arnold Duncan. 1961. *The Law of Treaties.* Oxford University Press.

McNeill, John H. 1994. 'International Agreements: Recent U.S.-UK Practice Concerning the Memorandum of Understanding.' *The American Journal of International Law* 88 (4):821–6.

Mearsheimer, John J. 1994/95. 'The False Promise of International Institutions.' *International Security* 19 (3):5–49.

Metcalfe, Les. 1978. 'Policy Making in Turbulent Environments.' In *Interorganizational Policy Making. Limits to Coordination and Central Control*, ed. K. Hanf and F. W. Scharpf. London: Sage.

MG-S-ROM. 2008a. 'MG-S-ROM (2008) 8. Committee of Experts on Roma and Travellers. 25th Meeting.' 2–4 April 2008. Strasbourg.

MG-S-ROM. 2008b. 'MG-S-ROM (2008) 2. Committee of Experts on Roma and Travellers. New terms of Reference Adopted by the Ministers' Deputies at their 1032nd Meeting in Strasbourg on 9 July 2008.' Strasbourg.

Mitterand, Francois. 1982. 'Speech to the Parliamentary Assembly of the Council of Europe. 30 September 1982. The Ultimate Question and the First Rule.' In *Annuaire Européen. European Yearbook, Volume XXIX, 1981*, ed. P. Drillien. The Hague: Martinus Nijhoff Publishers.

Ness, Gayl D., and Steven R. Brechin. 1988. 'Bridging the Gap: International Organizations as Organizations.' *International Organization* 42 (2):245–73.

Oliver, Christine. 1990. 'Determinants of Interorganizational Relationships: Integration and Future Directions.' *The Academy of Management Review* 15 (2):241–65.

Oreja, Marcelino, and Jacques Delors. 2001 [1987]. 'Arrangement between the Council of Europe and the European Community, Concluded on 16 June 1987.' In *Compendium of Texts Governing the Relations between the Council of Europe and the European Union*, ed. COE. Strasbourg

Ostrom, Elinor, Roy Gardner, and James Walker. 1994. *Rules, Games, & Common-Pool Resources*. Ann Arbor: The University of Michigan Press.

O'Toole, Laurence J. 2003. 'Interorganizational Relations in Implementation.' In *Handbook of Public Administration*, ed. B. G. Peters and J. Pierre. London: Sage.

O'Toole, Laurence J., and Robert S. Montjoy. 1984. 'Interorganizational Policy Implementation: A Theoretical Perspective.' *Public Administration Review* 44 (6):491–503.

PACE, Parliamentary Assembly of the Council of Europe. 1993. 'Recommendation 1203 (1993) on Gypsies in Europe.'

PACE, Parliamentary Assembly of the Council of Europe. 2005. 'Resolution 1427 (2005). Plans to set up a Fundamental Rights Agency of the European Union.'

PACE, Parliamentary Assembly of the Council of Europe. 2006a. 'Doc. 10892. 11 April 2006. Memorandum of Understanding between the Council of Europe and the European Union. Report.' Political Affairs Committee.

PACE, Parliamentary Assembly of the Council of Europe. 2006b. 'Recommendation 1743 (2006). Memorandum of Understanding between the Council of Europe and the European Union.' 13 April 2006.

PACE, Parliamentary Assembly of the Council of Europe. 2006c. 'Recommendation 1744 (2006). Follow-up to the 3rd Summit: the Council of Europe and the proposed Fundamental Rights agency of the European Union.'

PACE, Parliamentary Assembly of the Council of Europe. 2007a. '2007 Ordinary Session. (Second Part). Report. Seventeenth sitting.' Thursday 19 April 2007 at 3 p.m. ADDENDUM.

PACE, Parliamentary Assembly of the Council of Europe. 2007b. 'Opinion No. 262 (2007). Memorandum of understanding between the Council of Europe and the European Union.'

PACE, Parliamentary Assembly of the Council of Europe. 2008. 'Statement by Dick Marty, addressing the Committee on Civil Liberties, Justice and Home Affairs of the European Parliament in Brussels. 7 April 2008.'

PACE, Parliamentary Assembly of the Council of Europe. 2011. 'AS/Bur/AH EP PACE (2011) 05. Parliamentary Assembly, Council of Europe – European Parliament Joint Informal Body. 2nd meeting report.'

Paclii, Pacific Islands Treaty Series. 2012. 'Treaties Glossary Page.' http://www.paclii.org/oldpits/english/glossary.html, 1 June 2012.

Parker, George, and Sarah Laitner. 2005. 'Too many of us in the human rights business, European leaders are told. 7 February 2005.' *Financial Times*.

Patten, Chris, and Walter Schwimmer. 2001. 'Joint Declaration on Cooperation and Partnership Between the Council of Europe and the European Commision.' In *Compendium of Texts Governing the Relations between the Council of Europe and the European Union* ed. COE. Strasbourg.

Petaux, Jean. 2009. *Democracy and Human Rights for Europe. The Council of Europe's Contribution*. Strasbourg: Council of Europe Publishing.

Peters, Ingo. 1995. 'Europäische Sicherheitsinstitutionen: Arbeitsteilung Oder Konkurrenz?' In *Sicherheitspolitik für Europa zwischen Konsens und Konflikt*, eds. E. Forndran and H.-D. Lemke. Baden-Baden: Nomos.

Pettigrew, Thomas F. 1998. 'Intergroup Contact Theory.' *Annual Review of Psychology* 49:65–85.

Pevehouse, Jon C., Timothy Nordstrom, and Kevin Warnke. 2004. 'The COW-2 International Organizations Dataset Version 2.0.' *Conflict Management and Peace Science* 21 (2):101–19.

Pfeffer, Jeffrey, and Gerald R. Salancik. 2003. *The External Control of Organizations. A Resource Dependence Perspective*. Originally published 1978 ed. Stanford: Stanford University Press.

Polakiewicz, Jörg. 1999. *Treaty-making in the Council of Europe*. Strasbourg: Council of Europe Publishing.

Polakiewicz, Jörg. 2009. 'The European Union and the Council of Europe – Competition or Coherence in Fundamental Rights Protection in Europe?' In *The European Union at 50: Assessing the Past, Looking Ahead*, ed. P. Canelas de Castro. University of Macau: University of Macau Press.

PR Austria, Permanent Representation of Austria to the EU. 2006. 'Informal Contact Group of Intergovernmental Organisations and Institutions on Roma, Sinti and Traveller Issues.' Brussels, *Meeting Report*, 3 April 2006. Brussels.

PR Finland, Permanent Representation of Finland to the EU. 2006. 'Informal Contact Group of Intergovernmental Organisations and Institutions on Roma, Sinti and Traveller Issues.' Brussels, *Meeting Report*, 19 December 2006, Brussels.

PR France, Permanent Representation of France to the EU. 2008. 'Report of the Meeting of the Informal Contact Group (ICG) of International Organisations and Institutions Dealing with Issues Concerning Roma, Sinti and Travellers.' *Meeting Report*, 5 December, 2008, Brussels.

PR Germany, Permanent Representation of Germany to the EU. 2007. 'Informal Contact Group of Intergovernmental Organisations and Institutions on Roma, Sinti and Travellers.' Brussels, *Meeting Report,*11 June 2007, Brussels.

PR Netherlands, Permanent Representation of the Netherlands to the EU. 2004. 'Report of the meeting of the Informal Contact Group of International Organisations on Roma, Sinti and Travellers.' *Meeting Report*, 18 November 2004, Brussels. .

PR Portugal, Permanent Representation of Portugal to the EU. 2007. 'Informal Contact Group of Intergovernmental Organisations and Institutions on Roma, Sinti and Traveller Issues.' *Meeting Report*, 17 December 2007, Brussels. '

PR Slovenia, Permanent Representation of the Republic of Slovenia to the EU. 2008. 'Informal Contact Group of Intergovernmental Organisations and Institutions on Roma, Sinti and Travellers.' *Meeting Report*, 22 April 2008, Brussels.

PR Spain, Permanent Representation of Spain to the EU. 2010. 'Meeting of the Informal Contact Group of International Organisations and Institutions Dealing with Roma Issues.' *Meeting Report*, 10 February 2010, Brussels.

PR Sweden, Permanent Representation of Sweden to the EU. 2009. 'Report. Meeting of the Informal Contact Group of International Organisations and

Institutions dealing with Roma, Sinti and Traveller Issues.' 28 September 2009, Brussels.

PR UK, Permanent Representation of the United Kingdom to the EU. 2005. 'Informal Contact Group of Intergovernmental Organisations and Institutions on Roma, Sinti and Traveller Issues.' *Meeting Report*, 9 November 2005, Brussels.

Pressman, Jeffrey L., and Aaron B. Wildavsky. 1974. *Implementation. How Great Expectations in Washington Are Dashed in Oakland*. 2nd ed. Berkeley: University of California Press.

Quinn, Gerard 2001. 'The European Union and the Council of Europe on the Issue of Human Rights: Twins Separated at Birth?' *McGill Law Journal* 46:849–74.

Ram, Melanie H. 2010. 'Interests, Norms and Advocacy: Explaining the Emergence of the Roma onto the EU's Agenda.' *Ethnopolitics* 9 (2):197–217.

Rathbun, Brian C. 2008. 'Interviewing and Qualitative Field Methods: Pragmatism and Practicalities.' In *The Oxford Handbook of Political Methodology*, ed. D. Collier, H. E. Brady and J. M. Box-Steffensmeier. Oxford: Oxford University Press.

Raustiala, Kal, and David G. Victor. 2004. 'The Regime Complex for Plant Genetic Resources.' *International Organization* 58 (Spring):277–309.

Rechel, Bernd. 2008. 'What Has Limited the EU's Impact on Minority Rights in Accession Countries?' *East European Politics & Societies* 22 (1):171–91.

Redgwell, Catherine. 2000. 'Multilateral Environmental Treaty-Making.' In *Multilateral Treaty-making*, ed. V. Gowlland-Debbas. The Hague: Kluwer Law International.

Ring, Peter Smith, and Andrew H. Van de Ven. 1994. 'Developmental Processes of Cooperative Interorganizational Relationships.' *The Academy of Management Review* 19 (1):90–118.

Rittberger, Berthold. 2001. 'Which institutions for Post-war Europe? Explaining the Institutional Design of Europe's First Community.' *Journal of European Public Policy* 8 (5):673–708.

Santer, Jacques, and Daniel Tarschys. 2001 [1996]. 'Exchange of Letters between the Secretary General of the Council of Europe and the President of the Commission of the European Communities on 5 November 1996 Supplementing the "Arrangement" between the Council of Europe and the European Community, concluded on 16 June 2987.' In *Compendium of Texts Governing the Relations between the Council of Europe and the European Union*, ed. COE. Strasbourg.

Sasse, Gwendolyn. 2005. 'Securitization or Securing Rights? Exploring the Conceptual Foundations of Policies Towards Minorities and Migrants in Europe.' *JCMS* 43 (4):673–93.

Scharpf, Fritz W. 1978. 'Interorganizatzional Policy Studies: Issues, Concepts and Perspectives.' In *Interorganizational Policy Making. Limits to Coordination and Central Control*, eds. K. Hanf and F. W. Scharpf. London: Sage.

Scharpf, Fritz W. 1997. *Games Real Actors Play. Actor-Centered Institutionalism in Policy Research*. 1st ed. Boulder, CO: Westview.

Scheeck, Laurent. 2005. 'Solving Europe's Binary Human Rights Puzzle. The Interaction between Supranational Courts as a Parameter of European Governance.' In *Research in Question N° 15 – October 2005*. Paris: CERI Sciences Po.

Scheeck, Laurent. 2007. 'Competition, Conflict and Cooperation between European Courts and the Diplomacy of Supranational Judicial Networks.' In *The Evolution of the European Courts: Institutional Change and Continuity. 6th International Workshop for Young Scholars (WISH)*. University College Dublin, School of Law.

Schermerhorn, John R. 1975. 'Determinants of Interorganizational Cooperation.' *The Academy of Management Journal* 18 (4):846–56.

Schneider, Heinrich. 1977. 'Die Plattform wird errichtet: Europa in Strassburg.' In *Leitbilder der Europapolitik 1. Der Weg zur Integration*. ed. I. f. E. Politik. Band 9. Bonn: Europa Union Verlag.

Schopler, Janice H. 1987. 'Interorganizational Groups: Origins, Structure, and Outcomes.' *The Academy of Management Review* 12 (4):702–13.

Schruijer, Sandra G. L. 2008. 'The Social Psychology of Inter-organizational Relations.' In *The Oxford Handbook of Inter-organizational Relations*, ed. S. Cropper, M. Ebers, C. Huxham and P. S. Ring. Oxford: Oxford University Press.

Schwimmer, Walter. 2003. 'SG/Inf(2003)35. 25 September 2003. A Europe of Partners. Towards an associate partnership between the Council of Europe and the European Union. Memorandum by the Secretary General.'

Schwimmer, Walter. 2008. 'Die zukünftige Rolle und Funktion des Europarates.' In *Österreich im Europarat 1956–2006. Bilanz einer 50-jährigen Mitgliedschaft*, ed. W. Hummer. Wien: Böhlau.

SG, Secretary General. 2009. 'SG/Inf (2009) 6. External Relations of the Council of Europe in 2008. Report by the Secretary General to the Committee of Ministers.' In *Information Documents*, ed. C. o. M. COM: Council of Europe.

SG, Secretary General. 2011. 'SG/Inf(2011) 11 rev. 20 April 2011. Follow-up to the Strasbourg Declaration on Roma. First Progress Report (November 2010–April 2011) by the Secretary General of the Council of Europe.'

Sharfman, Mark P., Barbara Gray, and Aimin Yan. 1991. 'The Context of Interorganizational Collaboration in the Garment Industry: An Institutional Perspective.' *Journal of Applied Behavioral Science* 27 (2):181–208.

Simitis, Spiros. 2001. 'Data Protection in the European Union – the Quest for Common Rules.' *Collected Courses of the Academy of European Law* VIIII (Book 1):95–141.

Simon, Herbert A. 1961. *Administrative Behaviour. A Study of Decision-Making Processes in Administrative Organization*. 2nd ed. New York: Macmillan.

Smismans, Stijn. 2010. 'The European Union's Fundamental Rights Myth.' *JCMS* 48 (1):45–66.

Smrkolj, Maja. 2008. 'The Use of the "Disconnection Clause" in International Treaties: What does it tell us about the EC/EU as an Actor in the Sphere of Public International Law.' In *GARNET Conference 'The EU in International Affairs'*, 24–26 April 2008. Brussels.

Spanish Presidency, of the EU. 2010. 'Report on the II European Roma Summit. Promoting Policies in Favour of the Roma Population.' Held in Córdoba on 8 & 9 April 2010. Córdoba.

Stivachtis, Yannis A., and Mike Habegger. 2011. 'The Council of Europe: The Institutional Limits of Contemporary European International Society.' *Journal of European Integration* 33 (2):159–77.

Strasser, Wolfgang. 2000. '45 Jahre Menschenrechtsinstitutionen des Europarats – Bilanz und Perspektiven.' In *50 Jahre Europarat*, ed. U. Holtz. Baden-Baden: Nomos.

Tansey, Oisín. 2007. 'Process Tracing and Elite Interviewing.' *Political Science & Politics* 40 (4):765–72.

Taylor, Verena. 2008. 'Die Zusammenarbeit des Europarats mit der Europäischen Union.' In *Österreich im Europarat 1956–2006. Bilanz einer 50-jährigen Mitgliedschaft*, ed. W. Hummer. Wien: Böhlau.

Toggenburg, Gabriel Nikolaij. 2007a. 'Die EU-Grundrechteagentur: Satellit oder Leitstern?' *SWP-Aktuell* 8 (Februar 2007):1–8.

Toggenburg, Gabriel Nikolaij. 2007b. 'Die Grundrechteagentur der Europäischen Union: Perspektiven, Aufgaben, Strukturen und Umfeld einer neuen Einrichtung im Europäischen Menschenrechtsraum.' *MenschenRechtsMagazin* 12 (Heft 1):86–104.

Tsai, Wenpin. 2002. 'Social Structure of "Coopetition" Within a Multiunit Organization: Coordination, Competition, and Intraorganizational Knowledge Sharing.' *Organization Science* 13 (2):179–90.

Verbeek, Bertjan. 1998. 'International Organizations. The Ugly Duckling of International Relations Theory.' In *Autonomous Policy Making by International Organizations*, ed. B. Reinalda and B. Verbeek. London: Routledge.

Vermeersch, Peter. 2002. 'Ethnic Mobilisation and the Political Conditionality of European Union Accession: The Case of the Roma in Slovakia.' *Journal of Ethnic and Migration Studies* 28 (1):83–101.

Von Bogdandy, Armin. 2000. 'The European Union as a Human Rights Organization? Human Rights and the Core of the European Union.' *Common Market Law Review* 37 (6):1307–38.

Wallace, William, Helen Wallace, and Mark A. Pollack. 2005. *Policy-Making in the European Union*. 5th ed. Oxford: Oxford University Press.

Whetten, David A. 1982. 'Issues in Conducting Research.' In *Interorganizational Coordination: Theory, Research, and Implementation*, ed. D. L. Rogers and D. A. Whetten. Ames, Iowa: Iowa State University Press.

Wilkinson, Paul. 1986. *Terrorism and the Liberal State* 2nd ed. Basingstoke: Macmillen.

Xanthaki, Alexandra. 2004. 'Protection of a Specific Minority: The Case of Roma/Gypsies.' In *Minority Rights in Europe*, ed. P. Thornberry and M. A. M. Estébanez. Strasbourg: Council of Europe Publishing.

Young, Oran R. 1989. *International Cooperation: Building Regimes for Natural Resources and the Environment*. Ithaca: Cornell University Press.

Young, Oran R. 2002. *The Institutional Dimensions of Environmental Change: Fit, Interplay, and Scale*. Cambridge: MIT Press.

Zikmund, Renate. 2008. 'Der Europarat im Spiegel der Massenmedien.' In *Österreich im Europarat 1956–2006. Bilanz einer 50-jährigen Mitgliedschaft*, ed. W. Hummer. Wien: Böhlau.

Index

Printed and bound in Great Britain by
CPI Antony Rowe, Chippenham and Eastbourne